DATE DUE

NO. 1. '78			

DEMCO 38-296

Democratic Politics and Economic Reform in India

Successive Indian governments from a variety of political persuasions have remained committed to market-oriented reform since its introduction in 1991. In a well-argued, accessible and often controversial examination of the political dynamics which underlie that commitment, Rob Jenkins takes issue with existing theories of the relationship between democracy and economic liberalisation, while also engaging with key debates concerning the nature of civil society and the functionality of political institutions. He contends that while democracy and liberalisation are no longer considered incompatible, recent theorising overemphasises democracy's more wholesome aspects while underestimating its practitioners' reliance on obfuscatory tactics to defuse political resistance to policy shifts. By focusing on formal institutions such as party and electoral systems, existing research ignores the value of informal political institutions. In India these institutions have driven economic elites towards adaptation, negotiation and compromise, while allowing governing elites to divide opponents of reform through a range of political machinations. These include shifting blame, surreptitiously compensating selected interests, betraying the trust of political allies, and cloaking policy change in the guise of continuity. Rather than simply denouncing democracy's dark underside, Jenkins argues that promoting change routinely requires governments to employ the underhanded tactics and impure motivations which all politics breed, but only democracy can tame.

ROB JENKINS teaches in the Department of Politics and Sociology at Birkbeck College, University of London.

Contemporary South Asia 5

Editorial board
JAN BREMAN, G. P. HAWTHORN, AYESHA JALAL,
PATRICIA JEFFERY, ATUL KOHLI, DHARMA KUMAR

Contemporary South Asia has been established to publish books on the politics, society and culture of South Asia since 1947. In accessible and comprehensive studies, authors who are already engaged in researching specific aspects of South Asian society explore a wide variety of broad-ranging and topical themes. The series will be of interest to anyone who is concerned with the study of South Asia and with the legacy of its colonial past.

1 Ayesha Jalal, *Democracy and Authoritarianism in South Asia: A Comparative and Historical Perspective*   0 521 478626 (paperback)
2 Jan Breman, *Footloose Labour: Working in India's Informal Economy*
   0 521 560837 (hardback)   0 521 568242 (paperback)
3 Roger Jeffery and Patricia Jeffery, *Population, Gender and Politics: Demographic Change in Rural North India*
   0 521 46116 2 (hardback)   0 521 46653 9 (paperback)
4 Oliver Mendelsohn and Marika Vicziany, *The Untouchables: Subordination, Poverty and the State in Modern India*
   0 521 55362 8 (hardback)   0 521 55671 6 (paperback)

Democratic Politics and Economic Reform in India

Rob Jenkins

Birkbeck College, University of London

CAMBRIDGE
UNIVERSITY PRESS

Riverside Community College
Library
4800 Magnolia Avenue
Riverside, CA 92506

JQ281 .J46 1999
Jenkins, Rob.
Democratic politics and
economic reform in India

NDICATE OF THE UNIVERSITY OF

ı Street, Cambridge CB2 1RP United Kingdom

ss

The Edinburgh Building, Cambridge, CB2 2RU, UK
http://www.cup.cam.ac.uk
40 West 20th Street, New York, NY 10011–4211, USA http://www.cup.org
10 Stamford Road, Oakleigh, Melbourne 3166, Australia

© Cambridge University Press 1999

This book is in copyright. Subject to statutory exception and to the provisions
of relevant collective licensing agreements, no reproduction of any part may
take place without the written permission of Cambridge University Press.

First published 1999

Printed in the United Kingdom at the University Press, Cambridge

Typeset in Plantin 10/12pt [VN]

A catalogue record for this book is available from the British Library

Library of Congress Cataloging in Publication data

Jenkins, Rob.
    Democratic politics and economic reform in India/Rob Jenkins.
        p.   cm. – (Contemporary South Asia; 5)
    Includes bibliographical references.
    ISBN 0 521 65016 X (hardback)   ISBN 0 521 65987 6 (paperback)
        1. Democracy – India.   2. India – Politics and government – 1977–
3. Free enterprise – India.   4. India – Economic policy – 1980–
I. Title.   II. Series: Contemporary South Asia (Cambridge, England); 5.
JQ281.J46   1999
338.954'009'049 – dc21   99–11994   CIP

ISBN 0 521 65016 X hardback
ISBN 0 521 65987 6 paperback

Contents

For M.S.J.

Acknowledgements

Giving due recognition to everyone who has assisted me in the course of completing this book is impossible. Even trying to list them all would be a daunting task. Many, particularly those in government, cannot be named, as they provided information on condition of anonymity. This makes things easier, but only slightly.

I must first thank Jim Manor, who was an outstanding PhD supervisor, going far beyond the call of duty. In the nearly fourteen years since I took my first undergraduate course on Indian politics with him, he has been a great source of information, provocation, and guidance. I could not have wished for a better guru.

I am also grateful to the many people in India who invited me into their homes and offices, shared their thoughts, and parted with papers from their personal collections. Hundreds of people made time for me, but I can name only a few. First, E. Raghavan, who gave me my first on-the-ground introduction to Indian politics, in informal tutorials in his Bangalore office and on the campaign trail during *panchayat* elections in late 1986. He continued to enlighten me and assist me during the research for this book. Also in Bangalore, I have over the years received stimulating insights, as well as friendship, from Narendar Pani and Jamuna Rao.

In Rajasthan, I received critical guidance and support from the late Professor Iqbal Narain, Professor V. S. Vyas, and Dr P. C. Mathur. My association with the Institute of Development Studies, Jaipur, was invaluable. At IDS-Jaipur, I benefited from disussions with Shail Mayaram, K. L. Kochar, Ratna Reddy, Sunil Ray, and Pradeep Bhargava. I was also aided greatly by many hours spent in the Indian Coffee House discussing Rajasthan politics with Sunny Sebastian of *The Hindu*, who, perhaps because he belongs to Kerala, was able to combine insider knowledge with an outsider's perspective, and convey both with great flair. Sanjiv Srivastava of the *Indian Express* and the BBC also shared his intimate knowledge of political events and personalities in discussions in Jaipur, New Delhi, and London. I would like to thank S. Ramanathan, Surjit

Singh, and Kavita Srivastava (and her warm and welcoming family) for their ideas, friendship and many kindnesses.

In Maharashtra, my first thanks go to Gopal Guru of the University of Pune, who took time out of his own research to escort me personally around western Maharashtra, introducing me to his many friends in activism, politics, and journalism. Another Maharashtrian, Professor B. S. Baviskar, provided much needed advice. In Bombay, Kumar Ketkar of the *Maharashtra Times* patiently corrected me on my many misapprehensions on a number of occasions over the past several years. Mayank Bhatt of *Business India*, Sanjoy Narayan and Niranjan Rajadhyaksha of *Business World*, and Mahesh Vijapurkar of *The Hindu* were all extremely helpful. I am also indebted to Ramya Subrahmanian, Vandana Desai, and Dara Mehta for making Bombay seem more like home.

In New Delhi, Om Prakash Rana and his family have been gracious hosts to me over the years. Sanjaya Baru, formerly of the *Times of India*, has been extremely generous with his time and ideas. I have also benefited enormously from my ongoing informal relationsip with the Centre for the Study of Developing Societies in Delhi. I am particularly grateful to Yogendra Yadav, whose clear-headedness has helped me to re-think important aspects of my research. Others at CSDS who have, at one point or another, provided useful advice include Ashis Banerjee, Harsh Sethi, D. L. Sheth, and Giri Deshingkar. Discussions with E. Sridharan and Pran Chopra of the Centre for Policy Research have enlightened me in many ways.

This book would not have been possible without the help of many libraries and librarians. The first thanks must go to the friendly and efficient staff at the British Library for Development Studies. The staff at Bombay's Centre for Education and Documentation were extremely helpful, as were librarians at the University of Rajasthan, University of Pune, the Institute of Development Studies in Jaipur, the *Times of India* offices in Bangalore and Bombay, and the *Rajasthan Patrika* in Jaipur.

I am grateful to John Toye, Michael Lipton, Mick Moore, Mark Robinson, and Charles Harvey of the Institute of Development Studies, and Ian Duncan and Bruce Graham of the University of Sussex, for their comments on earlier versions of this and related work. Observations by David Potter and Gurharpal Singh also proved very helpful.

Other friends and colleagues from my time at IDS also contributed useful insights and a supportive environment, particularly Samer al-Samarrai, Sally Baden, Ulrich Bartsch, Lyla Mehta, Khalid Nadvi, Paul Shaffer, Arti and Saurabh Sinha, and Shen-Lang Tang. Many thanks also to my colleagues in the Department of Politics and Sociology at Birbeck College, especially Jane Tinkler, who has kept me abreast of events during my long periods outside of London, and Sunil Khilnani, who listened patiently to my half-formed ideas and also read the entire draft manuscript.

I have benfited from the reactions of seminar participants at the Centre for South Asian Studies, Cambridge; Queen Elizabeth House, Oxford; the Institute of Development Studies (Sussex and Jaipur); the Institute of Commonwealth Studies, London; the US Department of State; and conference programmes of the American Political Science Association, the UK Development Studies Association, and the European Association of South Asian Studies. Members of the Indian Administrative Service participating in the annual study courses organised jointly by the Institute of Development Studies and India's National Academy of Administration (Mussoorie) have been a source of constructive commentary. I also received useful feedback from Pranab Bardhan, Geoffrey Hawthorn, Loraine Kennedy, and Ashutosh Varshney – each of whom read all or most of the draft manuscript.

I gratefully acknowledge the generous financial support of the UK Department for International Development, the Nuffield Foundation, the Birkbeck College Small Grants Scheme, and the British Council. A grant from the Ford Foundation, related to a separate research project, also assisted this study by getting me to India for two final field visits in 1997 and 1998–99.

Elizabeth Heichler, Andrew Spooner, Bliss Austin, Patrick Barton, Jason Burns, Brian Schaffield, Claire Taylor, and Menno Ravenhorst all deserve hearty thanks for the sustenance their friendship has provided.

My brothers Ron and Joseph and my sister Tamara have done me a great service by setting high intellectual standards. They have also given me great love and encouragement. I have the best siblings there are. I am also indebted to Lillian and Douglas Annett for the many times they have gone out of their way to be supportive.

Anne Marie Goetz has helped me in more ways than I can say. Her proofreading services were the least of her contributions. She has been patient, loving, thoughtful, and kind. Though these things come naturally to her, they must have required great effort as this project dragged on. She deserves more gratitude than I can offer.

Finally, my thanks go to Max, just for showing up.

Map   States of the Indian federal union.

International boundaries are indicative
and do not represent any kind of endorsement
of actual territorial legitimacy.

1   Introduction

'India has fundamentally altered its development strategy', the World Bank announced in 1996. Government initiatives since 1991 to restructure the basis of the Indian economy 'ended four decades of planning and have initiated a quiet economic revolution'.[1] Whether this will produce the economic results hoped for by Indian and foreign advocates of liberal reform remains to be seen. But the wide-ranging reorientation of economic policy has already demonstrated a quality which has surprised many observers – staying power. As this book goes to press in mid-1999, the liberalisation process has not been reversed. New reforms continue to be unveiled on a regular basis, while with each passing day the early policy breakthroughs become further entrenched, as people and organisations operate in accordance with them. New approaches to policy on trade, foreign exchange, anti-trust regulation, banking, industry, foreign investment, and many others are now a familiar part of economic life. Because liberalisation is an open-ended process, the policy landscape continues to evolve. But many of the old landmarks have faded from view. Even two changes of government – towards the left in 1996, and then rightwards in 1998 – did not lead to retreat. In many ways economic reform was strengthened after each of these elections.

This is a transformation that requires explanation. The objective of this study is to account for the capacity of the Indian political system to sustain policy reform over an extended period of time in the face of formidable political obstacles. Dismantling a system of state control is a notoriously difficult task. Witness the on-again-off-again reform programmes throughout the developing world.[2] While most developing

---

[1] World Bank, Country Operations, Industry and Finance Division, Country Department II, South Asia Region, *India: Country Economic Memorandum – Five Years of Stabilization and Reform: The Challenges Ahead* (8 August 1996), p. i.

[2] Among the more recent reversals was the Tanzanian government's decision to re-launch its market-oriented reform programme, after many false starts. See 'Tanzania Returns to the IMF Fold', *African Business* (London), no. 218, January 1997. Another classic case of on-again-off-again reform has been Kenya. See 'Survey: Kenya' (special supplement), *Financial Times*, 10 May 1994, p. 3. The governments of Kenya and Ghana abandoned

countries, including India, fail to fulfil all of the obligations stipulated in the conditionality-based lending programmes of multilateral institutions,[3] many countries fail even to remain nominally committed to reform. By this standard, India's reforms have shown remarkable durability.

In India, as in most state-dominated economies, there are powerful groups and individuals with a strong interest in maintaining the status quo. Not least among the opponents of change are the bureaucratic and political elites who have prospered as gatekeepers. Their accomplices in the private sector are not only well off financially, largely as a result of the privileged positions they have occupied within the controlled economy, but extremely well organised. When any president or prime minister embarks on a programme of far-reaching reform, he will face resistance from opponents who are well positioned to thwart fundamental change. The groups that might stand to benefit from liberalisation tend to be poorly organised and lacking in influence. They are of little use to reformers seeking a constituency with which to counter the inevitable resistance.

Theoretically, democracy should add to the difficulties of bringing about sustainable policy reform. In democratic settings, powerful opponents of reform – farmers fearing the loss of subsidies, protected industrialists fearing foreign competition, party leaders fearing the loss of the illicit spoils of office – have usually forged strong vertical linkages with electoral constituencies which can be mobilised in opposition to policy reform. Powerful interests, and their junior partners, have many weapons at their disposal. Particularly effective are attacks on a reforming government's 'capitulation' to multinational corporations and western-dominated multilateral banks, and its 'betrayal' of the 'socialist' commitment to economic justice. Elected politicians are not known for their far-sightedness. Indeed, their vision rarely extends beyond the next election. They are disinclined to foment unrest among the powerful interests that fund their political activities and, often, their personal bank accounts. They do not relish conflict with public-sector unions over privatisation, or petty traders over tax reforms. Even when a particularly powerful politician launches a reform programme, it is difficult to sustain.

Like many other developing-country leaders, former Indian Prime Minister Rajiv Gandhi learned this lesson during the second half of the

economic reform in order to win their first multi-party elections in 1992. As the *Economist* put it, 'They threw money around like confetti, were duly re-elected and have never been able to get . . . back on track'. See 'The Rulers, the Ruled, and the African Reality', 20 September 1997, p. 85.

[3] See Paul Mosely, J. Harrigan, and J. Toye, *Aid and Power: The World Bank and Policy-Based Lending in the 1980s* (London: Routledge, 1991), two volumes.

1980s. His high-profile efforts to 'modernise' and 'liberalise' the Indian economy lasted less than three years before they were effectively abandoned in favour of the more comfortable path of state-led development. Powerful interests, both inside and outside the state, were credited with forcing Rajiv's retreat from liberalisation. Democracy's theoretical aversion to change seemed confirmed. That liberalisation eventually returned to India in a much more dramatic and lasting form under Prime Minister P. V. Narasimha Rao and Finance Minister Manmohan Singh is thus a puzzle worth untangling. The political durability of India's reform programme runs counter not only to much of the experience in the rest of the developing world, but also to India's own lacklustre track record.

How can we explain the ability of liberal reform to become rooted in India despite the daunting array of political obstacles placed in its path? India is not only a democracy; it has been one continuously for the past fifty years: unlike newly democratising countries in the developing world, or in the former Eastern Bloc, there are no discredited authoritarian regimes on which past failures can be blamed. The lasting ills of colonialism notwithstanding, the Raj has lost much of its usefulness as a scapegoat. Narasimha Rao's Congress Party, unlike so many other reforming governments, was never likely to be granted an extended 'honeymoon' with the electorate. Both had been married before, to each other, and not that long ago. By 1991, Congress had ruled India for all but four years since it attained independence in 1947. It had been out of power for less than two years before Rao and Singh took office. There was no national euphoria to distract people from the unpleasant economic tasks at hand, as there was in the countries emerging from authoritarian rule. Indian voters and powerful interests remained as cynical as ever. The two coalition governments which succeeded Congress – brought in by general elections in 1996 and 1998 – faced even more formidable odds. Both the centre-left United Front government and the coalition led by the Hindu nationalist Bharatiya Janata Party (BJP) had campaigned on anti-liberalisation platforms. That both ultimately pressed on with reform – substantially deepening its content – makes reform's political durability all the more intriguing.

In explaining the political sustainability of economic reform in India, we must address not only the deeply ingrained notion that democracy, particularly under developing-country conditions, constrains politicians from ushering in far-reaching reforms, but also a more recent set of thoughts on the matter. These hold that some variants of democracy may be conducive to sustainable policy reform because open competitive politics provides a forum within which governing elites can 'sell' the benefits of reform to individual constituencies and to the public at large.

This argument is popular among aid agencies, and has had its greatest impact as part of the 'good government' agenda, which seeks to establish links between democracy and market orientation. The good government agenda has been furthered by the findings of mainstream academic research on the politics of economic reform, which is more subtle than the good government literature, but suffers from many of the same shortcomings. Most importantly, both perspectives neglect the capacity of democratic governments to usher in policy reform by engaging in underhanded tactics, one of the salient features of the Indian case.

The unseemly underside of democracy is wished away by the architects of the good government agenda largely because foreign aid must be justified in highly moral terms. Such practical considerations are not the reason why democracy's unwholesome aspect is neglected by academic political economists. In this case the cause is a combination of methodological preoccupations and sample bias. A fixation upon a rather rigid form of rational-choice analysis leads much of the comparative literature to a conception of democratic institutions that is divorced from their actual functioning. Rational-choice political economists have become hostages to models and the model-building process. Concerned with cross-national comparability, the institutional variables selected in this portion of the literature are schematic, bland, and unenlightening. The result is an unfortunate blind spot when it comes to apprehending the complex calculus of survival – particularly its adaptive quality – by which political and socio-economic elites operate in times of change. The relative autonomy of democratically accountable governing elites in India, both today and in general over the past fifty years, is greater than many had expected, and for reasons that standard rational-choice models are unable to comprehend.

As for sample bias, India's status as a long-established democracy goes a long way towards explaining why the new-political-economy approach would have been unable to reveal the underlying reasons for its ability to sustain adjustment. Much of the literature is based on case studies of newly democratising countries. Few studies have examined the politics of economic reform in a long-established developing-country democracy, like India, largely because they are so rare. While democracies clearly can sustain reform (perhaps as well as authoritarian regimes), the sample's bias towards fledgling democracies has led theorists to emphasise the *wrong reasons why* they are able to do so. Preoccupied with the contrasts between new democracies and their authoritarian predecessors, the literature over-emphasises democracy's wholesome aspect – particularly the role of 'accountability', but also democratic governments' skill at selling reform to open-minded electorates. In an effort to assess the creation of political institutions in the new democracies, they have neglected to look elsewhere to determine how they might function in practice. 'Actually existing' democratic governments are often more 'accountable' to the powerful than to the powerless, a fact which affects their operation in times of reform no less than it does in times of stasis.

In short, there are two variants of conventional wisdom about the relationship between democracy and the promotion of policy reform, and both are wrong. Democracies are less constrained by unholy interest-group coalitions than was previously thought, but neither are they paragons of consensus-building. Democratically elected governments operate in a complicated world in which obfuscation and betrayal are routinely used to achieve political ends. Arguably democracy makes such tactics both necessary and possible. Advanced capitalist democracies rely on them all the time. Nevertheless, the explanation advanced in this book is not simply that India's reformers were Machiavellian enough to outwit opponents of liberalisation. Our concern is with the system within which reform was sustained. We identify three aspects of that system, around which the case material is structured: political incentives, political institutions, and political skills.

Two types of incentives are identified. First, governing elites at many levels of the Indian polity were attracted by the potential of liberalisation to provide new sources of patronage to substitute for some of those forfeited by the shrinkage of the state's regulatory role. Once it became clear to powerful political elites that economic reform did not have to conform to a rigid recipe, but that they themselves could write the rules of the transition as they went along, they were less inclined to press hard for a reversal of reform. They were also able to see the value of a second incentive: the inherent fluidity of India's interest-group structure. Interest groups themselves respond to new policy-derived incentives, and are vulnerable to divide-and-rule tactics. The ability to compensate narrowly defined groups, often clandestinely, and thus to magnify the 'feedback effects' that the new policy environment itself has on the fortunes and lobbying potential of various economic sectors, served to lessen the perceived political cost to governing elites of continuing with reform.

They were aided in this process by two types of political institutions – formal and informal. Many formal institutions were important in absorbing the political strain on reformers at the apex of the political system, but one institutional feature stands out, and is treated in detail – the federal political system. For a variety of reasons, the division of power between the central government and state governments tended to quarantine political resistance to reform within the confines of state-level political systems. Because the impacts of reform varied from state to state, politicians from states that did well economically were less inclined actively to oppose reform, while those from states that were not as fortunate had fewer allies and less clout with which to mount a campaign of resistance. Moreover, the responsibilities of governance forced state-level governing elites to adapt to liberalisation by competing with each other for private investment. Once reluctantly engaged in liberalising activities in their own right – even if not fully committed to reform – governing elites at the state level proved invaluable in tackling resistance among powerful interest groups, who were also subjected to the divisive impacts of the federal system.

Governing elites at the state level were also able to rely upon *informal* political institutions, particularly the regularised networks of influence, encompassing party and non-party organisational arenas, which are constructed around individual party leaders. These are a crucial feature of India's institutional environment, but one which most of the comparative and theoretical literature is ill-equipped to treat seriously. Because of the far-reaching scope of these informal political networks, politicians were able to arrange accommodations between a vast array of groups concerned with the effects of the new policy dispensation. Not all could be adequately compensated. But the openness of the democratic system allowed governing elites at the centre and in the states to use the intelligence-gathering capacities of their informal networks to gauge both the mood and the relative political worth of various constituencies, and to distribute whatever advantages were at their disposal with impressive *political* efficiency. The impacts on *economic* efficiency are less certain, but to the extent this political mechanism facilitated the transition to an ostensibly more efficient policy framework, it can be presumed to have had an indirect effect.

Sustaining adjustment also required political skills. Particularly critical was the tactical skill of governing elites at disarming opponents of reform. On some occasions this relied on the capacity to cloak policy change in the guise of continuity, while at others continuity with earlier liberal reforms was effectively disguised as a return to the status quo ante. Contrary to the conventional wisdom, the projection of an economic 'vision' for India played virtually no role in this process. By using informal political networks to negotiate compensation for powerful allies, and orchestrating the sequencing of reforms in ways that benefited themselves and their parties, governing elites contributed to an image of 'politics as usual', thus concealing the radical implications of reform. All of this bought India's besieged reformers valuable time, the one commodity that any reform programme requires if it is to become politically rooted and have at least a chance of success.

To recapitulate: the Indian state is more capable of producing system-maintaining change than theories of 'demo-sclerosis' would have us believe – indeed, less captured by powerful interests than was allowed for by most explanations of why Rajiv Gandhi failed to remain committed to reform in the late 1980s. Nevertheless, the contrary view, most visibly put forward as part of the good government agenda, is marred by inconsistencies, naïvety, and an overly schematic view of democratic institutions. Much of this shortcoming stems from the methodologically constrained analyses found in the theoretical literature on why some democracies have been able to promote reform, from which the good government literature has borrowed highlights. New-political-economy approaches are at times helpful in framing research questions, but tend systematically to discount the incentives facing governing elites to take limited risks, as well as the capacity for interest groups themselves to respond to new incentives, redefine their strategic objectives, and fall prey to the divisive tactics of governing elites. A selective application of the less dogmatic elements of rational-choice analysis can yield a more nuanced approach to both incentives and institutions, which in turn can allow us to appreciate the value of the *informal* institutions and political skills to which formal democracy can give rise. Indian politics, constructed around these institutions, induces socio-economic elites to engage in negotiation and compromise – and governing elites to engage in obfuscatory and manipulative tactics. These tactics include, in addition to outright pilfering: shifting unpleasant responsibilities and blame on to political opponents, surreptitiously compensating selected interests, concealing intentions, reassuring and then abusing the trust of long-time political allies, and obscuring policy change by emphasising essential continuity.

Before proceeding further, a few disclaimers are in order. First, this book is not arguing that India's reform programme is irreversible. The Indian government could announce a nationalisation of all industries tomorrow, though this or even less drastic forms of backtracking are unlikely. Even if a stark reversal in policy direction were to take place, it would not make the findings from this study any less relevant. The interpretation of events that is put forward is an attempt to explain not the irreversibility of economic reform in India, but its ability to last longer than many had originally predicted. Second, it must be recognised that economic factors are crucial to the sustainability of reform. Without producing at least some economic results, no reform programme, however well managed politically, can hope to retain the political support of state elites or resist the opposition of adversely affected interests. India has been blessed in this area. But positive economic results, while necessary, are not sufficient to ensure the continuation of reform. Third, and finally, what we are discussing in this book is *Indian* democracy, not democracy in the abstract. Lessons from one country cannot be translated to another. History matters. While the findings from the Indian case may allow us to take issue with generalisations in the existing literature, and to formulate questions about other democracies, they do not constitute a model with general applicability.

Methods and case-study regions

The questions that have arisen from the evolution of economic policy in India do not lend themselves to quantitative analysis. They are intimately bound up with the changing perceptions of interest groups, with backroom deal-making, and with the complex motivations underlying political decisions. It is therefore difficult, if not impossible, to subject such material to rigorous hypothesis-testing. What follows is an interpretive account of events in India. The goal has been to make sense of seemingly contradictory forces, and to do so by probing the actual functioning of political institutions. This, in turn, will allow us to transcend what have become sterile debates surrounding the relative capacities of authoritarian and democratic systems, and the impact of such institutional variables as party and electoral systems.

To achieve these objectives it has been necessary to rely on first-hand information provided in interviews with key informants – that is, with actors involved in the process of bargaining, protest, policy formulation, and other forms of political activity. The research included field visits in every year between 1992 and 1999, inclusive. Field research consisted primarily of close to 300 interviews with senior bureaucrats, elected officials, party functionaries, lawyers, and representatives of business associations, trade unions, and non-governmental organisations. Also contributing to the base of knowledge on which these key-informant interviews were conducted were conversations with local journalists, academics, retired bureaucrats, representatives of international organisations, and long-time observers of the political scene. One of the major sources of background and supporting information has been press reports. These have been combined with reviews of the academic literature and documentation provided by interviewees. The result is not political 'science'. But it is hoped that the insights provided by this approach will assist us in understanding the complex realities underlying the trends identified by other social scientists, particularly economists, which are often presented with little attention to the context of power relations.

This study has placed considerable emphasis on the state level of

India's federal system. The reasons for doing so are outlined in the analysis of the case material in Chapters 4, 5, and 6. In brief, the justification is as follows: though the decision to initiate economic reform was made by the national government, state governments must cope with many of its implications; they provide the first line of political defence. They play a large – perhaps decisive – role in defusing resistance to reform among socio-economic interests. The existence of well-institutionalised competitive political arenas below the national level is one of the defining characteristics of Indian democracy. The sustainability of adjustment has also been aided immensely by the ability of reformers in the central government to rely on the dynamics of inter-state competition to fragment opposition to reform from within the political elite.

Though evidence to support the propositions advanced in this study is drawn from a number of states, four states receive particular attention. Most of the case material concerns Maharashtra and Rajasthan, largely because the longest periods of field research were spent there. Developments in Karnataka and West Bengal are also featured prominently. Though any two (or even four) states are bound to be unrepresentative of a country as diverse as India, these four provide a relatively good cross-section of political and economic life. They cover the north, south, east, and west of India. This selection also includes a range of points along the spectrum of economic development, from industrially advanced Maharashtra to severely underdeveloped Rajasthan, with Karnataka and West Bengal fitting somewhere in between. While West Bengal's once formidable industrial base went into a period of decline in the 1970s and 1980s, as a combination of trade union militancy and government focus on rural areas took effect, Karnataka's economy, particularly around the capital of Bangalore, made significant strides towards diversification.

India's range of political parties is also well represented, with their fluctuating fortunes adding to the mix. The Hindu nationalist Bharatiya Janata Party (BJP) was the only elected ruling party in Rajasthan between 1991 and 1998.[4] Rajasthan has been the strongest bastion of the Indian right. The citadel of India's left, West Bengal, is also represented. The Communist Party of India-Marxist (CPI-M) heads a coalition government that has ruled for more than twenty years under the same chief

---

[4] The BJP government in Rajasthan was dismissed by the President of India, acting with the advice of the central government, in the wake of the destruction of a disputed religious structure in Uttar Pradesh in December 1992. President's Rule, in which the central-government-appointed governor heads the state administration, lasted until November 1993, when fresh elections were held. The BJP, though it did not win a majority of the state's assembly seats in those elections, managed to form a government with the support of independents and members of small parties.

minister, Jyoti Basu. Maharashtra had until recently been the most consistently Congress-dominated state in India. Its chief minister, Sharad Pawar, championed liberalisation in the state even before it became official party policy under Narasimha Rao. The Congress lost power in Maharashtra in the March 1995 assembly elections. A regional party, the Shiv Sena, took power in coalition with the BJP. The significant degree of policy continuity between the Congress and Shiv Sena–BJP governments in Maharashtra provided a useful context for analysing the political management of economic reform. In Karnataka, the shift from Congress rule to a government led by the centre-left Janata Dal, following elections in November 1994, furnished similar opportunities. These four states thus cover bastions of the left and right, as well as regions in which Congress was superseded by the right and the left, respectively.

Even if we could have chosen only one state, Maharashtra would have been a sensible choice. Because its economy, both agricultural and industrial, is among the most advanced and diversified in India, it faces some of the most difficult political challenges associated with liberalisation, such as mediating between powerful and well-organised interests in both urban and rural areas. It also affords us a bit of a glimpse into the future. As liberalisation of the state's economy began three years before the national trend (roughly in 1988), it has experienced many more of the economic and political implications.

Finally, it is worth noting that the explanation for India's ability to sustain adjustment has borrowed some of the conceptual tools of rational-choice analysis. It takes seriously the role of incentives and the way in which these are affected by the behaviour-shaping role of institutions. Moreover, tactical skill in politics is assessed largely in terms of the ability to influence the expectations of economic agents. And by focusing on the role of informal institutions in expanding the quantity and diversity of political transactions that are possible in a democratic setting, the types of concerns that preoccupy rational-choice political economists are never far from centre-stage. Rational-choice approaches can be useful, but they have their limits.

The next chapter provides an overview of reform since 1991, explaining what has happened and why it is significant. Chapter 3 situates the findings from the Indian case within the comparative and theoretical literature on the politics of economic reform. Chapters 4 to 6 detail the contribution of political incentives, institutions, and skills, respectively. Though for analytical reasons these are treated distinctly, they are part of a functioning system, and an attempt is made throughout to identify points of convergence and processes of interaction among them. Chapter 7 assesses some of the further implications of this interpretation of the

Indian case. It is meant to highlight the types of issues which the Indian experience with adjustment has raised for the study of Indian politics, comparative political economy, and development policy, as well as how the findings from this study might help to frame future research questions.

When the Narasimha Rao government, shortly after taking office in mid-1991, announced its intention to overhaul the workings of the Indian economy, many observers considered the plans of Finance Minister Manmohan Singh far too radical for what 'the compulsions of democratic politics' would allow.[1] At each stage of the reform process there was a vocal segment of opinion – for the most part ideologically opposed to liberalisation – ready to predict the imminent arrival of an ill-defined 'political reality' which would force the government to beat a hasty retreat to the well-trod path of Nehruvian socialism. The backlash never appeared. Curiously, as announcements of additional reforms became routine, and as economic and political life under the new (though always evolving) policy dispensation came to seem almost natural, the Cassandras' prophecies of political (as distinct from economic) doom grew even louder. But with a new twist: slowly their voices became almost indistinguishable from the laments of neo-liberal advocates who complained that each new reform measure was too little, not radical enough, a half-measure.[2] The prophets of the political backlash explained its failure to materialise by arguing that the government had yet to take the *really* tough decisions, and that what it had achieved thus far was mere window dressing. The government, according to this logic, had avoided the adverse political consequences of reform by, in effect, not reforming. Oddly, these voices bought into the neo-liberal true-believer's notion that everything short of extreme fiscal retrenchment, complete rupee convertibility, and a policy of hire-and-fire at will, was not truly economic reform at all, but simply tinkering at the margins. This conviction was supported with a circular form of reasoning which held that the absence of a political

---

[1] Interview with a former chief economic adviser to the finance ministry, 13 March 1992, New Delhi.
[2] This view was elaborated forcefully by Biplab Dasgupta, an academic economist and CPI-M MP, in seminars and informal discussion at the Institute of Development Studies, University of Sussex, during the autumn of 1994. Almost three years later, he voiced similar opinions at a seminar on Indian development policy at Birkbeck College, University of London, 10 October 1997.

backlash was, in fact, evidence that no reforms of genuine consequence had been effected. For those of this opinion, attempting to explain the political durability of economic reform in India is a pointless exercise. This is a misguided view.

It is only natural that international financial institutions, current and potential foreign investors, and advocates of specific reforms within India should attempt to prod the central and state governments to push forward with what is, after all, a continuous process with no predefined end-point. Nor is it surprising that these same groups should warn of the perils of complacency. Unfortunately, however, this advocacy has led to the impression in some quarters that what has been achieved thus far is relatively insubstantial, or that, in response to political factors, reform has 'stalled', been 'slowed down', or lost its 'momentum'.[3] In addition to the desire for more change, the other reason why this view has attained such currency is that many reforms have been progressing quietly. This fact has important implications. The understated nature of what has been taking place in India helps to conceal both the sheer magnitude of these reforms, as well as the chief reason why policy changes with such far-reaching implications could escape the political minefield that democracy lays in their path: that is, stealthily introduced reforms succeed largely because of the stealthy means through which they were introduced.

Indeed, much of the reform process after 1995 possessed far less drama than what are often portrayed as the really difficult reforms. IMF Managing Director Michael Camdessus, for instance, stated in April 1995 that Indian reforms are 'possibly slowing down'.[4] In one national business newspaper, the item which reported this statement was positioned alongside an article on the possibility that Congress Party reformers were getting 'cold feet' about whether to introduce new industrial-relations legislation in that session of parliament. This lent credence to Camdessus' assessment: because of the perceived power of the national trade unions, a thoroughgoing overhaul of the labour regime had long been considered the one act that would incontrovertibly demonstrate the government's reformist credentials. Yet, on the very same page another article reported statements by top finance ministry officials on proposed amendments to the State Financial Corporation Act, 1951. These would permit state governments to divest further their stakes in these patronage-ridden development banks. The significance of this journalistic juxtaposition is not simply that a fixation with the big issues (such as reforming the industrial-relations regime or adhering religiously to stringent deficit-reduction targets) allows less 'sexy' reforms to go unnoticed – though this

[3] See, for instance, 'Economic Reforms: Down to a Trickle', *India Today*, 15 October 1995, pp. 26–33.   [4] *Business Standard*, 25 April 1995.

is very common. Just as important is the failure to appreciate the sequencing pattern by which reforms are being introduced – and the effectiveness of the political strategy underlying this pattern.

The main feature of this pattern is gradual reform on any single issue. This involves a strategy of carefully laying a foundation by using less transparent means of initiating change in an effort to avoid direct political confrontation for as long as possible. The objective is to provide more conducive circumstances under which further changes can be effected at a later date, when potential supporters of change are more likely to prove politically useful, and opponents less capable of mounting resistance.[5] The case of industrial-relations reform – the biggest gripe of Camdessus and other critics – is perhaps the clearest illustration of the existence of this pattern. Since policy regarding organised labour is used as an illustration in two of the empirical chapters (5 and 6) that analyse how the Indian political system has contributed to making this strategy successful, we will not address that case here.

Fortunately, the proposed amendments to the State Financial Corporation Act also conform to this pattern. They were preceded over the course of two years by as many administrative changes as could be effected without new legislation – and therefore high-profile discussion and debate in parliament, the press, and informal political circles. These were introduced through official 'notifications' by the Industrial Development Bank of India, the administering agency. By April 1995, most state governments, including those run by non-Congress parties, had embraced at least the concept of economic liberalisation (for reasons to be discussed at length in Chapters 4 and 5), and were coming to terms with the need to raise resources.[6] For this and other reasons, the perceived political value of keeping tight control over state financial corporations had been reduced. Opposition MPs who would have vociferously (and possibly fatally) attacked the proposed legislative amendments to the SFC Act had they been introduced in 1992 or 1993 could (by 1995) no longer rely on state governments – even those controlled by their own parties – to support them on this issue. Shorn of their natural allies, opposition parties were conspicuous by their relative silence over the proposed amendments.[7]

---

[5] A strategy that was explicitly stated as such in numerous interviews with both elected officials and bureaucrats in the four main states in which field investigations were made, Karnataka, Maharashtra, Rajasthan, and West Bengal – as well as in New Delhi.

[6] By 1997 the reliance of SFCs on resources from central government financial institutions, particularly the Industrial Development Bank of India (IDBI), had been reduced substantially. One of the reasons why, according to an IDBI official, 'was that SFCs have been able to raise money from other sources'. *Indian Express*, 8 February 1998.

[7] *Business Standard*, 25 April 1995.

The willingness and capacity of the Indian government at the centre and in the states to use the institutional framework of its political system to effect such tactical victories within what is often considered the excessively constraining context of liberal democracy forms the basis for the main argument of this book: that democracies possess greater capacities for promoting change and breaking free of unholy interest-group coalitions than generally thought, but that they do so in ways that are more complex than prevailing theories of the relationship between democracy and development are capable of capturing.

The very nature of this process hints at another reason why the extent of economic reform in India thus far is significant and in need of explanation. This is that reform has taken on a life of its own by generating a chain reaction of demands for more reform from within the domestic political arena. It is in the creation of such momentum – in the sense not of increased pace but of being self-sustaining – that a programme can be considered relatively 'consolidated' politically. If political 'consolidation' is equated with the 'irreversibility' of reform, as it is in the influential collection of case studies edited by John Williamson, then the extent to which reform begins to rely on internal mechanisms of political self-propulsion should be a crucial factor in determining what constitutes consolidation.[8] According to this criterion, India's programme of economic reform is at least as consolidated as any of the others treated as such in Williamson's edited volume, one of the key aims of which was to understand which factors lead to consolidation.

As the next two sections of this chapter will help to demonstrate, there has been a sufficient degree of economic reform to warrant an investigation into the sources of its political sustainability. The first section furnishes an overview of the reform measures that have been implemented or partially implemented. Clearly, any such accounting of accomplishments is vulnerable to a critique of the 'glass-half-empty' variety.[9] This inexhaustive list is provided in the hope that the depth and diversity of reform measures, as well as an appreciation of their considerable downstream implications, will convince the reader that something substantial has taken place that is worthy of explanation. That less comprehensive reform programmes in other countries have generated a quantum of political resistance sufficient to snuff out (at least temporarily) the reforming impulse in their governments should serve as a powerful reminder of what has been achieved in India.

[8] John Williamson (ed.), *The Political Economy of Policy Reform* (Washington, DC: Institute for International Economics, 1994).

[9] See, for instance, Mrinal Datta-Chaudhuri, 'Liberalisation without Reform', *Seminar*, no. 437 (January 1996), pp. 32–5.

The second section of this chapter examines the efforts of Rajiv Gandhi's government to liberalise the Indian economy during the 1980s. The significance of that earlier attempt at economic reform for the arguments advanced in this book stems from the fact that it was cut short. Explanations offered by various political analysts for why the Rajiv-era reforms were *not* sustained provide an important context for our efforts to explain why those initiated by the Narasimha Rao government *were*. Not only were the latter reforms far more substantial; they were introduced by a minority government, and then extended by two coalition governments, one of the centre-left and the other under the leadership of the Hindu right. In brief, Rajiv's short-lived reforms dampened hopes for what was politically feasible in India, making the longevity of the current programme all the more puzzling, and opening a window on to some of the most fiercely debated questions in the study of Indian political economy.

What has been achieved: economic reform since 1991

While there are still many reforms that have yet to be initiated, and others that require further work, what has been achieved to date is very substantial. Since the tendency has been for critics of the government to shift the goalposts by continuously altering the definition of what might constitute a significant level of reform, it has escaped the notice of many commentators that a good number of those reforms that have been instituted were once considered politically unthinkable. That the direction of change has been consistent is the important point. As the CEO of US multinational General Electric told an audience of Indian executives, 'So what if India takes two steps forward and a half step back. It happens everywhere, including America'.[10]

Clearly the most far-reaching reforms have taken place in the area of trade and industrial policy. While it is true that India still has some of the highest tariff levels in the world, when compared to the earlier system (which had *the* highest) the current policy environment represents an enormous transformation of the trade regime. Successive rounds of tariff reductions brought maximum tariff levels down from over 300 per cent in early 1990–1 to 65 per cent by 1994–5,[11] and then down to 40 per cent by 1997–8.[12] Nominal weighted average import tariffs decreased from 87 per cent in 1990–1 to 33 per cent in 1994–5,[13] before dipping all the way

[10] *Asian Age*, 25 January 1995.
[11] World Bank, Country Operations, Industry and Finance Division, India Country Department, South Asia Region, *India: Recent Economic Developments and Prospects* (27 May, 1994), p. v.
[12] Economist Intelligence Unit, *Country Forecast – India*, 1st Quarter, 1998 (London 1998), p. 4.   [13] World Bank, *India: Recent Economic Developments*, p. v.

to 20 per cent for 1997–8.[14]

While these statistics are impressive, in the sense that many observers once considered such steep tariff reductions politically unfeasible, it is the substantial dismantling of the system of bureaucratic controls governing international commerce that represents the more difficult political feat, for it affected not only various economic sectors, but also the politicians and bureaucrats who have profited from their privileged positions as gatekeepers. The import-licensing system was abolished, with the exception of imports of most consumer items. The Cash Compensatory Scheme for exports, which had been a major subsidy item on the federal budget, was withdrawn in an effort to both restore fiscal discipline and promote a greater degree of allocative efficiency. These were combined with successive devaluations of the rupee. The government then ended a year-long experiment with a dual exchange-rate system and announced a further liberalisation of foreign exchange dealings, though not full convertibility. The latter received a setback from the East Asian economic crisis, starting in mid-1997, which provided ammunition to opponents of full capital-account convertibility. India, they argued, was spared the same meltdown because of the shield provided by foreign-exchange controls. Right or wrong, this created an unhelpful political environment for such a splashy reform.

As usual, however, things began to proceed in a more subtle way, laying the groundwork for later action. In early 1998, the Reserve Bank of India (RBI) showed quietly but unmistakably that it was heading towards full convertibility: it decided to allow foreign institutional investors to bring in funds that could later be repatriated, while Indian companies were permitted to borrow on international capital markets with fewer RBI restrictions.[15] By mid-1998, it was clear that the BJP-led coalition would become the third government in succession to pursue a more open trade regime. Despite criticisms that he had not been bold enough, and that the finance minister's subsequent budget statement imposed a special additional duty on imports, Commerce Minister Ramakrishna Hegde did shift a large number of items from the restricted list to 'open general license'. The best evidence that progress continues to be made on the trade front are the outraged reactions from both hardline economic nationalists[16] and business associations from sectors newly subjected to

---

[14] World Bank, *India: Sustaining Rapid Economic Growth* (Washington, DC: The World Bank, 1997), Table 10, p. 46.

[15] Economist Intelligence Unit, *Country Forecast – India*, 1st Quarter, 1998 (London 1998).

[16] See, for instance, the highly critical response of the Swadeshi Jagran Manch, an organisation promoting economic nationalism which is effectively an offshoot of the BJP-affiliated RSS. *The Hindu*, 28 April 1998.

foreign competition.[17] A broader review by the World Bank concluded that India had reduced its tariff rates in 'striking fashion'.[18]

In terms of industrial policy, progress has also been gradual, but it began with a big bang. The centrepiece of reform was the drastic scaling back of the industrial licensing system for all but eighteen 'core' sectors, announced at the beginning of the reform process in 1991. By 1992 the system had been effectively dismantled, with several notable exceptions, such as sugar production. It was this rapid action, which has been strengthened by a range of refinements to policies relating to capital mobility, that grabbed the attention of industrialists, domestic and foreign. Combined with substantial relaxation of the Monopolies and Restrictive Trade Practices (MRTP) Act, which had severely restricted the activities of large business houses, industrial delicensing resulted in a spurt of private-sector investment and corporate restructuring. This higher level of business activity, in turn, led to further regulatory anomalies that necessitated additional reforms in policies relating to taxation, share markets, foreign joint ventures, and infrastructure. Every quarter has registered movement in each of these areas, to the point that by 1998, constant refinements were expected.[19]

Abolition of licensing freed firms to make independent decisions regarding plant capacity and investment levels. But its most important implication in political terms has been to take decisions about the siting of new projects out of the hands of bureaucrats in New Delhi, and to place them under the control of individual business concerns. While the complex impacts of this change will be discussed at length in the section of Chapter 5 that deals with the nature of the federal system, for the present we can mention that one important result has been to increase the salience of state governments as facilitators of new investments. Since businesses can choose where to locate new ventures, state governments have been forced to compete with one another to create investor-friendly climates. While this burdens them with additional responsibilities, it also opens up opportunities for innovative state-level leaders, and tends to draw even reluctant chief ministers actively into the process of liberalisation.

The government of India also opened up to the private sector industries that had previously been the sole preserve of state-owned enterprises.

[17] See, for instance, the remarks of spokesmen for spice, fruit, and horticulture producers in the *Economic Times*, 17 April 1998. For a broader survey, see *Financial Express*, 18 April 1998.

[18] World Bank, *World Development Indicators 1998* (Washington, DC: The World Bank, 1998).

[19] For an indication of the extent to which expectations of change had become second nature, compare the Economic Intelligence Unit's quarterly *Country Forecasts* and *Country Reports* for 1991 with those of 1998.

This is distinct from industrial delicensing: in effect, sectors that had been highly regulated through licensing were deregulated, while sectors that were once completely off-limits to the private sector moved into the highly-regulated-but-available category. The implications of each of these policy shifts differed from sector to sector. There is insufficient data to chart the net impacts on individual sectors; and even if there were, this breakdown would not find clear political correlates because of the political dominance of the traditional family-owned business houses that represent the heart of the Indian corporate sector. The extent to which these conglomerates have diversified over the past several decades – a process fuelled in large part by the system of economic controls – means that what the Tata Group (to take one example) might lose from increased domestic competition in one sector, it might more than gain back by entering into previously restricted industries.

The cost–benefit calculus even for sector-specific industrial associations is significantly complicated by the numerous and constantly shifting changes to the tax system; by policies which affect demand for their products; by macroeconomic variables that may or may not affect their industry with particular intensity; and by calculations as to the future intentions of governments at the centre and the states. Indeed, there have also been innumerable reforms that affect specific industries or industrial subsectors. Some of these have come in the form of regulatory changes that do not require authorising legislation, while others have been included in important acts passed by both parliament and state legislatures. The most important industry to be thrown open to private investors was the power sector. The response has been massive, though not without difficulties. The notion of electricity generation and certain telecommunications subsectors in the hands of private enterprises was considered unthinkable by many Indian business professionals, intellectuals, and bureaucrats in the late 1980s.[20]

Liberalisation of foreign direct investment and foreign portfolio investment is another area in which advocates of reform are constantly demanding further actions, denigrating government measures as inadequate. While some of these assessments may be correct in so far as they relate to India's capacity to compete for foreign investment from faster-

---

[20] This emerged in conversations between the author and a range of informed insiders, including a Supreme Court advocate specialising in commercial law, during field visits to India during 1986, 1987, and 1989. Most commentators considered the nexus of interests too deeply entrenched to be uprooted by Rajiv Gandhi's men, such as non-resident Indian entrepreneur Sam Pitroda, who had been installed as telecommunications 'czar'. The notion that a subsequent minority government, lacking the charismatic authority of the Gandhi name, would prove capable of taking such steps would have been greeted with derision.

liberalising countries in East and South-East Asia, this represents the imposition of a *comparative* framework, the ultimate aim of which is *prescriptive*. They are thus not relevant in understanding the extent to which, *within the Indian context*, the reforms to regulations governing foreign ownership have flown in the face of conventional wisdom about what is politically feasible. As non-resident Indian industrialist Swraj Paul put it, 'If you look at the reforms from India's point of view, there has been great change . . . If you look from the international point of view, there is still a lot to be done'.[21] To argue that India's reforms are half-hearted, and therefore not in need of a political explanation, because foreign investment laws are twice as lax in Indonesia, does not capture the capacity of India's political system to absorb changes that not long ago were considered beyond its competence.

For example, it had long been considered political suicide even to contemplate relaxing the controls on foreign capital imposed by the Foreign Exchange Regulation Act (FERA), 1974. But the government did just that fairly early in the reform process, permitting automatic approval of foreign investment up to 51 per cent of equity holdings in thirty-four industries. That the ceiling should be set at the seemingly irrational figure of 51 per cent (once it has conceded majority ownership, why not allow 100 per cent?) highlights the continued political sensitivity on this issue. It signifies the government's willingness to allow foreign control over joint ventures, but also its desire to be seen to be doing so only grudgingly. As with other areas of reform, the initial push towards reform of policies governing foreign investment gave way to a quieter period, in which less sensational (yet functionally vital and politically fraught) regulatory changes took place. Some affected only one industry. Others were so complex that the impacts were ambiguous and fiercely debated by politicians, business leaders, and trade union officials. The resulting lack of clarity gave some observers and participants in the process the impression of a reforms process adrift. In fact, the bickering over *how* reform measures should be refined and implemented, or what their impacts might be, obscured the extent to which the debate over *whether* reform measures should, would, and perhaps most importantly, could take place had become moot.

The same is true of financial-sector liberalisation. Like most other areas of reform, policy changes in this sector have also occurred in a phased manner. And despite criticism from external agencies as well as foreign investors that the government was proceeding with excessive caution, the Indian government took actions (and continues to take them) which

---

[21] Quoted originally in the *Observer of Business and Politics*, reprinted in *Business World*, 26 January–8 February 1994.

would have been hailed as revolutionary had not expectations been raised by the many other reforms it has enacted. It has, for instance, substantially lowered the statutory liquidity ratio and the incremental cash reserve, instruments through which the government has access to the resources of commercial banks. Interest rates have, with important exceptions, been given relative freedom to seek their natural market levels.

The government has also taken numerous steps to create the conditions under which deregulated financial markets could operate. It has enhanced the capital base of public-sector banks to meet Basle international norms. This has led to a snowball effect whereby quasi-autonomous government agencies – including public-sector financial institutions – have adapted to the logic of a liberalising economy, often in an effort to preserve their own positions in the new environment. The Reserve Bank of India (RBI) created a Board of Financial Supervision, which commenced its activities in late 1994. The RBI also set up a dealer network that could provide liquidity to government security markets. After the post of Controller of Capital Issues was abolished in 1992–3, many reforms were introduced which strengthened the regulatory capacity of its successor, the Securities and Exchange Board of India (SEBI). As a result of many committee reports, the regulations governing primary public issues as well as secondary market trading have been rationalised to bring them closer into line with international norms.

The most recent policy changes in this area have been driven largely by the desire to increase levels of foreign portfolio investment. To term them simply liberalisation would be to mischaracterise what has taken place. In some areas, such as the types of information that company promoters must provide, regulation has actually increased. But when combined with new rules designed to increase effective market liquidity, the net effect will be to create a more transparent and efficient market system.

It is on fiscal policy that critics focus when attempting to portray India's economic adjustment programme as half-hearted. To many economists, a government's capacity to meet targets for reducing the fiscal deficit (measured as a percentage of GDP) is the *sine qua non* of true structural adjustment. The rise in India's fiscal deficit to 7.3 per cent of GDP in 1993–4 was often cited as a watershed, the point at which the Narasimha Rao government abandoned fiscal retrenchment as an objective of state policy. It was portrayed as the first step on a slippery slope back to populism. Nevertheless, when measured over the longer term, the fiscal deficit as a percentage of GDP has come down significantly, and has certainly broken free from the escalating trend that was evident in the pre-reform period. It hovered between 5–6 per cent for most of the period since 1993–4.

But a fixation upon this one statistic is misleading, for it obscures many others of great importance. For instance, net bank credit to the government was reduced by 44 per cent (from Rs. 21.3 billion to Rs. 12 billion) between 1992–3 and 1993–4 – that is, in the year of greatest fiscal 'backsliding'.[22] This allowed credit to flow more freely throughout the economy, contributing significantly to India's emergence from recession into growth, particularly in the industrial sector. Over the longer haul, the amount of general government debt held by the RBI has been reduced from 15 per cent of GDP in 1990–1 to around 10 per cent in the provisional figures for 1996–7, with proportionate declines in both the state and central government subheadings.[23] Back in 1990–1, more than a third of the central government budget deficit was financed by the RBI; by 1997–8 (according to budget estimates), the RBI accounted for less than a quarter of a substantially reduced deficit,[24] and the net general government debt held by the RBI (that is, including both state and central governments) had declined from 15.6 per cent of GDP in 1991–2 to 9.8 per cent in the provisional figures for 1996–7.[25] Over the same period, net external borrowing also declined by a third in terms of its proportional weight among all sources of government finance.[26] Filling the gap have been marketable securities and other domestic borrowing, sources considered less distortive of the economy than the central bank, an institution whose other stabilising functions could easily be threatened.

Other measures reinforce this picture. The ratio of direct to indirect taxes increased from an average of 1:3 during 1985–90 to an average of 2:3 during 1990–5.[27] This is considered an important ingredient of economic restructuring, since direct taxes are considered less distortionary than indirect taxes. A more narrow measurement of this shift can be found by looking at patterns in the four main components of central government revenue during the reform period. The combined take from corporation and income tax rose from 2 per cent of GDP in 1990–1 to 3 per cent by 1997–8, while the combination of excise and customs duties fell from 8.5 per cent in 1990–1 to 7.2 per cent in 1997–8.[28] Non-interest expenditure decreased from 15.8 per cent of GDP to 13.3 per cent between 1990–1 (the last pre-reform year) and 1993–4 (the year of greatest profligacy).

One of the main scourges of the Indian economy, according to neo-liberal economists, is the prevalence of subsidies. And, indeed, even

---

[22] *The Asian Age*, 4 February 1995.
[23] World Bank, *India: Sustaining Rapid Economic Growth*, Table 4, p. 40.   [24] Ibid.
[25] Ibid., Table 14, p. 49.   [26] Ibid., Table 4, p. 40.
[27] Government of India, Ministry of Finance, *Economic Survey 1994/95* (New Delhi, 1995).
[28] World Bank, *India: Sustaining Rapid Economic Growth*, Table 4, p. 40. The 1997–98 figures are government 'budget estimates', though the same figures had been reached in the government's 'revised estimate' for 1996–97.

several years after the initiation of reform subsidies were still ubiquitous. But while outlays for the two largest subsidy items – for food and fertiliser – have remained level or continued to rise, the growth in the overall subsidy burden of the central government has been arrested. Total subsidies grew from Rs. 122 billion in 1990–1 to Rs. 137 billion in the 'revised estimate' for 1995–6. This is an increase of only 12 per cent; but with an average annual inflation rate of roughly 9 per cent, this represents a significant decrease in real terms. Moreover, as a percentage of total central government expenditure, subsidies accounted for just 7.5 per cent in 1995–6, as opposed to 11 per cent in 1990–1. The share of subsidies in GDP, according to one estimate, was reduced from 3.5 per cent in 1990–1 to 2.8 per cent in 1995–6.[29] The World Bank's review of India's reform programme perceives an even greater decline, from 2.3 per cent of GDP in 1990–1 to 1.3 per cent for both 1996–7 and 1998–9.

Expenditure on fertiliser subsidies increased by 44 per cent from 1990–1 to 1995–6. This is about even with inflation, but it is important to recognise that increases in this line-item had been even higher in the years preceding economic reform. The fertiliser subsidy doubled in the three years between 1987–8 and 1990–1 – from Rs. 22 billion to Rs. 44 billion. And had the government fully compensated farmers for the higher prices paid on fertilisers whose prices were allowed to float to market levels in 1992–3, the subsidy level would have been much greater indeed. In other words, subsidy growth was lower during a phase in which important first steps towards liberalisation of the fertiliser market were taken than in the years in which the system was left unchecked. This must count as an accomplishment, even if a limited one. Moreover, the increases revealed in the figures for 1995–6 represent the populism that inevitably precedes an election campaign. Earlier years showed a capacity for a marked reduction, when measured as a percentage of GDP. According to one estimate, the fertiliser subsidy declined from 0.82 per cent of GDP in 1990–1 to 0.56 per cent by 1993–4. Though it had increased again by 1995/96 (to 0.68 per cent of GDP), arresting the escalating cost of this mainstay of the subsidy system is a substantial achievement.[30] The World Bank's review suggests a clear reduction as a percentage of GDP – from 0.8 per cent in 1990–1 to 0.6 per cent in 1996–7 and 1997–8.[31]

[29] The data in this paragraph, unless stated otherwise, are drawn from an analysis of government budget documents performed by the Business Standard Research Bureau, with commentary from the EPW Foundation (Bombay). It was reported in *Business Standard*, 12 August 1996.

[30] Ashok Gulati, 'Agricultural Sector and Liberalisation', *Economic and Political Weekly*, 13 April 1996, pp. 929–30.

[31] World Bank, *India: Sustaining Rapid Economic Growth*, Table 4, p. 40. The 1997–98 figures are government 'budget estimates', though the same figures had been reached in the government's 'revised estimate' for 1996–97.

A similar story is in evidence for the food subsidy. Despite more than doubling in sheer rupee terms during the first five years of reform, the food subsidy has remained remarkably steady throughout the reform period, beginning and ending at 0.5 per cent of GDP, and deviating from that figure in only two of the intervening years, once down by a point and once up by two. The food subsidy, moreover, must be placed in the context of other politically sensitive measures. In particular, it must be recognised that in an effort to placate farmers concerned about other losses, the central government has been rapidly raising the price at which it procures foodgrains. Had the government not also effected similarly unprecedented increases to the prices at which foodgrains are sold through the government-run Public Distribution System (PDS), the food subsidy (the difference between the cost of procurement and the 'issue price' obtained from PDS consumers) would have grown astronomically. While placating farmers might seem a return to populism, the government's willingness to take the highly unpopular decision to continue hiking the price of subsidised food shows a firmer side to the Indian state. As we will see in Chapter 6, the political management of this strategy reveals the political skill, and underhanded tactics, of Indian reformers, as well as the adaptability of Indian political institutions.

One of the major areas in which subsidy savings were made was in debt relief for farmers. In 1994–5, the government finished paying for the massive loan-forgiveness programme for farmers that it inherited from the previous non-Congress government. Resisting the temptation to extend this populist measure was more than many commentators had expected of either the Narasimha Rao government or the 'pro-farmer' United Front government that succeeded it. A subsidy that accounted for Rs. 15 billion in 1990–1 was thus completely phased out by 1995–6. Reductions in subsidies for export and market development also declined dramatically, even in absolute terms. Smaller savings were made in interest subsidies and subsidies to handloom cloth producers.

As for India's slippage on overall deficit reduction targets, even World Bank analysts concede that much of the blame must be attributed to other aspects of economic reform. As the 1994 Country Economic Memorandum stated, 'the 1993–4 fiscal outcome accommodates the considerable fiscal cost of the structural reform programme underway, such as forgone revenues because of lower tariffs, higher interest payments on the government debt because of the liberalization of interest rates, and retrenchment costs associated with public enterprise reform'.[32] In other words, not only does an obsession with deficit statistics mask other important reforms; it

---

[32] World Bank, *India: Recent Economic Developments*, p. ii.

obscures the extent to which the far-reaching nature of other reforms *militated against* the achievement of deficit-reduction targets. Similar factors – combined with some political ones – were cited in the World Bank's 1996 Country Economic Memorandum for the government's failure to meet the fiscal deficit target in 1995–6, though by then it had been reduced to 5.9 per cent of GDP.[33] When considered alongside the 1990–1 figure of 8.3 per cent (and growing), it is clear that India has made significant progress in the area of fiscal responsibility. Even if it has not reformed the system which produced wayward spending habits – and the financial positions of state governments continue to be a source of great uncertainty – India has made progress. No greater claim is required for the premise of this book to be valid.

Reforms in the agricultural sector have been limited. Some consider this a shame, others a blessing. Among the former are analysts who consider neglect of the rural sector the greatest threat to the sustainability of economic reform.[34] Either way, it is worth emphasising that even in this neglected sector, more has been accomplished than almost anyone had expected at the outset of the reform process. Key reforms include abolition of central government restrictions on the movement of agricultural commodities between government-defined zones; the freeing of prices on some types of fertiliser; the substantial abandonment of canalisation of agricultural trade through state trading corporations, though with important exceptions; and the dismantling of quantitative restrictions on agricultural trade. While these measures do not add up to a revolution in agriculture, it is important that we not ignore the substantial efforts made in many Indian states to alter the ways in which governments treat cultivators, agricultural labourers, and the conduct of trade in agricultural commodities. A number of these will be examined in Chapters 5 and 6. We will also probe the significance of efforts by state governments to cope with policy changes that, while marginal in relation to the Indian agricultural sector taken as a whole, have a deep impact on important constituencies in individual states.

[33] World Bank, Country Operations, Industry and Finance Division, Country Department II, South Asia Region, *India: Country Economic Memorandum – Five Years of Stabilization and Reform: The Challenges Ahead* (8 August 1996), p. iii. By 1996, however, the list of reform-related causes of fiscal slippage was expanded to include the rationalisation of the excise system to make it resemble a value-added tax. World Bank analysts also estimated that liberalisation of financial markets had increased the cost of government interest payments by 1 per cent of GDP, demonstrating the complexities which prevent a true appraisal of the extent to which fiscal retrenchment has progressed.

[34] Narendar Pani has been among the most vocal of these critics, arguing that when reformers look at agriculture they see only subsidies, when in fact addressing the agrarian economy from a broader perspective is critical to advancing a sustainable developmental transformation. See his: 'The Services Factor' (21 April 1995), 'Rural Banks without Patronage' (6 September 1996), and 'When Farm Policies Turn Suicidal' (3 April 1998), all from the *Economic Times*.

The political bargains struck by key elites in Karnataka in response to the central government's liberalisation of the coffee sector is just one example of the adaptive strategies that have helped to make reform politically sustainable by filtering it through the integrative mechanisms of regional politics (a central argument of Chapter 5).

As indicated in the introductory chapter, reforms at the state level – particularly those designed as adaptations to either the economic or the political implications of national policy changes – are one of the focal points of this book. Much of what state-level reformers have achieved, it must be said, lacks the sort of sex-appeal that grabs headlines. This tends to obscure the extent to which the liberalising tendency has become rooted politically in India. Arguably, it is when mundane micro-reforms begin to affect the lives and interests of diverse constituencies operating at more localised levels that the cumulative weight of economic liberalisation becomes effectively irreversible. For instance, for the central government, restoring previous tariff levels would be a relatively simple matter administratively, international commitments notwithstanding; undoing all of the complicated reforms at the state level, on the other hand, would be far more difficult. Complex sales-tax reform in Rajasthan, for instance, has simplified administration, reduced evasion, and increased state revenues – but has been achieved only because of elaborate political trade-offs calculated and effected by a state government that is in no position to go back on them. Similarly, the deliberately unheralded 'commercialisation' of public-sector firms in Maharashtra (which has been termed 'backdoor privatisation') and the reorganisation of the State Electricity Board in Orissa are just the type of nuts-and-bolts reforms that any economic liberalisation programme needs if it is to stand a chance of becoming sustainable over the long haul. The same holds true for the substantial reduction in the amount of time required for private investors to obtain bureaucratic clearances from state governments – whether for land acquisition, pollution-control board approval, or tax registration.[35]

A good number of the reform episodes that will be examined in Chapters 4 to 6 are of this type: not headline material (except in the business and trade press), but integrally related to the liberalisation process, to the extent that without them even the big reforms would be unable to deliver the economic benefits that are the basic prerequisite for avoiding a political backlash capable of convincing governing elites to reverse course on reform. To use a convenient shorthand, each type is necessary though

---

[35] A survey of the attitudes of foreign investors in Karnataka, Rajasthan, Maharashtra, and Haryana conducted by the Delhi-based Centre for Research and Planning revealed that state-level bureaucracies had become substantially faster in each of these regions. *India Today*, 15 March 1996, p. 60.

(on its own) insufficient to ensure the political sustainability of reform. To take one particularly arcane example, we will briefly assess the significance of how state governments forged political compromises among interests affected by the central government's reforms to the system of molasses pricing. Without this sort of complementarity, it is maintained, the reform process would have faced far greater (and politically more potent) resistance. The arguments advanced in this book rely on many such examples – relating to the rules governing small-scale industry, amendments to land-reform legislation, the implementation of state-mandated credit targets, and many others – all of which required prolonged deliberation and complex negotiation.

One potential methodological shortcoming of building an argument around such obscure case studies is that it is impossible to assign each successful episode of political management a numerical weighting which signifies its contribution to the political sustainability of reform as a whole. The overall argument rests on an assumption – the accuracy of which is only sometimes demonstrated explicitly – that these region-specific (or sector-specific) reforms are sufficiently linked to larger processes of policy reorientation that they can justifiably be regarded as vital to the creation of a political climate conducive to a continued commitment to the path of change. To argue for the *cumulative* significance of these sometimes obscure episodes in the absence of quantitative indicators for each individually may strike some readers as methodologically unsound.

Two factors may assist in combating this objection. First, a similar assumption is, in effect, built into all studies which seek to explain a political system's capacity to implement policy or institutional reforms. A good example is the cross-national literature which examines why various economic adjustment programmes were cut short, rather than sustained. Because they cannot isolate which individual factors influenced governments finally to bail out of reform commitments, such studies inevitably rely on multi-causal explanations which do not assign individual values or rigorously demonstrate the motivations of governing elites. In this literature, even in the more scientifically phrased studies, there is as much informed speculation, based upon strong suspicions and reasonable assumptions, as is found in this book. The second reason is more straightforward: it is hoped that in discussing each of the 'minor' (or to use a term which highlights their integral role, 'supporting') reforms, the way in which the specific context is portrayed will strongly support the claims of political relevance.

To recapitulate: this section has argued that economic adjustment in India to date has, despite many criticisms, been substantial. It has not satisfied the *hopes* of some, but more importantly it has exceeded the *expectations* of practically everyone. The view that the level of foreign investment in India – more than $5.1 billion in 1996–7[36] – is insufficient refers to a notion of sufficiency based on a prescriptive view of economic need. It in no way undermines the validity of the assertion made in this chapter: that the degree of change represented by that level of inflow (an increase of thirty times over the 1990–1 figure of $165 million[37]) is sufficient cause for an investigation into how the policy shifts which caused it were made politically palatable.

The preceding discussion has also proposed that, in examining the reasons why the overall realignment of economic strategy has become politically sustainable, it is important to give due weight to the many less-visible reforms which are essential components of this process. While it is always possible to highlight what has been left undone, or what was promised but not delivered, such an attitude ignores the significance, in terms of Indian standards of political viability, of those reforms that *have* been implemented. It also deprives us of an opportunity to use the reorientation of economic policy as a lens through which to examine the ways in which an established democracy copes with the perceived need for change. It is worth revisiting the words of the World Bank: 'India has fundamentally altered its development strategy.' It has 'ended four decades of planning and . . . initiated a quiet economic revolution'.[38] Surely, this is a profound reorientation that demands explanation. As we shall see in future chapters, the notion of a 'quiet' revolution is integral to the explanation offered in this book.

Explaining the abandonment of Indian economic reform in the 1980s

We now turn to India's short-lived experiment with economic liberalisation under Prime Minister Rajiv Gandhi in the mid-1980s. It was launched in the budget of 1985–6 and lasted, by most accounts, until some time in 1987, when reform was effectively abandoned. The literature which examined this brief attempt at reform has a direct bearing on the structure of the argument advanced in this book. First, the fact that analysts considered the failure of Rajiv Gandhi's government to sustain reform worthy of explanation implies that our endeavour to explain the sustainability of a far more consequential reform programme under Narasimha Rao is justified (at least as much, if not more so) as an

---

[36] Government of India, Finance Ministry, *Economic Survey 1996/97* (New Delhi, 1997).
[37] Reserve Bank of India, *Report on Currency and Finance*, 1992 (New Delhi, 1992).
[38] World Bank, *India: Country Economic Memorandum*, p. i.

analytical exercise. This is particularly true given that most explanations of Rajiv's failure to remain committed to reform cited domestic interest-group opposition as the main cause. If the cautious and limited reform programme of the Rajiv Gandhi government provoked a political back-lash that sealed its fate, surely it is worth asking why the later, wide-ranging liberalisation programme has not been stopped in its tracks by the same (or similar) political dynamics.

Second, the literature which examined the causes for the Rajiv Gandhi government's abandonment of reform drew conclusions about the nature of Indian democracy which are now open to criticism. Not only were various social groups and economic interests held responsible for effec-tively vetoing any move towards a greater reliance upon markets as the foundation of economic policy; these constraints were held to be sympto-matic of a larger malaise. The Indian state was portrayed as incapable of promoting a reorientation of the policy environment. Depending on the theoretical perspective of the author, the critiques of India's failed effort at adjustment were attributed to one or another *structural feature* of the Indian political system. The implication was that the character of the Indian state made the politically inspired demise of reform *inevitable*.

With the benefit of even greater hindsight, however, we can see the folly of such an assertion: the success of the Narasimha Rao government and its successors in sustaining their reform programmes clearly demonstrates that Indian political conditions are not intrinsically inhospitable to the introduction and consolidation of a market-oriented direction for econ-omic policy. The natural rebuttal that things were different by 1991 – particularly the notion that the force of necessity brought on by the balance-of-payments crisis created a political opening – is unconvincing. The existence of a crisis is no guarantee that a government will respond, and more importantly, that it will be successful in convincing interest groups that 'something must be done'.[39] Indeed, the only convincing rebuttal is that Rajiv Gandhi's liberalisation programme *was* sustained: that is, Narasimha Rao's reform programme was a continuation of some-thing initiated six years earlier, but temporarily delayed by teething pains. There is merit in this view. But, crucially, it does not account for the extreme conclusions concerning the nature of the Indian state which were drawn from what turned out to be a short hiatus in the reforms process. This is an important point, because these conceptions, which were them-selves based upon earlier notions of the constraints on India's develop-mental performance, continue to influence thinking about the nature of

---

[39] I have developed this point in greater detail in Robert S. Jenkins, 'Theorising the Politics of Economic Adjustment: Lessons from the Indian Case', *Journal of Commonwealth and Comparative Politics*, vol. 33, no. 1 (March 1995), pp. 1–24. See especially, pp. 9–10.

Indian politics in particular, and the change-promoting capacities (and mechanisms) of democracy in general.

Let us briefly consider a few of the explanations for the failure of Rajiv Gandhi's government to build a durable reform programme. Some authors had, in fact, predicted the political troubles that lay in store for liberalisation before they had assumed full-blown form. This is our first clue that theoretical biases were in widespread operation. Before serious signs of backsliding by the government were evident, Mrinal Datta-Chaudhuri, arguing from a perspective that emphasised both rational-choice logic as well as flaws in the sequencing of reform, highlighted the potential for individual interests to escape from reforms of such limited scope.[40] The argument was that with so many powerful enemies still at large, even well-meaning efforts at economic reform were doomed: politicians would fall prey to the corrupting influence of rent-seeking interests, while other social groups would learn the lesson that reform was not for real. Another forecast of a political backlash came from Barnett Rubin, who (like the pessimists of the Narasimha Rao years) emphasised that the difficult parts of reform had been delayed, and only the popular measures implemented. He cited particularly the pro-middle-class bias of the policies, maintaining that this represented an unreliable constituency upon which to undertake a major reorientation of development policy.[41]

Because of his established position as a critic of the class bias of the Indian state, it was not particularly surprising to find John Harriss' analysis stressing the state's impotence to carry through a reform programme in the face of the same nexus of privileged classes that had been thwarting redistributive policies since independence.[42] Harriss' analysis conveys the impression of someone whose long adherence to the notion of a 'compromised' state, beholden to class power, caused him to find irresistibly ironic the idea of the same state unable to implement pro-capitalist policies. His underlying conclusion – that decisive action either to the left or right appeared impossible – allowed him to deflect criticism from those who might dismiss his analysis of the failure of redistributive projects as too reliant upon wooden Marxist political economy. Indeed, it was not. The subtlety of both Harriss' framework and his writing is apparent, especially in accounting for the move towards liberalisation in the first place. Yet, for Harriss, the fundamental problem was *structural* – that is, built into the mechanisms of representation and competition.

---

[40] Mrinal Datta-Chaudhuri, 'The New Policy', *Seminar* (December 1985), pp. 18–22.
[41] Barnett R. Rubin, 'Economic Liberalization and the Indian State', *Third World Quarterly*, vol. 7, no. 4 (October 1985), pp. 942–57.
[42] John Harriss, 'The State in Retreat: Why Has India Experienced Such Half-Hearted Liberalisation in the 1980s?', *IDS Bulletin*, vol. 18, no. 4 (1987), pp. 31–8.

James Manor also blamed the abandonment of reform on the power of vested interests, but (crucially) without the same deterministic edge. Manor assigned a good deal of culpability for liberalisation's demise to the personal qualities associated with Rajiv Gandhi, most notably his lack of resolve.[43]

One of the most widely cited accounts of the failure of economic reform to take root in what was considered India's infertile political soil came from Atul Kohli. In two very similar publications,[44] Kohli argued that the efforts of Rajiv Gandhi and his technocratic team ran into a predictable array of political obstacles. While stressing that it was the hard-to-document sense of 'diffuse disillusionment with the national leadership' from within the Congress' ranks that was particularly 'damaging politically',[45] Kohli also gives prominence to the outright hostility of rural groups, as well as leftist economists. His account of the complex layering of intellectual opinion, the general disgruntlement among Congressmen at the brash style in which reform was put forward, and the ever-present danger of a disaffected and volatile rural electorate is cogently argued and generally plausible.

Nevertheless, it is striking that the empirical material Kohli cites to support the political role played by these three forces in applying the brakes to economic liberalisation returns to the interest-group gridlock conception of pluralist democracy. This view has captured the imagination of students of Indian political economy since the 1970s, when efforts increased to explain the country's various economic crises (of investment, of fiscal imbalance, of sectoral bias).[46] Kohli cites the importance of trade unions as a lobby – a group which can be found in both his 'Congress rank and file' and 'moderate left opinion' categories of political resistance to 1980s-era liberalisation. While the occupants of his categories differ substantially, Kohli's explanation of interest-group machinations shares the pessimism regarding the prospects for change found in the most elaborate and influential approach to the political economy of India's arrested development – that of Pranab Bardhan.

Bardhan's work has been so often cited, in the service of so many

---

[43] James Manor, 'Tried, then Abandoned: Economic Liberalisation in India', *IDS Bulletin*, vol. 18, no. 4 (1987), pp. 39–44.

[44] Atul Kohli, 'The Politics of Liberalisation in India', *World Development*, vol. 17, no. 3 (1989); and chapter 11 ('Managing the Economy: Halfhearted Liberalization') of his book, *Democracy and Discontent: India's Growing Crisis of Governability* (Cambridge: Cambridge University Press, 1990), pp. 305–38.

[45] Kohli, *Democracy and Discontent*, p. 323.

[46] For a useful discussion of the development of this phenomenon, see Prabhat Patnaik, 'New Turn in Economic Policy: Context and Prospect', *Economic and Political Weekly*, vol. 21, no. 23 (1986). For a comparative perspective, see John O'Connor, *The Fiscal Crisis of the State* (New York: St. Martin's Press, 1973).

different arguments and prescriptions, that its attractiveness is itself worthy of explanation. Doing so is beyond the scope of this chapter; but clearly its style and forceful logic have contributed greatly to its ubiquity. (John Toye calls it a 'minor masterpiece of compression'.[47]) The point of discussing it here is to trace the aura of *inevitability* which links the many explanations for Rajiv Gandhi's abandonment of reform to a common intellectual ancestor. Not all of the authors specifically rely upon Bardhan; indeed, many take issue with his depiction of civil society.[48] But in explaining the origins of the systemic economic problems that liberalisation was intended to rectify, his ability to straddle Marxist and new-political-economy conceptions of the state[49] made his account very attractive to a diverse array of scholars.

His eclectic model, presented originally as a series of lectures in 1983, includes 'dominant proprietary classes' as the units of analysis and 'rent-seeking' as their mode of economic activity.[50] The result of these groups' combined power and growing greed, according to Bardhan, was a diversion of public expenditure from development (investment) into subsidies (current consumption). This is deemed to be the main culprit behind India's depressing growth performance since 1965. The crucial *deus ex machina*, however, is Bardhan's vaguely game-theoretical explanation of how the tripartite structure of rich farmers, public-sector professionals, and industrial capitalists has perpetuated this sad state of affairs: conflicts among them ensured that none was powerful enough to dominate the state, while their mutual apprehensions concerning the distribution of benefits that might arise from alteration to a system which was collapsing under their combined (and growing) weight meant that change was *structurally* inhibited. Each class was able to veto the initiatives of the others or the state.

With such an elegant yet gloomy narrative in the intellectual air – one that recalled fables like the goose that laid the golden egg – it is perhaps no surprise that explanations for why economic reform was not sustained in

---

[47] John Toye, 'Political Economy and the Analysis of Indian Development', *Modern Asian Studies*, vol. 22, no. 1 (1988), p. 113.

[48] For instance, in a paper which treats the politics of liberalisation in the 1990s, Manor takes issue with Bardhan's failure to include labour as a separate constituency. See James Manor, 'The Political Sustainability of Economic Liberalization', in Robert Cassen and Vijay Joshi (eds.), *India: The Future of Economic Reform* (Delhi: Oxford University Press, 1995).

[49] For an extremely good account of the overlap between various approaches to the study of economic liberalisation in India, see E. Sridharan, 'Economic Liberalisation and India's Political Economy: Towards a Paradigm Synthesis', *Journal of Commonwealth and Comparative Politics*, vol. 31, no. 3 (November 1993), pp. 1–31. He describes Bardhan's approach as a 'fusion of a modified Marxism with neo-classical political economy' (p. 28).

[50] Pranab Bardhan, *The Political Economy of Development in India* (Oxford: Basil Blackwell, 1984).

the 1980s possessed a strong streak of determinism. It is this sense of resignation that made it very difficult for many academic analysts and other commentators to believe that 1990s-vintage economic reform would be able to escape such formidable obstacles.

Oddly, it is Pranab Bardhan himself who provides the careful reader a lifeline out of this despair. This is because, while discounting the possibility of internally generated change – a movement spearheaded by the three dominant proprietary classes themselves – he does not consider the state to be 'captured'. Bardhan, in *some* of his writings, allows much greater scope for creative state autonomy than those who drew on his framework in their analyses of the political demise of economic liberalisation in the late 1980s. Indeed, when economic reform emerged as part of the 'taking India into the twenty-first century' rhetorical enthusiasm of Rajiv Gandhi, Bardhan was among the first to probe the political possibilities this unanticipated kick-start might generate. He argued that '[a]s opportunities to take cuts from deals in foreign trade and agreements with multinational corporations increase, the dependence on domestic capital for contributions to the party funds may diminish, and the autonomy of the national leadership from domestic class interests may rise'.[51]

Nevertheless, Bardhan's various writings reveal a failure to appreciate two further implications of his own arguments. The first concerns the way in which he extends his explanation for 'why the dominant classes, who have so much to gain from economic growth, do not pull together in their long-run collective interests and cooperate in dredging the silted channels' of surplus mobilisation and investment, which were in danger of being overrun by 'patronage and subsidies'.[52] In general, his argument stresses the difficulties of collective action in 'large and heterogeneous coalitions': 'For any single partner in such coalitions, the risks and sacrifices of what may turn out to be one-sided dismantling of carefully cultivated patronage structures may be too costly'.[53] In arguing the particular intensity of this syndrome in the Indian case, however, Bardhan unwittingly reveals one of the reasons why it may be *less* relevant to Indian circumstances. His point is that these 'general [collective action] problems are, of course, far more acute in a country of India's size and bewildering crisscross of interest alignments within the dominant coalition'.[54]

---

[51] Pranab Bardhan, 'Dominant Proprietary Classes and India's Democracy', in Atul Kohli (ed.), *India's Democracy: An Analysis of Changing State-Society Relations* (Princeton: Princeton University Press, 1988), p. 224 (fn 9).

[52] Pranab Bardhan, 'The "Intermediate Regime": Any Sign of Graduation?', in Pranab Bardhan, Mrinal Datta-Chaudhuri, and T. N. Krishnan (eds.), *Development and Change: Essays in Honour of K.N. Raj* (Bombay: Oxford University Press, 1993), p. 343.

[53] Ibid., p. 344.   [54] Ibid.

In other words, greater diversity results in greater difficulty in coordinating an 'elite pact' to save the economic system that laid the golden egg. While this may be true if one assumes a passive state, awaiting coherent instructions from a dominant coalition, it does not capture a situation in which holders of state power are capable of initiating policy reform without a specific mandate to do so. Under such circumstances, which prevail in India, a government which takes the initiative may, in fact, be able to exploit the social divisions represented by the 'bewildering crisscross of interest alignments', even within one segment of the dominant coalition. This is where Bardhan's 'schematic but undoubtedly ingenious'[55] representation of India's dominant proprietary classes begins to look decidedly less ingenious.

As P. N. Dhar has pointed out, Bardhan's classification system has 'under-estimated the economic and political role played by the small-scale industrialists and middle peasants', while virtually excluding 'unionised labour' (particularly in the public sector) from his analysis.[56] Had Bardhan taken proper account of these three groups, then each of his dominant proprietary classes would have looked rather less monolithic, as indeed they do after more than seven years of economic reform in the 1990s. He might then have been more receptive to the potential for such a situation to stand the collective-action dilemma on its head: instead of stressing the difficulties of getting the dominant economic interests to act in concert to save their collective skins, he would have seen that their mutual antagonisms (and internal divisions) would have rendered them ill-prepared to orchestrate a campaign of opposition to a government which had precipitated matters by unveiling a programme of liberalisation without explicit prompting.

Indeed, for all the conceptual elegance of Bardhan's marriage of Marxist and rational-choice elements, the sustainability of liberalisation in the 1990s suggests that the messy realities of interest-group pluralism may have far more explanatory power. Such an explanation also has the great advantage of avoiding determinism, the primary flaw of the literature which mistook the failure of Rajiv's reform efforts for a systemic failure of Indian democracy. While a diversity of interests may provide even a cautiously reform-minded government with room for manoeuvre, it does not guarantee a result. Human agency (in the form of political skill and the willingness to respond to political incentives) and historical contingencies (in the form of institutional legacies) can either facilitate or thwart the reformist ambitions of a government possessing only short- or

---

[55] Toye, 'Political Economy', p. 113.
[56] P. N. Dhar, 'The Political Economy of Development in India', *Indian Economic Review*, vol. 22, no. 1 (1987), p. 1.

medium-term autonomy. This book is not arguing that Indian conditions *had* to produce a sustainable policy reform, only that certain mechanisms proved extremely helpful.

Bardhan's second oversight concerns the nature of reform programmes themselves. He again fails to appreciate the ambiguous implications of another of his statements in support of the collective-action hypothesis. His argument is that the 'crowded agenda and the weight of the pre-existing list of complex understandings in large lobbying coalitions make any negotiation on changing the basic rules of the game excruciatingly slow'.[57] This statement makes three key presumptions concerning the way in which a state will introduce policy reform, none of which are valid *ex ante*. Indeed, upon closer examination, it is clear that none of them conform to the specific case of liberalisation in 1990s India. First, it assumes negotiation, and reaching consensus, *before* the initiation of reform. As we have seen, however, governments can seize the initiative to turn the tide of events. Second, it assumes that a government will signal its intention of 'changing the basic rules of the game', when in fact the Indian government found it politically expedient to pile one piecemeal reform on top of another while underplaying the radical implications of what it was doing. And third, Bardhan's pejorative depiction of the 'pre-existing list of complex understandings' as possessing an inhibiting 'weight' blinds him to the potential for these 'complex understandings' to function as political 'institutions'. As the case material discussed in Chapter 5 demonstrates, institutions of this sort were crucial in providing governments at both the national and state levels the means to negotiate side deals and to allay fears among various interests regarding the radical consequences of its reforms.

Bardhan's assumption that reformist ambitions must be stated unambiguously is also apparent in his analysis of why East Asian countries have been able to solve the 'paradox of liberalism' – in which strong states are required to impose 'the discipline of dynamic market competition, resisting the inevitable forces of clientelistic pressure' – while India has not.[58] Unlike 'the well-developed networks of MITI in Japan or IDB in Taiwan, which allow industry experts within the State apparatus', in India 'a social contract between the State and the dominant classes on a project of national economic transformation is rare and increasingly so'.[59] Given that Bardhan is operating within a model based upon dominant coalitions of monolithic interests, it is understandable that he would find it difficult to grasp that nothing so grand as a 'social contract' is necessarily required, or even desirable, if a government proclaims intentions that are more

---

[57] Bardhan, 'The "Intermediate Regime"', p. 344.   [58] Ibid.   [59] Ibid., p. 345.

modest than 'a project of national economic transformation'. The Indian reform programme has succeeded largely because it proceeded by stealth. The ambiguity surrounding the long-term consequences of reform, and the government's capacity to exploit divisions between interests, were major advantages for reformers seeking a sustainable reorientation of policy. Democracy's disorder helped to quiet discontent.

Bardhan himself eventually conveys a tacit recognition of the potential contribution of interest-group realignment to adjustment's political sustainability. Discussing the prospects for the reforms begun in 1991 to result in a *durable* reshaping of the economy', he notes that we 'should not overlook some perceptible changes [in the underlying political economy] . . . that have come about in recent years'.[60] He emphasises the creation of a more broad-based 'middle class', which acts as a new, though vague, social and political identity:

Its members certainly belong to different parts of what I have described earlier, as the three dominant classes in India. One significant difference may be that in recent years some parts of these dominant classes have come a bit closer in their class interests as well as their life-styles.[61]

He cites two developments as critical: the diversification of rich-farmer families into private trade, real-estate, and small industry, and the emergence of new technologically oriented medium-scale firms into the 'industrialist class'. The former leads to a blurring of the lines between the rural rich and industrialist categories, while the latter undermines the structural integrity of the industrialist class itself by creating increased competition within it. Under the weight of liberalisation, Bardhan's neat groupings have begun to look less neat. It is difficult not to wonder whether they were ever coherent members of a 'dominant coalition' to begin with.

We may also wonder whether, without acknowledging it, Bardhan the synthesiser of Marxist class analysis and new-political-economy approaches to determining the incentives and constraints facing these classes is giving way to Bardhan the liberal-pluralist. The processes of fusion and fragmentation that he discusses are made possible by the combination of a relatively autonomous state, which initiates policy changes that generate new economic niches, and a wider political system that permits such groups to organise freely in pursuit of non-market gains through public and private lobbying. By clinging to the language of 'class interests', Bardhan appears to remain consistent with his previous framework, even if now allowing for the effects of unpredictable change. But a

[60] Bardhan, 'The "Intermediate Regime"', p. 350 (emphasis added).   [61] Ibid.

deeper understanding of the forces at work in Indian political economy –
one which requires fewer conceptual somersaults to avoid contradiction –
would be better served by taking as our frame of reference Lloyd and
Susanne Rudolph's work.[62]

Of particular concern is the Rudolphs' focus on the oscillations between constrained and autonomous action by the Indian state. They do
not posit a grand theory, noting that there is no clear correlation in
post-Independence India between positive economic policy-making
habits and either periods of relative autonomy ('command politics') or
those in which the state was constrained by 'demand politics'. What they
have provided is a conception of Indian politics that recognises the
centrality of contingency and unforeseen consequences, while stressing
the central mediating role of the state. Moreover, the state's capacity to
act as a 'third actor' – between labour and capital – stems from the fact
that these 'two traditional adversaries in class politics . . . are marginal
forces in the Indian political arena'.[63] This is a far cry from Bardhan's
dominant-proprietary-class model, in which big business held effective
veto power over important areas of policy.

The range of the Rudolphs' study is formidable, but what is relevant for
the present are the special circumstances which they consider to have
given rise to this 'third actor' role. In particular, they cite the consensus on
the broad framework of socialism. With this consensus clearly threatened
by liberalisation, the ability of the state to continue acting with relative
autonomy would seem to be commensurately endangered. And yet this
book argues that it is still managing to do so. There are three inter-related
reasons why this is a valid proposition. First, the state continues to occupy
the central role in managing the politics of identity. To the extent that
issues associated with reconstituted identities are the primary forces
driving the organisation of political parties and the contesting of elections, class politics will remain marginal, and the state will derive considerable autonomy in relation to economic policy.

The second reason concerns one of the other distinctive features of
Indian politics highlighted by the Rudolphs – the existence of 'demand
groups' such as students and farmers, which they liken more to social
movements than organised interests. It is not the existence of such
groups, but the tendency of Indian politics to continue producing new
ones, that provides plausible grounds for expecting the state to maintain
its ability to carve out significant niches for autonomous activity. Demand
groups provide a constant source of fresh material from which regional

[62] Lloyd I. Rudolph and Susanne Hoeber Rudolph, *In Pursuit of Lakshmi: The Political
Economy of the Indian State* (Chicago: University of Chicago Press, 1987).
[63] Ibid., p. 259.

politicians in particular fashion new electoral constituencies. It is the ever-present prospect of such realignments that provides state-level politicians the capacity to resist the demands of established 'organised' interests. Bardhan's framework does not allow for such change, his late and implicit conversion to liberal-pluralism notwithstanding.[64]

The third reason why we can rely upon the liberalisation-threatened notions advanced by the Rudolphs, and yet still expect state autonomy to persist, stems from the way in which they characterise interest-group representation in India. Their notion of 'involuted pluralism' is particularly relevant to the way in which this book approaches the case material on Indian economic reform in the 1990s. They define involution as 'the excessive multiplication of less effectual units',[65] using examples from both labour unions and business associations which have splintered, weakening themselves in the process. The Rudolphs argue that it is the centrality of the state (and its ability to use incentives) that produces this dysfunctional replication, and that '[i]nvoluted pluralism as a form of representational mediation strengthens command politics and weakens demand politics'.[66] In other words, the tendency for interests to fragment allows the state considerable autonomy. Again, the relative retreat of the state would seem to threaten this niche, as its ability to deploy resources in ways that lead to 'excessive multiplication' declines. But this need not be the case. If we conceive of economic reform as something initiated and directed by the state, then it may not come as a surprise that governing elites in many corners of the state are able to orchestrate its implementation in a manner capable of dividing interests long enough to forestall

---

[64] His one reference to liberal pluralism is to state that in an 'open pluralist polity with the slow but growing assertiveness of some of the subordinate groups the liberal policy changes announced from above cannot acquire durable political legitimacy until and unless some serious attempts are made by the elite in striking downward alliances with some of these groups in the form of trying to work out some minimal social security safety net and extensive public works programme' (Bardhan, 'The "Intermediate Regime"', p. 351). In fact, the level of expenditure on public works programmes increased dramatically during the reform period. Bardhan deflects attention away from the significant implications of interest-group proliferation for the political sustainability of economic reform by stating, rather breezily, that 'these changes and realignments in the composition and attitudes of the dominant coalition do not mean that the political resistance to far-reaching reforms in economic policy is *likely to wither away*' (p. 351, emphasis added). He cites the reluctance of 'political heavyweights', 'unionized workers', 'newly mobilized social groups', the 'affluent classes', and 'small propertied interests' to resign themselves peaceably to changes that will negatively affect them. Yet, no one would have expected these voices of resistance to 'wither away'. The important dynamics are: (1) the ways in which interest-group proliferation and conflict undermines their capacity to provide *effective* resistance (of the kind which would cause reformers to reverse course); and (2) the role of governing elites in actively fomenting such discord while managing its most pernicious effects by striking individual bargains.

[65] Rudolph and Rudolph, *In Pursuit of Lakshmi*, p. 257.   [66] Ibid.

resistance to reform until it is too late. Interests that the state created and manipulated through state planning have, during the gradual introduction of quasi-market conditions, also been subjected to the sort of tactics that can create multiple channels of representation. The political sustainability of reform has not undermined the conditions which the Rudolphs considered instrumental to the creation of relative state autonomy; in fact, it has relied on them.

It is for this reason that we are able to chart a course away from the excessive determinism of political economy explanations derived from Pranab Bardhan's theory-driven model of a conflict-ridden dominant coalition and an impotent state. We are able instead to read the events of the past eight years through a lens which reaffirms the validity of Stanley Kochanek's empirically derived observation of more than twenty years ago:

Policy initiatives usually come from government . . . not from the larger society . . . so most groups are forced to take a negative or defensive rather than a positive stance . . . [T]he pattern of public policy . . . has concentrated vast powers in the hands of government officials. This power enables them to control and regulate the internal affairs and external conduct of business, trade unions, and other organisations . . . . Far from being an outcome of interest group activity, as group theory would have it, public policy in India exerts a significant impact on group mobilization and on behaviour.[67]

Moreover, it is not only the American political science tradition of studying political change in terms of liberal interest-group pluralism that supports a view of the Indian state as a creative initiator in the process of change. Sudipta Kaviraj, India's leading exponent of Gramscian analysis, comes to similar conclusions. Kaviraj has argued that many conceptions of the state in India have a 'tendency to underestimate the political functions of the state, and to view the state as merely an *expression* of class relations rather than a *terrain*, sometimes an independent actor in the power process'.[68]

Before proceeding to the next chapter, which examines the experiences of other countries with economic reform and the theoretical conclusions

---

[67] Stanley Kochanek, *Business and Politics in India* (Berkeley: University of California Press, 1974), p. xii. Quoted in Rudolph and Rudolph, *In Pursuit of Lakshmi*, p. 256.

[68] Sudipta Kaviraj, 'A Critique of the Passive Revolution', *Economic and Political Weekly*, November 1988, Special Number, p. 2431 (emphases in original). I am grateful to Satyajit Singh for alerting me to this source. For a useful discussion of how theoretical conceptions of the Indian state stand up to empirical data relating to the evolution of irrigation policy, see Chapter 3 ('The State, Classes and Irrigation Development') of his *Taming the Waters: Political Economy of Large Dams in India* (Delhi: Oxford University Press, 1997).

drawn from those experiences in the literature on the politics of adjustment, let us briefly address one potential criticism: that the arguments in this book regarding the capacity of Indian democracy to effect change suffer from an excessive reliance upon features of Indian politics which are patently undemocratic. In other words, India faced an easier task in so far as its elites were able to *subvert* democracy. Its capacity to sustain policy reform is thus less worthy of explanation, because the political system's crypto-authoritarian tendencies provide most of the explanation. While the discussion in the next chapter should help to deflect this criticism by citing evidence which illustrates the extent to which archetypical democracies such as the United States and Britain rely upon similar tactics, for the present it is worth briefly outlining a case for why sustaining structural adjustment in India should have been even *more* difficult than in most other democracies in the developing world and former Eastern Bloc. The objective is to support further the contention that what has transpired in India since July 1991 is worthy of explanation.

The Indian government faced three additional obstacles.[69] First, the Narasimha Rao government, for almost half of its term, was a minority government, reliant upon the support of elements outside the Congress Party. The United Front government that took office in the wake of the 1996 general election had to rely to an even greater extent on support from outside its ranks, while the BJP government that succeeded it was saddled with an even more fractious coalition. Because they lack a clear mandate, and their ideological inconsistency breeds public suspicion, such governments find themselves robbed of the traditional 'honeymoon period', during which democratic governments are allegedly given the benefit of the doubt by sectoral interests and the public at large.[70]

Second, the Narasimha Rao government which carried the reform baton for the first five years was not able to associate the previous policy dispensation with a discredited authoritarian predecessor, or even a rival party. While it could blame the non-Congress National Front government of 1989–91 for poor stewardship of the economy, and for fuelling unrealistic expectations of the state through widespread populism, the state-controlled economy that the Narasimha Rao government inherited

---

[69] These three are drawn from Stephan Haggard and Steven B. Webb, 'What Do We Know About the Political Economy of Economic Policy Reform?', *The World Bank Research Observer*, vol. 8, no. 2 (July 1993), pp. 143–68.
[70] See John Williamson and Stephan Haggard, 'The Political Conditions for Economic Reform', in J. Williamson (ed.), *The Political Economy of Policy Reform* (Washington, DC: Institute for International Economics, 1994), pp. 568–9; and Robert H. Bates and Anne O. Krueger, 'Generalizations Arising from the Country Studies', in R. H. Bates and A. O. Krueger (eds.), *Political and Economic Interactions in Economic Policy Reform: Evidence from Eight Countries* (Oxford: Blackwell, 1993), p. 459.

was clearly a product of the same democratic political regime. In fact, and in the public mind, it was the legacy of the Congress Party's official commitment to 'socialism'. What Narasimha Rao's government was unable to take advantage of was a phenomenon aptly summarised by Haggard and Webb: '[n]ew democratic governments taking over from authoritarian regimes are in an especially good position to trade political gains against short-term economic losses. Spain in the late 1970s and Eastern Europe in recent years demonstrate this pattern'.[71] In India there were no 'usurping generals' to demonise.

The third impediment posed by the contingencies of India's political history was the legacy of earlier abandoned reform programmes. The failure of both Indira Gandhi in the early 1980s and Rajiv Gandhi in the mid-1980s to remain committed to liberalisation made many political and economic actors sceptical of reform's staying power, causing them to hedge their bets. The risks posed by this attitude were not inconsiderable. Dani Rodrik, among others, has argued that since successfully sustaining reform requires a response from economic agents, which in turn relies upon confidence that reform will be sustained, reforming governments can be held hostage to a vicious cycle in which lack of faith in the capacity to effect change becomes a self-fulfilling prophecy.[72] Since economic agents often have few cues on which to base their assessments of sustainability, they often extrapolate from the previous experience. In such a situation, past failures can doom present efforts. This, obviously, is not an iron-clad rule. Otherwise, very little in the world would be subject to change.

For economic agents to calculate that present reform efforts will not meet the same fate as earlier ones, they require (at the least) indications of a more conducive set of circumstances. In the Indian case, however, the two characteristics listed above – a minority government and continuity of political regime – were clearly less likely to convince anyone that things would be different this time around. And indeed the Cassandras heavily outweighed the Pollyannas during at least the first three years of the adjustment process. Had Indians been more aware of the frequency with which reform programmes in other countries had been thwarted by political pressures, their pessimism would likely have been strengthened. We turn now to the comparative and case-study literature which details these experiences and the theoretical literature which attempts to draw conclusions from observed patterns of success and failure in sustaining economic reform.

---

[71] Haggard and Webb, 'What Do We Know'.
[72] Dani Rodrik, 'How Should Structural Adjustment Programs be Designed?', *World Development*, vol. 18, no. 7 (1990), pp. 933–47.

3 Theoretical and comparative perspectives on the politics of economic reform

Chapter 2 presented an overview of the major changes in Indian economic policy during the period 1991–8. The objective was to establish that something substantial had indeed taken place, and that it requires explanation. These reforms were also situated within the context of reform episodes that took place during the 1980s, in which a pattern of 'reform and retreat' was clearly in evidence. We then examined various attempts in the literature on Indian political economy to explain this pattern – that is, to explain the inability of earlier Indian governments to sustain economic reform. The literature explained this failure largely with reference to *structural features* of the Indian political system. The culprit was a sclerotic democracy, captured by powerful interests and unable to extricate itself from a deep-seated malaise stemming from the predominant pattern of state–society relations.

Yet, liberal economic reform, as we know, made a comeback only four years after its demise in late 1987. During the next five years its principles seeped further into economic policy than many had previously thought possible. If economic reform has returned from the grave more healthy than ever, then the coroners who passed judgement on its earlier much-exaggerated death have a lot to answer for. Renewed attempts in the 1990s to reform the Indian economy do not completely invalidate the explanations for why the efforts of the 1980s were abandoned. Clearly, the power of vocal interests had a bearing on the decision to reverse course. But the broad theoretical implications drawn from these rather unremarkable observations were unwarranted. Democratic politics is not the enemy of change – otherwise how could the process of economic reform have reached the level of consolidation found in India today? We need an explanation for why reform is succeeding, instead of one which enumerates reasons for why it is doomed to fail.

In this chapter we will situate this problematic within the comparative and theoretical literature on the politics of economic adjustment. In the years since the reversal of India's late-1980s reform programme was explained with reference to complex, though excessively mechanistic, models of the Indian state, there arose among scholars studying a wide range of adjustment programmes throughout the developing world a theoretical interest in why some reform programmes are sustained while others are not. The consensus that has emerged is that a democratic political system need not be an impediment to reform. It is important to note that there is no general belief that democratic political systems are *better* at implementing liberal economic reforms. Nor is this book making any such argument. For those who believe that democracy is a good in itself, however, it is worth attempting to understand the *means* by which a preferred political system can, in some cases, realise what are also considered desirable policy objectives.

Thus, the present chapter situates our explanation for why reform has been able to surmount political obstacles in India within the literature which attempts to understand the mechanisms at work in other countries where reform has been sustained amidst democracy. The objective of this exercise is to identify those theoretical generalisations about the interaction between democratic politics and economic reform which are called into question by a close reading of the Indian case. This survey of the comparative literature seeks to highlight analytical approaches that fail to capture the complexities inherent in processes of change, as well as those that contain useful insights, concepts, and methods which have informed our analysis of the Indian case. These are drawn from the case-study literature on both authoritarian and democratic regimes.

We will examine, first, the literature with which our findings from the Indian case have led us to take issue, beginning with the form in which these ideas have had the most influence: as part of the agenda of multilateral financial institutions and bilateral donors which aims to foster democracy and 'good government' in aid-recipient countries. We will then examine the theoretical approaches from which aid-agency conceptions of the relationship between politics (particularly democratic politics) and economic reform have been drawn. The final section of the chapter examines country case studies in which sometimes surprising parallels with the Indian case have emerged. To the extent that these shed light on the value of one or another analytical approach, their implications will be discussed.

Assessing democracy's powers of persuasion

Since the early 1980s, when conditionality-based lending programmes began to spread rapidly throughout the developing world, debates concerning the interactions between economic and political factors in the process of market-oriented policy reform have become considerably more subtle. The great variation in country cases instilled an appreciation for the unpredictability of such complex events. There was also a profound change in the thinking about the capacity of democracies to permit, or even to assist, the process of market-oriented economic reform. In fact, it is fair to say that the pendulum has swung from one extreme to the other: from the conventional wisdom that democracies – with their tendency towards collusion between vote-seeking politicians and rent-seeking interests – were obstacles to reform, to a new, and fairly widespread consensus that democratic politics can be a positively useful ingredient in promoting policy change. It has been a long and uneven road from democracy's demonisation to its apotheosis, with many false turns, much backtracking, and still considerable debate concerning the current state of play and the way ahead.

Indeed, large multi-country studies have been unable to establish significant correlations between regime type and either the economic success or political sustainability of reform (leaving aside for a moment the question of the relationship between economic success and political sustainability). Thus, while individual country cases have led to a significant shift of opinion with respect to generalisations about the potential practical utility of democratic politics – that is, democratic politics does not necessarily obstruct, and *sometimes* actually facilitates, policy change – there has been no rush to insist that economic liberalisation *requires* a democratic political system in order to avoid the many political pitfalls into which it might slip.

Regardless of the inability to formulate such generalisations on the basis of large-sample studies, the one area of inquiry where the shift of opinion has acquired the dimensions of a pendulum-like swing concerns the manner in which democratic political systems adapt to the pressing need for change. Of particular interest is the way in which they structure relationships between governing elites and sectoral interests. In general, the conception of political change that has emerged is one of committed reformists using the open sphere of competitive politics to make a persuasive case for the merits of general policy reorientation as well as for the advantages of specific reforms. While the terms in which this conception is put forward vary from author to author, it clearly represents an underlying belief in the 'salesmanship' function of democratic politics. This is particularly true when the studies from which these conclusions are drawn concern newly democratising countries, rather than cases in which democracy has long been entrenched. Preoccupied with the contrasts between new democracies and their authoritarian predecessors, the literature over-emphasises democracy's wholesome aspect – particularly democratic governments' skill at 'selling reform' to open-minded electorates.

The display of such skills is prompted, according to this logic, by governments' need to enter into a more balanced 'public debate'. Van de Walle argues that this can even be the case in authoritarian regimes, such as mid-1980s Nigeria, where 'Babangida had no intention of tolerating an open-ended policy debate, but sought rather to gain support for a program he had already come to believe was necessary'.[1] Without citing any supporting evidence, Van de Walle then goes on to argue that '[d]emocratic governments may be better equipped to handle such national public debates and indeed to "steer" them in the desired direction'.[2] Especially when they develop 'effective' political parties, he argues, democratically accountable governments 'may find it less difficult to sell economic reform programs than the more authoritarian regimes they replace'.[3] This tends to conjure up a rather unrealistic high-school civics-lesson image of democratic politics: open flows of information allowing public opinion, prodded by a committed governing elite, to coalesce around optimal solutions. In this construction, democracy hands elected governments the tools with which to guide electorates towards the light of truth, and (just as importantly) to discredit the self-serving rhetoric of sectoral interests who oppose well-intentioned reform.

Blinded by historical amnesia, analyses of this type suffer from two main shortcomings. First, they blatantly ignore the extent to which democratic governments have themselves been responsible for drawing their economies into the populist tailspins from which adjustment is designed to extricate them. Surely, if persuasive powers were enough to overcome the power of vested interests, democratically elected governments would never have led their countries into such messes to begin with, or would at least have changed course much earlier. And second, they presuppose a clear case of neo-liberal 'conversion' on the part of democratic governments, who are then expected to proselytise their followers in national public debates. In fact, many executive elites, operating in either democratic or authoritarian contexts, embark upon adjustment programmes for political reasons of their own. They may not have been convinced by (or even fully understand) the World Bank's logic for effecting adjustment measures. Robert Bates, for instance, has argued that Latin American and sub-Saharan African governments may be operating under a radically different 'utility function' than World Bank economists:

[1] Nicolas Van de Walle, 'Political Liber[aliz]ation [sic] and Economic Policy Reform in Africa', *World Development*, vol. 22, no. 4 (1994), p. 491. [2] Ibid., p. 492.
[3] Ibid.

It is my deepest suspicion . . . that structural adjustment does not mean the expansion of the private sector and the retrenchment of governments. Rather, it may well mean the opposite, and represent an attempt by the public sector to revive an old order which proved unsustainable . . . In the 1980s, the existing structures of power were crumbling in many developing countries; structural adjustment represents policy reform, conducted by governments; and it is therefore likely more to represent a reassertion and underpinning of the previous ways of doing business than any sort of fundamental reform.[4]

A similar sentiment is found in Jean-François Bayart's study, *The State in Africa*. Bayart argues that economic impacts of structural adjustment, intended or otherwise, can often yield political results that, depending on the specific context, may require no further 'adjustment':

By drying up the principal channels of autonomous accumulation without creating a true market, [structural adjustment] suits the hand of the president who finds himself restored to his position of principal distributor of sinecures. Abdou Diouf (in closing down ONCAD, the unofficial cashbox of the 'barons' of the Parti Socialist), Sassou Nguesso (in launching a 'structural adjustment plan') and Houphouet-Boigny (in dissolving the State companies, in abolishing the posts of directors-general, in accepting the demand of the World Bank for separating the functions of management and accounting in the civil service and in attaching the Department of Public Works to the Presidency of the Republic) have all three recovered their freedom of action with regard to a political class and a bureaucracy which had cut loose financially from the centre, and they have regained their control over a patrimonial machine which had run out of hand at the expense of a wild and runaway foreign debt. The policies of structural adjustment are thus not so very different from the policies of nationalism during the two previous decades.[5]

Bates and Bayart may be understating the unpredictable implications and ultimate imperatives of even modest changes in the structure of economic ownership and regulation, as well as the effects of greater integration into the world economy.[6] In other words, 'tactical' liberalisation programmes can take on a life of their own which is beyond the ability of their initiators to control. But the basic point, which is nowhere to be found in the

---

[4] Robert Bates, 'The Reality of Structural Adjustment: A Sceptical Appraisal', in Simon Commander (ed.), *Structural Adjustment and Agriculture: Theory and Practice in Africa and Latin America* (London: Overseas Development Institute, 1989), p. 223.

[5] Jean-François Bayart, *The State in Africa: The Politics of the Belly* (Harlow: Longman, 1993), pp. 225–6.

[6] Indeed, the strong pressures for democratisation that followed adjustment programmes in Kenya and Malawi, two of the cases cited by John Toye in his analysis of the complex factors which influence the preferences of governmental elites (in these cases, direct Presidential ownership stakes in agribusiness), illustrate that reforming elites can sometimes find themselves hostage to a reforming logic which they thought they could control. See John Toye, 'Interest Group Politics and the Implementation of Adjustment Policies in Sub-Saharan Africa', *Journal of International Development*, vol. 4, no. 2 (November 1992), pp. 190–1.

theoretical literature, is well worth contemplating: that state elites enter into the adjustment process believing that they can steer it towards their own ends. This perhaps explains why they decide to adjust at all. And if they begin with their own objectives, they are likely to have their own ways of deciding when these objectives have been met.

Thus, many governments choose to put a halt to their reform programmes, despite what are seen as efforts to 'sell' them to their publics in a 'national debate'. Babangida's government, after all, backtracked on its commitment to reform not long after the conclusion of the 'public debate' it engineered. The great majority of India's governing elites, including the prime minister who initiated reform, were not 'converted' to the neo-liberal faith. Indeed, they were not even committed politically to liberalisation until they perceived the possibilities of responding to illicit incentives, manipulating formal and informal political institutions, and exercising their considerable political skills in support of both.

That democracy's powers of persuasion should be considered the chief reason for its ability to promote policy change is a recurrent theme in commentaries on the politics of economic reform in India. The news magazine *India Today* began a scathing editorial on the Narasimha Rao government's flirtation with pre-election populism by stating that, '[t]ill sometime back, Prime Minister P. V. Narasimha Rao had seemed to have realised that sticking tenaciously to a successful economic-reform programme was a saleable election platform'.[7] What the various allegations of corruption against his government should have taught the prime minister, it argued, 'is that the reform process must not be carried out either by stealth or by executive muscle'.[8] Yet, there is little evidence that the prime minister ever actually believed in the direct vote-winning potential of economic reform, and even less evidence that such a strategy was ever followed. As the same editorial admits, 'intellectual arguments in favour of reform are unlikely to go down well with the electorate'.[9] Protestations by well-meaning economists to the contrary notwithstanding,[10] the political sustainability of Indian economic adjustment can largely be explained by the government's ability to pursue a strategy of 'reform by stealth', though this would not have been possible in the absence of a conducive

---

[7] 'Fiscal Responsibility' (editorial), *India Today*, 15 September 1995, p. 3. See also 'Create a Political Base for Reform' (editorial), *Observer of Business and Politics*, 3 February 1994.

[8] 'Fiscal Responsibility' (editorial), *India Today*, 15 September 1995, p. 3.   [9] Ibid.

[10] Amit Bhaduri and Deepak Nayyar argue that '[t]ransparency combined with debate, which highlights both the consensus and dissensus, will give our economic policies the essential element of stability, where both continuity and change are an integral part of a long-term view. The present set of policies is not characterized by such stability because the government has been neither open nor transparent about economic liberalization'. See Amit Bhaduri and Deepak Nayyar, *The Intelligent Person's Guide to Liberalization* (New Delhi: Penguin, 1996), p. 178.

constellation of political incentives, institutions, and skills.

In a similar vein, Jagdish Bhagwati argued that the political storm surrounding the Enron power project in Maharashtra had taught reformers a lesson, and that henceforth 'transparency' would be the watchword with respect to investment policy.[11] There is no reason to believe that this will be true. While governments at both the centre and in the states will increasingly rely upon competitive tendering for investment in infrastructure projects – indeed, they had already been doing so long before the Enron project was cancelled by the subsequent Maharashtra government's review committee – there are many ways to favour particular interests in the organisation of such procedures, as we will see in the discussion of political incentives in Chapter 4. Indeed, once they came to power in Maharashtra, the parties which had spearheaded the anti-Enron protests while in opposition re-negotiated the deal with as little transparency or public debate as had their predecessors in office. This naturally raised suspicions of corruption, and at the very least indicated that, contrary to Bhagwati's pronouncement, reformers had not learned the lesson he hoped they had.

The notion of relying upon the educative function of democratic government is echoed in a broad cross-section of the literature which attempts to formulate generalisations from case-study evidence, including studies devoted to specific sectoral issues. Carol Graham's study of the politics of protecting the poor during economic adjustment – which examined the cases of Chile, Bolivia, Peru, Zambia, Senegal, and Poland – argued that the first lesson to emerge from these countries' experiences was 'that open political environments are more likely to be places in which there is a broad base of support for economic reform and therefore a policy atmosphere in which effective poverty reduction can take place'.[12] Graham's reasoning is that '[i]n an open environment, the government is more likely to communicate with the public and increase popular understanding of the reform process, an effective means to create a political base of support for change'.[13] While there may be some merit in thinking of governments as proselytisers, Graham overstates the extent to which democratic governments rely upon their powers of persuasion.

At least as important are tactics which mask governments' true intentions. These do not appeal to the reasonableness of electorates. They rely instead on the ability of governments to outmanoeuvre them. Democratic governments face a difficult dilemma: they must deliver relief to extremely vulnerable social groups at a time when more vocal (but less deserving)

---

[11] *India Today*, 15 September 1995, p. 80.
[12] Carol Graham, *Safety Nets, Politics, and the Poor: Transitions to Market Economies* (Washington, DC: Brookings Institution, 1994), p. 252.   [13] Ibid.

interests are demanding compensation for losses suffered due to adjustment. Their capacity to do so relies crucially on the extent to which they are capable of devising mechanisms for allowing anti-poverty programmes to deliver benefits to groups occupying the middle deciles of the income ladder as well as to the genuinely poor. In this sense, some of the politically inspired manipulations of 'anti-poverty policy' found in India conform more closely to the model elaborated by Joan Nelson in her study of which countries were most successful at protecting the poor during adjustment.[14] This involves intended leakages of resources to groups other than the 'targeted' beneficiaries. Such strategies, naturally, are not openly advertised. But, in India at least, they are 'designed-into' policy, and this intent is communicated through a range of informal institutions to the 'unofficial beneficiaries'.

Once again, politically sustainable solutions are delivered through less-than-wholesome means. And to the extent that *all* functioning democracies are systemically reliant upon them,[15] it is pointless to condemn governments that employ such devious devices as operating a form of 'low-intensity democracy'.[16] Call India undemocratic, and you must level the same charge against most if not all advanced capitalist democracies. While such a charge might form the basis of a radical critique of democracy's crisis of representation worldwide, this is certainly not on the agenda of the international aid agencies, which, whether they admit it or not, are still tethered to the fundamental modernisation premise that OECD countries possess the appropriate models of governance to which their counterparts in the developing world should aspire.[17]

---

[14] Joan Nelson, 'The Politics of Pro-Poor Adjustment', in Joan M. Nelson (ed.), *Fragile Coalitions: The Politics of Economic Adjustment* (New Brunswick, NJ: Transaction Books, 1989), pp. 95–113.

[15] For an illustration of this point in the context of US presidential election campaigns, see Kathleen Hall-Jamieson, *Dirty Politics: Deception, Distraction and Democracy* (Oxford: Oxford University Press, 1992).

[16] See Barry Gills, Joel Rocamora and Richard Wilson (eds.), *Low Intensity Democracy: Political Power in the New World Order* (London: Pluto Press, 1993).

[17] This is an intentionally provocative statement, which takes one 'premise' of modernisation theory as 'fundamental', while acknowledging the current marginalisation of some of the more extreme propositions of authors within this 'school' – particularly claims concerning the *inevitability* of historical trajectories or developmental 'end-states' (which aid agencies do not in general adhere to), as opposed to recommending historical models worth *emulating* (which they do). While there are many variants of modernisation theory, a good number of which posit trade-offs between various development goals (equity and growth, stability and participation, national autonomy and growth, etc.), the thrust of current aid policy is, to paraphrase Albert Hirschman, that '(some if not) all good things go together' (Albert O. Hirschman, 'The Case Against "One Thing at a Time"', *World Development*, vol. 18 (August 1990), pp. 1119–22). Hence the governance agenda's emphasis on the mutually reinforcing properties of democracy and market-oriented economic policy. For a useful analysis which places the evolution of thinking on the relationship among various objectives in historical perspective, see Samuel P. Hunting-

An insider's account of the policy-making process in the Reagan administration details the stealthy ways in which tax increases were introduced during Reagan's second term in order to compensate for the Laffer curve's failure to produce higher tax revenues from lower rates during his first term.[18] Paul Pierson's study of social policy reform in the United States under Reagan and in the United Kingdom under Thatcher argues that there are three broad strategies for dismantling the welfare state: 'obfuscation', 'compensation', and 'divide-and-rule'. Obfuscation is seen as the most likely to succeed. It involves a conscious strategy of refusing to tackle problems head-on (and thereby averting direct and concerted political resistance); concealing aims and actions to the greatest extent possible; and shifting blame. Successful obfuscation accounts for 90 per cent of what Reagan and Thatcher 'accomplished', according to Pierson.[19] In India, all three tactics have been utilised by reformers at various levels of the political system, something which its practitioners have understandably not been keen to advertise.

That tactics of this type are not unique (or peculiarly suited) to what are generally considered economically conservative policy reforms is supported by the findings of a study on 'the politics of redistribution in Latin America' by William Ascher.[20] Examining various sequences of reform and reaction in Peru, Argentina, and Chile, Ascher concluded that redistributive objectives were most successfully achieved by 'pragmatic' progressives[21] whose efforts are too easily derided by more 'radical' political opponents as 'merely reformist': 'More subtle attempts meet the ironic fate of greater success but far less recognition; as a result, the true record of redistribution is considerably better than the apparent record based on more prominent episodes'.[22] The reasons for this discrepancy in outcome find strong echoes in the India of the 1990s, where 'cautious' reformers were charged with lacking the ideological fervour required for the enormous task of reversing the tide of Nehruvian socialism. For market-oriented reform in India, as much as for state-interventionist reform in

---

ton, 'The Goals of Development', in Myron Weiner and Samuel P. Huntington (eds.), *Understanding Political Development* (Boston: Little Brown, 1987), pp. 3–32.

[18] Richard Darman, *Who's in Control? Polar Politics and the Sensible Center* (New York: Simon and Schuster, 1996), pp. 72–119; cited in Garry Wills, 'A Tale of Two Cities', *New York Review of Books*, vol. 43, no. 15 (3 October 1996), p. 16 (fn 3).

[19] Paul Pierson, *Dismantling the Welfare State* (Cambridge: Cambridge University Press, 1995).

[20] William Ascher, *Scheming for the Poor: The Politics of Redistribution in Latin America* (Cambridge, Mass.: Harvard University Press, 1984). I am grateful to Paul Shaffer for bringing this source to my attention.

[21] For an account of the success of one such political leader in India, see James Manor, 'Pragmatic Progressives in Regional Politics: The Case of Devaraj Urs', *Economic and Political Weekly*, annual number, vol. 15, 1980.

[22] Ascher, *Scheming for the Poor*, p. 19.

Latin America, '[t]he virtues of forthrightness, openness, ideological consistency, and courage to face attack often turn out to be liabilities'; success as a reformer, in fact, 'may be more readily effected when regime leaders indulge in improvisation, obfuscation, and even insincere threatening'.[23] Narasimha Rao's famous penchant for indecision and conflict-avoidance thus finds justification of a sort in political precedent. To the extent that both types of reform entail redistribution of resources and political influence, the comparison is not in the least far-fetched. As Ascher points out:

[i]n case after case the masters of redistribution prove to be the tacticians rather than the warriors. The best records of redistribution are held by the pragmatic politicians whose familiarity with the policy process enables them to manipulate the political atmosphere to lull, disarm, or intimidate the potential opposition, and to isolate the direct victims of specific redistributive measures from their potential allies among all other groups fearing drastic redistribution.[24]

To quote Ascher is not to claim a general applicability of these tactics, or to assert that Indian policy reform conforms to some iron law that can be inferred from an examination of the comparative literature. Indeed, Ascher himself argues that tactics must 'match' their context.[25] The point is to demonstrate the importance of tactical skill as a factor which cuts across other comparative variables, including culture, regime type, level of development, and even the objectives of the policy reforms themselves.

Politics, economic reform, and the good government agenda

Much of the rose-tinted perspective on the persuasive powers of democracy – which casts it as the secret weapon that compensates for democracy's inability to coerce agents into accepting change – has filtered into the development policy discourse and what has come to be termed the 'good government' agenda. This is supported by a large and growing body of official and non-official literature, and there is insufficient space to address its many shortcomings here. For the present, we are concerned only to highlight the link between the more mainstream academic literature on the politics of adjustment (discussed in the next section) and the intellectual orientations of key staff members within multilateral financial institutions and bilateral aid donors. In particular, it is striking that a number of World Bank and IMF publications speak of the need for 'vision' and 'political will' (read: the will to persuade, rather than the will

---

[23] Ibid., p. 18.   [24] Ibid., pp. 18–19.
[25] Ibid., see Chapter 2, 'Matching Tactics, Context, and Theory'.

to [exercise] power) in order to make adjustment politically sustainable. The irony is that a policy agenda premised upon a cynical view of power – one that considers rent-seeking an almost inevitable consequence of state intervention, and democracies inherently prone to interest-group grid-lock – relies upon a conception of democratic 'governance' that is cripplingly naïve about the manner in which governments actually go about achieving their policy objectives.

The answer to the question of how reform has been sustained amidst the difficulties posed by a democratic political system reveals a tension between two of the central tenets of the good government agenda, as defined by international financial institutions and aid donors. On the one hand is what the UK's Overseas Development Administration (ODA[26]) terms 'competence': 'the capacity to formulate policies and strategies; to take timely decisions both on the longer term and on more immediate issues which arise; to implement policy decisions'.[27] Competence in this usage is often called capacity by other donors. On the other hand is the concept of 'accountability', which among other things requires 'transparency of decision-making and relationships'.[28]

This book attempts to explain the Indian government's 'competence' in allowing policy reforms to take root amidst the political minefield of India's liberal democracy. Yet one of the main explanatory factors cited is the state elite's ability to employ political tactics that have little to do with 'transparency'. These include strategies to soften the edge of political conflict by promoting change in the guise of continuity, and to arrange clandestine compensation for groups who perceive reform as a threat. In other words, the governance capacity of democracies need not rest solely, or even primarily, on the transparency of decision-making or relationships.[29]

The World Bank's primary policy statement on governance argues that economic reforms tend to generate a parallel effort at restructuring governmental institutions, and goes on to assert that '[t]o nurture a political consensus in support of these reforms, governments require political

---

[26] The ODA was in 1997 renamed the Department for International Development (DFID).

[27] Overseas Development Administration (Government and Institutions Department) 'Taking Account of Good Government', *Technical Note No. 10* (London, 1993), section 2.9.   [28] Ibid., section 2.7.

[29] Even leaders of the developing world's 'new' democracies have displayed this talent. Yoweri Museveni, darling of aid donors despite his insistence on party-less democracy, Uganda's quelled resistance to an IMF-sponsored reform programme among newly assertive elected leaders by spreading rumours of a cabinet reshuffle, and individually promising many more MPs than could possibly have been accommodated that their ascendancy to ministerial office was imminent. Inevitably, most were disappointed. See 'The Rulers, the Ruled and the African Reality', *Economist*, 20 September 1997, p. 85.

skill'.[30] A 1994 World Bank assessment of India's structural adjustment programme stated that the 'skill with which reforms have been introduced thus far has few parallels elsewhere'.[31] Yet the skill referred to in both statements involves mechanisms of elite compromise, the operation of which often involves a decided lack of transparency, and even corruption. (These will be discussed in detail in Chapters 4 to 6.) Rather than explore the role that formal and informal institutions might play in this process, World Bank analyses revert to admiration for the democratic stereotype.

One of the best examples of this literature is the series of publications authored or co-authored by the World Bank's Chief Economist for the Africa Region, Ishrat Husain. In considering the findings from seven country case studies, Husain announced his intention to move 'a step beyond the Bank's adjustment study[32] by undertaking to identify the causal linkages underlying whether or not adjustment policies are sustained'.[33] After sifting the evidence, he argued that the primary lesson to be derived from these cases was that

> strong, committed and visionary leadership that places these policy reforms in the context of [the] long-term development path of the country can provide the bonding and cementing of diverse and divergent viewpoints and nurture a shared vision for the future.[34]

This statement projects an extremely sanitised vision of politics. It is based on misapprehensions about the workings of democracy which are at the heart of what is wrong with the good government literature. There are two main problems. First, Husain (and many others besides him) seems to assume that there are clear 'losers' in the process of reform who can be 'neutralised' politically, presumably before all of the 'bonding and cementing' takes place. In fact, those interests which find themselves among the losers will, in most cases, suffer relative, and perhaps short-term, losses. Moreover, they will usually be sections or fragments of larger 'interests': small-scale rather than large-scale steel producers, for instance, or labour union officials in the private rather than public sector. Just as importantly, those potential losers who are spared often find themselves in this position by virtue of individual bargains arranged by governments eager to avoid alienating too many groups at once.

---

[30] World Bank, *Governance and Development* (Washington, DC: World Bank, 1992), p. 5.

[31] World Bank, Country Operations, Industry and Finance Division, India Country Department, South Asia Region, *India: Recent Economic Developments and Prospects* (27 May 1994), p. 3.

[32] World Bank, *Adjustment in Africa: Reforms, Results and the Road Ahead* (New York and Oxford: World Bank/Oxford University Press, 1994).

[33] Ishrat Husain, 'Why Do Some Economies Adjust More Successfully Than Others? Lessons from Seven African Countries', *Policy Research Working Paper*, no. 1364 (World Bank, Africa Regional Office, October 1994), p. 2.   [34] Ibid., p. 43.

The requisite 'visionary leadership', then, turns out to rest upon the capacity to strike under-the-table bargains; to divide interests (and thus create new, independently minded ones); and to find ways of rationalising, within the broad framework of liberalisation, what are often patently unjustifiable 'exceptions'. This conception of statesmanship, if one probes beneath the surface, consists largely of manipulation and casuistry. Not only is this not acknowledged, but the failure to see such leadership for what it is obscures the factors which allow reform to be sustained in the face of daunting political odds. Indeed, the evidence presented in this book is an overwhelming refutation of two of the 'lessons' concerning the politics of policy change set forth in an essay by John Williamson and Stephan Haggard: that a national leader of vision is required to facilitate policy change, and that 'voodoo politics', in which politicians dissemble about the aims of policies (and indeed the policies themselves), is seldom useful.[35] Unfortunately, Williamson and Haggard (as well as Husain) appear to have swallowed the rhetoric of reforming politicians themselves.[36] For instance, in a self-serving analysis of 'the challenge of reform', former prime minister of the Czech Republic Vaclav Klaus argues (without any supporting evidence) that

[t]he reforming politician must . . . be able to formulate a clear and lucid vision of a future which is both attractive and achievable; he must explain this vision to his citizens and defend it against populists of all shades; he must implement a consistent reform strategy and introduce unpopular reform measures as and when they are needed; and he must not defer to rent-seekers and lobbyists who pursue their own short-term advantage to the detriment of society as a whole.[37]

More objective analysts of the Czech case have a substantially less elevated view of the means by which economic reform has been introduced under Klaus' leadership.[38]

The second problem with the literature on good government and economic reform, of which Husain's work is just one prominent example,

[35] John Williamson and Stephan Haggard, 'The Political Conditions for Economic Reform', in J. Williamson (ed.), *The Political Economy of Policy Reform* (Washington, DC: Institute for International Economics, 1994), pp. 527–96.

[36] Their findings have also directly influenced popular discourse on the matter, by finding their way into reports in the mainstream media. See, for instance, 'Democracy and Growth: Why Voting is Good for You', *Economist*, 27 August 1994, pp. 17–19.

[37] Vaclav Klaus, 'So Far, So Good', *Economist*, 10 September 1994, p. 45.

[38] See the Economist Intelligence Unit's quarterly Czech Republic *Country Reports*, which reveal a far more complicated picture, one punctuated by tales of favouritism, blame-shifting, and duplicity. The Czech government's privatisation programme also involved a process in which the existence of continued state involvement and poor oversight mechanisms were underplayed in public discourse in favour of a 'returning assets to the people' image. See Cheryl Gray, 'In Search of Owners: Privatization and Corporate Governance in Transition Economies', *World Bank Research Observer*, vol. 11, no. 2 (August 1996), p. 192.

is the artificial dichotomisation of secrecy (bad) and consultation (good): 'The current practice of secrecy and inadequate communication and consultation accentuates the feeling of mistrust and suspicion',[39] argues Husain, in what he (and others) portray as a major conceptual shift from the bad old days when the World Bank supported governments which engaged in unannounced 'shock therapy'. Husain and others[40] like the idea of reforming governments consulting with interest groups because it can 'involve' them in the reform process, and instil a sense of 'ownership',[41] perhaps even contributing to a reform strategy that is economically (and not just politically) more efficacious.[42] 'Secrecy', on the other hand, can undermine the working relationship between governments and economic interests, fomenting unnecessary conflict. What this logic ignores is that much of the secrecy for which governments are condemned in the formulation and implementation of adjustment programmes relates directly to the process of consulting with favoured interests.

While Husain argues that consultation with 'professional associations . . . and other interest groups . . . will be helpful in understanding their viewpoints and concerns and arriving at mutually acceptable solutions',[43] he neglects the extent to which closed-door diplomacy is necessary in order to avoid attracting dissent from suspicious electorates, opposition

---

[39] Husain, 'Why Do Some Economies Adjust More Successfully Than Others?', p. 41.

[40] See, for instance, Charles Harvey and Mark Robinson, 'The Design of Economic Reforms in the Context of Political Liberalization: The Experience of Mozambique, Senegal and Uganda', *IDS Discussion Paper*, no.353 (Brighton: Institute of Development Studies, November 1995).

[41] Husain highlights two senses of the term 'ownership': first, in the sense of building a domestic political consensus in support of reform, such that it ceases to be seen as a programme 'imposed' by outside agencies; and second, in terms of the constituent building blocks of support within the domestic political economy who must feel that they have a stake in (and influence over) the reform process. For an example of the first sense, see Ishrat Husain, 'The Macroeconomics of Adjustment in Sub-Saharan African Countries: Results and Lessons', *Policy Research Working Paper*, no. 1365 (World Bank, Africa Regional Office, October 1994), p. 18; and for the second sense, stressing the need for 'broadly based ownership', see Rashid Faruqee and Ishrat Husain, 'Conclusions', in Ishrat Husain and Rashid Faruqee (eds.), *Adjustment in Africa: Lessons from Country Case Studies* (Washington, DC: The World Bank, March 1994), p. 430.

[42] The case for discussion and negotiation improving the 'technical quality of reform programs' is made in Luiz Carlos Bresser Pereira, Jose Maria Maravall, and Adam Przeworski, *Economic Reforms in New Democracies: A Social Democratic Approach* (Cambridge: Cambridge University Press, 1993), pp. 208–9. The authors also make the point that the issue of 'credibility' makes it impossible fully to distinguish between the economic and political inputs into the design of reform programmes: the perception among economic agents of whether the programme will ultimately be sustained (as opposed to whether they would like it to be sustained) will influence their investment decisions. A programme that emerges from a process of consultation 'may be more, not less, credible, because it creates the political conditions for the continuation of reforms' (p. 209). This, however, will be true only in a limited number of circumstances.

[43] Husain, 'Why Do Some Economies Adjust More Successfully Than Others?', p. 32.

politicians, and most of all those interest groups who find themselves cut out of these bargains. Indeed, the 'accommodated' interests require this secrecy as much as governments do. The organised interests that deride governmental secrecy are usually those that were unable to arrive at a suitable compromise, and may even have engaged in *sub rosa* negotiation with political leaders before 'going public'. This has certainly been a pattern in India, and it is difficult to believe that such goings on are so completely absent in the adjusting countries evaluated in this segment of the good government literature. Indeed, studies of the politics of reform in Zimbabwe and Indonesia suggest that economically defined interests do not simply respond to new economic incentives.[44] Their lobbying strategies are critically affected by the tactics employed by holders of state power, such that changing definitions of self-interest can incline groups towards bandwagoning, rather than opposing reforms.[45]

It is understandable that multilateral agencies would be reluctant openly to recommend individual negotiations and favouritism – not only because it seems to violate democratic norms, but because it also undermines adjustment's message of reducing governmental discretion at all costs. The irony is that Husain, like many other analysts, admits that compensatory gestures towards powerful interests may be necessary to 'cushion them from abrupt and large shocks'. He cites Jennifer Widner's work on East Asia,[46] where (in Husain's summarisation) 'liberalizing economic reform was a consequence of more or less explicit "deals" negotiated between leaders, technocrats and the heads of the networks or groups that structure political life'.[47] Like most attempts to explain the political sustainability of economic liberalisation, however, Husain associates negotiated pacts with authoritarian regimes, while democracies are linked with effective political salesmanship. What the Indian experience illustrates quite clearly is that both strategies apply in both contexts. As the discussion of the Chinese and Mexican cases later in this chapter will

[44] Tor Skalnes, 'The State, Interest Groups and Structural Adjustment in Zimbabwe', *Journal of Development Studies*, vol. 29, no. 3 (April 1993), pp. 401–28; and Richard Robison, *Power and Economy in Suharto's Indonesia* (Manila: Journal of Contemporary Asia Publishers, 1990).

[45] The notion of interest 'learning' has emerged as a major area of empirical research. On business lobbies, see Sandra L. Suarez, 'Interest Learning: Explaining the Political Behaviour of Business', and Peter R. Kingstone, 'Corporatism, Neoliberalism, and the Failed Revolt of Big Business in Brazil: The Case of IEDI', both presented at the Annual Meeting of the American Political Science Association, Washington, DC, 28–31 August 1997. On labour, see Joan Nelson, 'Organized Labor, Politics, and Labor Market Flexibility', *World Bank Research Observer*, vol. 6, no. 1 (January 1991), pp. 37–56.

[46] Jennifer Widner, 'Reform Bargains: The Policies of Change', in D. Lindauer and M. Roemer (eds.), *Asia and Africa: Legacies and Opportunities in Development* (Cambridge, Mass.: Harvard Institute for International Development, 1994).

[47] Husain, 'Why Do Some Economies Adjust More Successfully Than Others?', pp. 32–3.

help to demonstrate, regime-type is a less important variable than most of the theoretical literature acknowledges, not only in terms of determining outcomes, but also in terms of predicting strategic behaviour. The strategy of selective compensation requires effective political institutions, which help to convince interests of the practicality of engaging in negotiations.

It also requires political skills. These tend to be ignored by analysts seeking 'structural characteristics' which may help to explain variations in the capacity of political systems to sustain reform politically over the long haul. Husain, like other World Bank analysts who have studied the Indian case directly,[48] fails to recognise the specialised nature of political skills, and the extent to which political institutions instil certain types of skills. Even when acknowledging that 'the mediation of conflicts in the civil society' is critical to the political sustainability of adjustment, Husain (writing with Rashid Faruqee) categorises this function as of a piece with the 'technical and administrative skills' required to resolve 'infrastructure problems' and maintain 'a framework of macroeconomic policies'.[49] This misunderstands the nature of political skills (the subject of Chapter 6), particularly their relation to political incentives (Chapter 4), and the way in which they are shaped by formal and informal political institutions (Chapter 5).

As the disclaimers routinely attached to policy analyses like those discussed above make clear, the views contained are not to be attributed to the World Bank or its executive directors. Yet, they do represent an important strand of thinking within the Bank – indeed, the development practitioner community at large – on the political dimensions of structural adjustment. And these views are generally consistent with those found in policy papers published by the IMF, again subject to the same disclaimer. These, however, project a slightly different emphasis, picking up on another of the conceptual orientations found in mainstream academic theorisation on the political sustainability of adjustment programmes (to be discussed in the next section). One policy analysis produced by the IMF's research department that sought to draw lessons from the theoretical literature attempted 'to examine how economic factors interact with political and institutional ones in determining whether an adopted reform program will be continued'.[50] Where Husain's work exemplified the good government agenda's preoccupation

---

[48] See, for instance, the various World Bank Country Economic Memoranda on India.
[49] Faruqee and Husain, 'Conclusions', pp. 427–8.
[50] Carlos M. Asilis and Gian Maria Milesi-Ferretti, 'On the Political Sustainability of Economic Reform', *Paper on Policy Analysis and Assessment*, IMF Research Department (Washington, DC: January 1994), p. 1.

with the virtues of openness and transparency, the authors of the IMF research study, Asilis and Milesi-Ferretti, have shown a partiality to rational-choice explanations of policy change.

This book, by focusing largely on incentives and institutions in analysing the Indian case, does not seek to dismiss entirely the value of rational-choice approaches. Clearly, there are advantages to thinking in terms of changing configurations of interests and the way these are shaped by both the motivations of utility-maximising actors and the pattern of relationships within which the actors are embedded. Moreover, the continuous refinements to the rational-choice toolkit make the wholesale rejection of such techniques, on the basis of their allegedly economistic or deterministic bias, appear ideologically motivated, perhaps even more so than rational-choice techniques themselves are alleged to be. Nevertheless, there are a number of shortcomings to the way in which rational-choice assumptions have been applied by those studying the politics of economic reform in developing countries. One of these, concerning the way in which 'winners' and 'losers' (two of the key rational actors) are conceived, has already been hinted at above. As we will see in the discussion of some of the literature on the Mexican and Chinese cases, interests are as much created as given. Rational-choice proponents would of course argue that these flaws could be accommodated by establishing more complex assumptions.

The more troubling aspect of rational-choice analysis that the IMF research paper has picked up from the mainstream academic theorising concerns the nature of political institutions and the nature of political systems. Drawing on the large literature in this field, Asilis and Milesi-Ferretti attempt to transcend the democratic–authoritarian divide by distilling three key variables associated with political systems. Their objective is to assess 'the impact of political fragmentation, political polarization, and the timing of elections on macroeconomic policy formulation', and then to examine 'the consequences for the sustainability of reforms'.[51] To summarise briefly, they follow the rational-choice (and empirically demonstrated) logic that associates *fragmentation* with the creation of 'blocking coalitions' which can hinder policy change; *polarisation* with instability, resultant policy uncertainty and, ultimately, adverse effects on investment decisions; and *election timing* with a greater willingness (if elections are far away) or greater reluctance (if they are relatively close at hand) to introduce potentially painful policy reforms. By focusing on these three variables – which are fairly typical of the academic literature as a whole – Asilis and Milesi-Ferretti are able to assess the worth of

[51] Ibid., p. 6.

the 'new political economy' approach, which 'highlights the interplay between initial economic, political and institutional conditions and economic policy choices in determining the political sustainability of reforms'.[52] That is, they are concerned to understand how the three variables listed above may heighten or lessen such political obstacles to sustainable reform as distributional conflict and adjustment programmes that are deemed to lack credibility by economic agents. These are not unimportant questions. But the political-system variables used to answer them are not particularly illuminating. Indeed, they offer such banal insights as that distributional 'conflicts are likely to emerge in cases in which the "winners and losers" from reform are difficult to identify ex-ante', and that '[i]f the political system is fragmented or a large degree of consensus is needed for the continuation of reforms, these conflicts will make it more difficult to sustain politically the reform process'.[53]

Using game-theoretical models based on such assumptions as a 'war of attrition' among interest groups, the literature from which Asilis and Milesi-Ferretti attempt to derive conclusions for donor and multilateral policy produces generalisations which are of dubious validity in relation to any individual country. Moreover, by citing Wyplosz[54] (and other such rational-choice practitioners), Asilis and Milesi-Ferretti feed the IMF policy-making process on a steady diet of highly questionable generalisations – for instance, 'that in the presence of uncertainty about the distributional consequences of reforms, it is harder to sustain them politically over time than it is to start them'.[55] Our reading of the Indian case arrives at exactly the opposite conclusion: that the skill of Indian politicians at playing upon the ambiguity of the reform process – in the context of an ongoing set of institutionalised relationships with economic elites – has helped to disarm potential opponents of reform, until it became too late for them to resist, or until some among them began to see its benefits.

This is why tactics of obfuscation and manipulation are of such great value: they disrupt the utility-enhancing calculus of interest groups in ways that provide breathing space for governing elites. Using variables such as fragmentation, polarisation, and election timing is attractive to quantitatively oriented political scientists because it allows them to make generalisations across large numbers of countries – in other words to ignore particular circumstances in favour of 'essential' features. In a very important respect this represents a problem highlighted by Samuel Huntington in his analysis of the way in which two sets of political scientists in

[52] Ibid., p. 9.   [53] Ibid., p. 19.
[54] Charles Wyplosz, 'After the Honeymoon: Economics and Politics of Economic Transformation', *European Economic Review*, vol. 37 (April 1993), pp. 379–86.
[55] Asilis and Milesi-Ferretti, 'On the Political Sustainability of Economic Reform', p. 20.

the 1950s and 1960s analysed the relationship between political and economic development:

Area specialists believed that explanation lay in the particular, that in order to understand and explain what happened politically in a society one had to have deep knowledge of its history, language, culture, and social institutions. The comparative politics scholars, on the other hand, believed the explanation could be found in empirical generalizations, that in order to understand and explain what happened politically in a society one had to have a broad knowledge of how social, economic, and political variables interacted generally and then had to apply the appropriate generalizations to the particular case.[56]

While Huntington was placing this analysis at the service of a different analytical end – namely, to justify his move towards studying the influence of culture, defined in terms of civilisations, on developmental trajectories – his point is as valid today as it was more than a decade ago, when it was written, or even thirty-five years ago, when the disciplinary division he describes assumed concrete form. Theorisation on the politics of adjustment has become, if anything, less bound by the contingencies of particular cases, a tendency which has only been accentuated by the vast increase in the number of adjustment programmes, which makes large sample sizes for comparative study (even on once-peripheral issues) ever more available. What this book hopes to demonstrate is the value of close scrutiny of individual country experiences. These must take into account historically contingent relationships whose influence would otherwise be obscured – particularly if we were to examine bland variables full of testability and comparability, but signifying nothing in any particular case.

Theoretical approaches to the politics of economic adjustment

There is a super-abundance of case studies along the lines of 'the politics of economic reform in country X'. Because this has been a growth industry among academics for over a decade, individual authors have, over time, changed their areas of inquiry and preferred lines of explanation, and refined their techniques for understanding the many issues that arise in attempting to explain puzzling outcomes. Even if we narrow our concern to the issue of political sustainability it is very difficult to ensure that one is comparing like with like. Some authors are concerned with sustainable adjustment taken generally (as is the present study), while others focus on how the sequencing of reforms contributes to the sus-

[56] Huntington, 'The Goals of Development', pp. 3–32.

tainability of individual components of the reform agenda. To summarise this literature would exceed the scope of this chapter, and there is a great risk of setting up straw men.

In an effort to reduce, though probably not eliminate, the chances of falling prey to such analytical pitfalls, the following discussion will focus on a cluster of studies which represent the most influential approaches to studying the political sustainability of economic reform.[57] These approaches are stated most clearly in the analytical introductions to collections of case studies. In these, the editors set forth the parameters within which (in some cases, the hypotheses against which) case-study authors were expected to approach the empirical material. Some of the most widely cited among these conceptual orientations possess serious shortcomings. The purpose of the following critique, then, is to highlight some of what we might have missed had a more restrictive conception of politics been used in analysing the Indian case. Corroborating insights drawn from a different set of empirical literature will then be presented in the chapter's final section.

One collection of case studies, edited by Haggard and Webb, and funded and co-published by the World Bank, generated an extremely rich set of empirical findings and a useful sifting of the issues.[58] In an effort to provide a consistent framework for the findings, however, the editors

[57] Indeed, many of the same authors appear in each of these collections as either editors, case-study contributors, or commentators on questions of theory. Volumes in which conceptual frameworks have significantly shaped the approaches of case-study authors include: Joan M. Nelson (ed.), *Fragile Coalitions: The Politics of Economic Adjustment* (New Brunswick, NJ: Transaction Books, 1989), to which Haggard and Kaufman have contributed a chapter; Joan M. Nelson (ed.), *Economic Crisis and Policy Choice: The Politics of Adjustment in the Third World* (Princeton: Princeton University Press, 1990), which was part of the same research project from which the 1989 volume emerged, and thus included many of the same authors; Gerald Meier (ed.), *Politics and Policy Making in Developing Countries: Perspectives on the New Political Economy* (San Francisco: ICS Press, 1991), in which Nelson, Haggard, and Bates co-authored a critical analytical chapter; Stephan Haggard and Robert R. Kaufman (eds.), *The Politics of Economic Adjustment: International Constraints, Distributional Conflicts, and the State* (Princeton: Princeton University Press, 1992), in which Nelson and others from earlier cited volumes have contributed chapters; Robert H. Bates and Anne O. Krueger (eds.), *Political and Economic Interactions in Economic Policy Reform: Evidence from Eight Countries* (Oxford: Blackwell, 1993), in which Haggard co-authors a chapter on South Korea, and other mainstay authors from these collections are present, including Merilee S. Grindle, Barbara Stallings, and Paul Collier; John Williamson (ed.), *The Political Economy of Policy Reform* (Washington, DC: Institute for International Economics, 1994), in which Bates, Krueger, Webb, Haggard, and Nelson all appear; and Stephan Haggard and Robert R. Kaufman (eds.), *The Political Economy of Democratic Transitions* (Princeton: Princeton University Press, 1995), in which many of the previously mentioned authors are represented.

[58] Stephan Haggard and Steven B. Webb (eds.), *Voting for Reform: Democracy, Political Liberalization, and Economic Adjustment* (New York: Oxford University Press/The World Bank, 1994).

imposed an approach to the study of economic reform's political sustainability that, in effect, severely constrained the types of issues which the case-study authors were able to probe. Haggard and Webb's approach, it must be stressed, is taken as paradigmatic of one important strand in the mainstream academic literature. There are, of course, important points of divergence between theorists represented in this literature; between the earlier and later works of individual theorists; and between the comparative frameworks set forth by the volumes' editors and some of the case-study authors who deviated (fortunately, as it turns out) from the prescribed approach.

There are three important deficiencies which must be highlighted. The first concerns the way in which the Haggard/Webb framework delimits the area of inquiry to specific reform measures, rather than to reform conceived broadly as a redirection of policy orientation. It focuses on four types of reform, relating to fiscal, monetary, exchange rate, and trade policy – what have come to be known as 'the big four'. The editors' rationale for this limited focus is clearly stated: 'Other policy reforms were equally important in many cases, but only these seemed to have enough universal importance to support cross-country comparisons' – that is, they permitted the editors to maintain their focus on 'the testing of a common set of hypotheses'.[59] Haggard and Webb pose this as a trade-off between the general and the particular: what the coordinated research project gains in the way of consistency, it loses in terms of its ability to convey the specificities of individual cases.

In fact, much more is lost than that. By paring down their concerns to only near-universal features, they deprive the case-study authors of the chance to put forward a convincing explanation for why individual countries are able to sustain a *general* reorientation of economic policy. This matters enormously, since many less visible reform measures contribute to the political sustainability of the 'big four' reforms themselves. This happens when, for instance, politicians operating at lower levels of the political system – a major threat to reform's sustainability in any democratic country – get implicated in the reform process. These actors are often forced by political implications stemming from the 'general' reorientation of policy to pursue 'minor' reforms within their jurisdictions.

Indeed, a serious shortcoming of the Haggard/Webb framework is the extent to which it renders unimportant the lower-level political actors responsible for these 'small' (or, 'important but not universal enough') reforms. As close scrutiny of the Indian case makes plain, the conflict-mediating activities of politicians at the state level proved exceptionally

---

[59] Haggard and Webb, *Voting for Reform*, p. xiv.

important in taking some of the interest-group pressure off liberalisers at the apex of the political system – pressure that in other countries endangered the sustainability of the big four reforms. Moreover, the enthusiasm with which many non-Congress state governments took to liberalisation helped to deflate the heated anti-reform rhetoric emanating from non-Congress MPs in the national parliament. Even in non-federal systems, these subnational power centres have at least the potential to play a key role in undertaking the sorts of micro-reforms upon which overall policy reorientation, not to mention successful economic outcomes, crucially depends. Under the Haggard/Webb framework, however, they disappear from the conceptual radar when a fixation upon testable hypotheses effectively restricts the analytical scope to only those issues identified as 'central' to economic reform, and therefore easily comparable.

The second major deficiency of the Haggard/Webb framework concerns its approach to democratic institutions. Their comparative study was designed to assess the contribution of three institutions. The case-study authors were instructed to examine 'how differences in the party and electoral system and in bureaucratic organization affect the choice of policy'.[60] Party systems, electoral systems, and bureaucratic organisations are all institutions worthy of study. Unfortunately, the way in which they have been conceptualised does not help to advance our understanding of why the aims of reformers are sometimes thwarted and sometimes achieved. Party and electoral systems are analysed in terms of their fragmentation or polarisation. Relying upon a model elaborated by Alesina in one of the book's theoretical chapters,[61] the editors intended the case studies to test the veracity of his key hypothesis: 'that polarized party systems, in which wide ideological differences separate the main political contenders, encourage bidding wars between competing political forces and produce destabilizing swings in policy'.[62]

In general, the case studies themselves, as well as the synthetic analysis provided by Haggard and Webb, seem to uphold this assertion. In particular, they cite the cases of Turkey and Chile, in which changes to the electoral and party systems were introduced, allowing 'comparisons between the performance of different party systems within the same country'. Turkey was an economic basket case in the late 1970s largely because of 'an increasingly polarized political system'.[63] After 1983, when new electoral regulations transformed the nature of the party system, the

[60] Ibid., p. 5.
[61] Alberto Alesina, 'Political Models of Macroeconomic Policy and Fiscal Reform', in Haggard and Webb, *Voting for Reform*, pp. 37–60. See also Alberto Alesina, 'Macroeconomics and Politics', *NBER Macroeconomics Annual* (Cambridge, Mass.: National Bureau of Economic Research, 1988), pp. 13–52.
[62] Haggard and Webb, *Voting for Reform*, p. 9.   [63] Ibid., pp. 9–10.

Turkish government pursued a more economically responsible course of action. A similar effort to remove polarisation in Chile also led to consensus around less destructive economic policies.

The details of the Indian case do not conform to these generalisations. At the time when economic reform was initiated India's party politics at the national level were certainly characterised by 'wide ideological differences' between 'the main political contenders'. And, yet, reform eventually received tacit, and eventually more explicit, backing from left-leaning and communist parties which ruled at the state level in many parts of India. While such flexibility might be cited as evidence that the party system was in fact not polarised, and that the ideological differences were mere rhetoric, this is unconvincing, for it raises a key methodological shortcoming of this approach to institutions. If the only means for determining polarisation is to judge actions, rather than words or manifestos, then any verification of Alesina's hypothesis is simply a truism. There is no way of disproving the hypothesis, because any polarised system that is alleged to have generated a working consensus in favour of structural reform will have its credentials as a polarised system called into question by virtue of its proven consensus-generating capacity. By this logic, even a government's capacity to neutralise party-political opponents of reform can be taken as evidence that the system was, because of the manifest weakness of the anti-reform parties (they lost the battle, after all, didn't they?), *de facto* un-polarised – that is, clearly dominated by those groups committed to responsible fiscal (or trade, or monetary, or exchange-rate) policy. While this logic has a ring of authenticity – the existence of radical socialist parties in America does not render its party system, in the main, ideologically polarised – it is also clearly circular. The terms in which the discussion is cast make responsible policy the *sine qua non* of un-polarity.

Haggard and Webb themselves acknowledge that '[g]auging the actual extent of polarization and fragmentation within the party system can be difficult if one looks simply at the number of parties or their ideological stance'.[64] Yet, in order to explain away the existence of a seemingly hypothesis-disproving case – Thailand's 'relatively consistent economic policy', and the ability of the Thai government to initiate 'important reforms during a period of political liberalization', *despite* political fragmentation – they argue that Thailand's 'apparently fragmented system' is really a 'single dominant coalition' consisting of three individual parties.[65] In other words, when the outcomes do not match the model's predictions, one may simply redefine the data to reach a functional equivalent of

[64] Haggard and Webb, *Voting for Reform*, p. 10.   [65] Ibid., p. 11.

the required variable. Or, alternatively, as with the editors' reading of the Mexico case-study evidence, where a clearly one-party-dominant system devoid of either ideological polarisation or a proliferation of parties did not 'prevent Mexico from getting into serious economic trouble in the early 1980s', it is possible to assert that such a country 'constitutes an important limiting case in this analysis of the party system'.[66]

The third problem with the approach taken by Haggard and Webb of interest to us here has to do with the way in which they treat the issue of 'building coalitions for reform'.[67] Their approach to this critical issue represents a clear improvement in terms of sophistication over earlier approaches to the fundamental question of how to construct a base of political support for policy reforms that have direct costs to articulate, well-organised interests, while only the promise of potential gains for what, at the beginning of the reform process, are diffuse and relatively powerless socio-economic groups. By emphasising the iterative nature of reform, Haggard and Webb have landed upon the crucial dynamic at work:

If interest groups determine policy, and interests in the period before reform tend to favor the status quo, how is reform ever possible? The answer to this paradox is that interests are not fixed but rather change in response to features of the programme itself.[68]

The nature of interest group realignment in the Indian case supports this basic conclusion. In our analysis of the Indian case, however, we will attempt to ground this process in theory by situating it within the general literature on 'policy feedback'. This will be discussed with reference to the malleability of interest groups in Chapter 4. The point that needs to be made at present is that, despite this retreat from the literature's earlier fixation upon collective-action dilemmas facing economic interests,[69] Haggard and Webb have constructed an analytical framework that, had it been followed in studying the Indian case, would have obscured many of the complex factors that contributed to sustainable policy reform. The reasons why relate to the first two deficiencies, and the way in which they are magnified when the Haggard/Webb framework takes up the question of 'compensating' negatively affected interest groups in order to build a

[66] Ibid., p. 9.
[67] This is one of the four political variables that comprise their framework for comparative analysis. The other three are institutions, international influences, and democratisation processes.   [68] Haggard and Webb, *Voting for Reform*, p. 5.
[69] A more elaborate version of this critique, focusing on the way in which the literature treats the question of why governments initiate (as opposed to sustain) reform, can be found in Robert S. Jenkins, 'Theorising the Politics of Economic Adjustment: Lessons from the Indian Case', *Journal of Commonwealth and Comparative Politics*, vol. 33, no. 1 (March 1995), pp. 1–24.

coalition for reform. By focusing on the four 'near universal' reforms – concerning trade, exchange-rate, fiscal, and monetary policy – Haggard and Webb (and the case-study authors working within their framework) are inclined to search for instances of compensation almost exclusively within the ambit of these four issue areas. The main types of compensation which the case-study authors uncovered were export subsidies to cushion import-dependent businesses from the blow of currency devaluation in Turkey and Thailand, and the expansion of access to the import trade (through delicensing) in Nigeria to help mute the cries of protest from the privileged business groups for whom trade policy reform was a major loss.[70]

In India, the types of compensation were far more varied, offered in many cases to rather narrowly defined sections of large and diverse interest groups. Above all, they involved policy arenas far removed from the big four. Therefore, had the analysis focused only on reform to fiscal, monetary, exchange-rate, and trade policy, it would have missed the extent to which the bargains that help to reduce political resistance to liberalisation involve a wider array of policy arenas and a more diverse set of issues. In short, a major finding would have slipped through the cracks of the Haggard/Webb framework. And, as a result, its theoretical implications regarding the nature of democratic politics would have remained unexamined. The reason why the strategy of compensation has proved so effective in defusing resistance to reform is that concessions to threatening interests were politically well targeted. The openness of Indian democracy – along with its federal structure – allows governing elites to gauge the strength of potential allies and opponents with much greater acuity and at much lower levels of aggregation. To emphasise the point, we can put it in rational-choice terms, though it perhaps overstates the case: given lower information costs, governing elites are better able to invest their political capital in narrowly defined constituencies in which the political payoffs from compensatory measures are relatively higher.

Because Haggard and Webb have narrowed the issue focus, and conceptualised institutions so restrictively, they are unable to appreciate the extent to which in India this process has been aided by networks of influence constructed around individual political leaders that encompass a diverse array of interests. (For reasons outlined in Chapter 5, these have been classified as informal political institutions.) Instead, in advocating institutional reform, Haggard and Webb maintain the rather stale preoccupation with 'insulating key parts of the bureaucracy from political

[70] The only other area in which compensatory measures were examined was in government promises to encourage wage restraint in Senegal as part of trade policy reform, which in the end proved fruitless. Haggard and Webb, *Voting for Reform*, pp. 19–20.

pressure'.[71] Once, however, we grasp the importance of complex forms of compensation – often decidedly untransparent, yet paradoxically relying upon the openness of the political system – it becomes increasingly untenable to focus upon 'insulation':[72] bureaucracies themselves have been instrumental in negotiating and implementing some of the most creative compensatory measures to have underwritten the political sustainability of India's economic reforms. This is particularly true at the state level – which, it will be recalled, tends to be relegated to the margins under the Haggard/Webb logic of comparability.

Because the Haggard/Webb framework depicts to a large degree the state of the art, it has been singled out for such close scrutiny. But its flaws are shared by other segments of the theoretical literature, such as the study by Goren Hyden and Bo Karlstrom, which 'treats the policy context as an explicit and independent variable'.[73] In the course of analysing the Tanzanian experience they highlight the importance of a variable which has been clearly in evidence in the Indian case: 'we argue that a policy situation where *ambiguity* rather than conflict prevails is more congenial to effective policy implementation'.[74] In studying India, however, we conceptualise the relationship between ambiguity and conflict differently than Hyden and Karlstrom have. Their model views them as separate factors whose intensity may vary among 'policy situations', such that the policy issue involved may be characterised in one of four ways: 'technical' (low ambiguity, low conflict); 'institutional' (high ambiguity, low conflict); 'political' (low ambiguity, high conflict); or 'ideological' (high ambiguity, high conflict).[75]

This model is at odds with what a close reading of the Indian case material reveals. As a good deal of the evidence in this book will demonstrate, these two 'variables' – conflict and ambiguity – are linked dynamically and interactively, rather than statically and in isolation from one another. An issue that seems to have the makings of a 'high conflict' scenario can, through the *intentional application of ambiguity* in the way in which it is handled, serve to lessen the chances for conflict. Ambiguity, in other words, is not a fixed variable. Conversely, a low-conflict, low-ambiguity 'technical' issue can become highly politically charged, de-

---

[71] Ibid., p. 13.

[72] An indication of how widespread this view is can be found in Joan Nelson's summary of the literature on the politics of economic reform, in which she states that sustained reform programmes have 'typically . . . been launched by governments . . . independent of or hostile to economic interests'. Joan Nelson, 'The Politics of Economic Transformation: Is Third World Experience Relevant in Eastern Europe?', *World Politics*, vol. 45 (April 1993), p. 433.

[73] Goren Hyden and Bo Karlstrom, 'Structural Adjustment as a Policy Process: The Case of Tanzania', *World Development*, vol. 21, no. 9 (1993), p. 1395.

[74] Ibid., p. 1396 (emphasis added).   [75] Ibid., p. 1401.

pending on a range of contingent factors that may be completely out of the control of political or bureaucratic elites. Indeed, the way in which Hyden and Karlstrom characterise 'political issues' is troubling, as is their understanding of how they can be dealt with. In their view, '[a] "political" issue . . . is low in ambiguity (the parties know where the battle lines are drawn) but loaded with conflict. It can only be implemented through the application of power'.[76] In fact, many actors (at least in the Indian case) are not at all sure where precisely their interests lie given the rapid unfolding of events and the considerable overlap between issue areas. The natural rebuttal to such a criticism is that situations in which actors have ambiguities do not constitute 'political' issues.

The problem with this response is that, given the frequency with which ambiguities in any adjustment process are at fairly high levels, it confines very few issues to the category of the 'political', when the reality (at least in the eyes of the main actors themselves) is that the overwhelming majority of reforms possess distinct political overtones in so far as they involve decisions on when to employ ambiguity and when to opt for conflict. The drawing of sharp distinctions between 'institutional' and 'political' issues, and between both of these and 'ideological' issues, ignores the role of institutions themselves as instruments in defusing conflict. In short, while Hyden and Karlstrom's analysis is helpful in suggesting concepts which have a bearing on the determination of outcomes, the relationships among them which their model posits do not capture the variability inherent in this process. This is a common problem among studies which attempt to define fixed relationships among policy measures, economic interests, and outcomes.[77]

This analytical shortcoming is all the more surprising since the authors maintain their adherence to Lindblom's dictum that interests are 'created', not given.[78] As they state later in their study, '[w]hat people want, and what interests they want to pursue, is something that grows out of commitment and will. Thus, interests do not create decisions, but decisions create interests'.[79] The Indian case provides ample testimony to the view that '[t]he relatively high level of ambiguity associated with the concept of structural adjustment is likely to serve as a potential advantage for those actors who wish to "seize" the issues and formulate new

[76] Ibid.
[77] See, for instance, Chung-in Moon, 'The Politics of Structural Adjustment in South Korea: Analytical Issues and Comparative Implications', *Korea Journal*, Autumn 1991, Table 1, p. 64.
[78] See Charles E. Lindblom, *Politics and Markets* (New Haven, Conn.: Yale University Press, 1977).
[79] Hyden and Karlstrom, 'Structural Adjustment as a Policy Process', p. 1402.

strategies'.[80] This conception, with its emphasis on the fluidity of social and economic interests, has much in common with the variety of political autonomy found in the writings of Antonio Gramsci, for whom:

The active politician is a creator, an initiator [who] . . . bases himself on effective reality . . . on a relation of forces in continuous motion and shift in equilibrium. If one applies one's will to the creation of a new equilibrium among the forces which really exist and are operative – basing oneself on the particular force which one believes to be progressive and strengthening it to help it to victory – one still moves on the terrain of effective reality, but does so in order to dominate and transcend it.[81]

Parallels with country case studies

An awareness of the complexities of the Indian case cannot help but raise suspicions that issues and events of great importance are lurking beneath the surface in the countries from which the theoretical literature has derived its rather unenlightening conclusions. Scattered evidence from individual countries, such as the sources cited earlier in connection with the Czech case, corroborates the importance of the issues and variables highlighted in this book. Two countries in particular reveal striking parallels with this book's reading of the Indian case: China and Mexico. That neither has been considered a paragon of democracy is not without its ironies.

China is generally viewed as the perfect case for political comparisons with India: a populous, highly diverse, predominantly rural Asian country in which, however, political freedoms and competition are severely restricted. Jean Dreze and Amartya Sen, among others, have exploited the analytical opportunity to cast India as China's democratic foil.[82] The greater levels of foreign investment, higher rates of economic growth, and booming international trade are often interpreted as a direct result of China's illiberal political system. Certainly, in terms of economic outcomes China's programme of economic reform is far more extensive than India's. Initiated in the late 1970s – since when India has initiated at least three separate reform efforts – its programme has shown greater staying power. However, there always exists the danger that a crisis arising from the social dislocation accompanying rapid growth and/or demands for

[80] Ibid., pp. 1402–3.

[81] Antonio Gramsci, *Selections from the Prison Notebooks*, edited and translated by Quinton Hoare and Geoffrey Nowell Smith (New York: International Publishers, 1971), p. 172.

[82] With reference to famine, see Jean Dreze and Amartya Sen, *Hunger and Public Action* (Oxford: Clarendon Press, 1989); and with reference to social development in a context of economic reform, see Chapter 4 of Jean Dreze and Amartya Sen, *India: Economic Development and Social Opportunity* (Oxford: Oxford University Press, 1996), pp. 57–86.

democratisation could create disorder, endanger China's economic success, and reveal reform's durability as more ephemeral than it seems today. This view casts India as the slow, sure tortoise, and China as the impetuous hare.[83]

What is striking, however, are the similarities between the countries suggested by some parts of the literature on the politics of adjustment in China. This is not to suggest that the Indian government is behaving in an authoritarian manner reminiscent of the one-party state in China, though the Indian case does in general serve to remind us that democracy as it is practised in India (and in the west) deviates from the immediately accountable, welfare-optimising model which textbooks (and western aid agencies) often represent as synonymous with the term. Similarly, the process of economic reform in China has in some cases illustrated the way in which a formally non-competitive political system can present opportunities for a defiance of central authority. The main way in which it has done so is through the gradual empowerment of provincial and local governments and the enterprises under their jurisdictions.[84] The most important implication of this for the arguments presented in this book concerns the impact of these developments for the political sustainability of reform in China.

A study by Montinola, Qian, and Weingast examines three puzzles that seem to confound the conventional wisdom about economic reform in China, two of which concern us here: first, that '[e]conomic reform appears to have been successfully pursued without any political reform'; and, second, that '[t]he central government seems to retain considerable political discretion, including the ability to reverse suddenly the reform process'.[85] The authors argue that what the conventional wisdom ignores is that there has been *de facto* political reform. While there has not been 'democratisation' in terms of the usual measures, there are other types of political reform, and these can often be potent agents of change. The most important, from our perspective, concerns relations between levels of the political system: 'not only has political decentralisation enhanced the powers of local government, but it has also altered central-local govern-

---

[83] See, for instance, Vincent Cable, *China and India: Economic Reform and Global Integration* (London: Royal Institute of International Affairs, 1995), pp. 6–8.

[84] James Manor, among others, has argued that there has been a greater degree of provincial autonomy over economic decision-making in Communist China since the revolution than much of the literature on Chinese politics would lead one to believe. See his 'India's States, China's Provinces and the Question of Central Autonomy', paper presented to the China-India Seminar, Fairbank Center for East Asian Studies, Harvard University, 1986 (typescript), especially pp. 3–6.

[85] Gabriella Montinola, Yingyi Qian, and Barry R. Weingast, 'Federalism, Chinese Style: The Political Basis for Economic Success in China', *World Politics*, vol. 48, no. 1 (October 1995), pp. 50–81.

ment relations in several critical ways that are difficult, though not impossible to reverse'.[86] While the disparities between China's booming southern and coastal provinces and those receiving little economic benefit from the policy of 'market socialism' are considered, perhaps justifiably, potentially explosive by some China watchers, according to Montinola *et al.* the underlying logic behind the emergence of greater provincial autonomy has 'resulted in a new political system that we characterize as federalism, Chinese style. This system, in turn, *provides considerable political protection for China's reforms*, including limits on the central government'.[87] While Indian and Chinese forms of federalism differ substantially, particularly in so far as they have differing perspectives on what the literature terms 'market-preserving federalism',[88] there are four important similarities.

The first is the extent to which economic reform in the context of a federal system creates 'competition among jurisdictions' for investment. Second, the system of competing jurisdictions, by dividing regions into those that benefit from reform and those that do not, tends to undermine the capacity of political elites from this tier of the system effectively to oppose economic restructuring. Political elites from regions that do well are less inclined to resist reform, while those from areas which lose out have less clout with which to do so. Third, federalism creates incentives for provincial and local governments to experiment with new policies, with the successful experiments becoming models for other regions to follow. Fourth, and most importantly, a virtuous cycle is created: economic reform tends to entrench further the authority of provincial and local politicians, while this relative loss of political autonomy for the central government makes it less possible for it to retreat away from markets.[89] As the authors put it with reference to China:

These changes [in the relationship between central and provincial political authority] endow the economic reforms with a degree of political durability. Each serves to raise the costs of a recentralization of political authority and an economic retrenchment, although this effect was unintended . . . Our argument does not imply that a retrenchment is impossible, but that it would be costly and might fail, thus making it less likely.[90]

As we will see in the next three chapters, a similar dynamic is at work in India. It is worth dwelling in particular on the role of unintended conse-

[86] Ibid., p. 52.   [87] Ibid. (emphasis added).
[88] See Barry R. Weingast, 'The Economic Role of Political Institutions: Market-Preserving Federalism and Economic Growth', *Journal of Law, Economics, and Organization*, vol. 11 (Spring 1995); and Ronald I. McKinnon, 'Market-Preserving Fiscal Federalism', *Working Paper*, Department of Economics (Palo Alto, Calif.: Stanford University, 1994).
[89] For a less zero-sum approach to centre–provincial relations, see Linda Chelan Li, *Centre and Provinces: China 1978–93* (Oxford: Oxford University Press, 1998).
[90] Montinola *et al.*, 'Federalism, Chinese Style', p. 52.

quences, as these are critical to the logic by which reforms become politically rooted in any country, particularly in a democracy. One potential objection to the arguments advanced in this book is that they attribute too much foresight to India's reformers and political managers. On the contrary: many of the explanations offered in the chapters that follow rely upon the logic of unintended consequences. For instance, there is no contention that when India's initial package of economic reforms was unveiled in July 1991 that either the finance minister or the prime minister had counted upon the federal political system to smooth the political path for the continued implementation of reform. Theirs was not a premeditated strategy. Yet, once the reform programme was further under way, the benefits of federalism became clear to at least some policy analysts and political managers in New Delhi. Inclined to take the path of least political resistance – given the perceived need to do something about the country's perilous economic condition – their reliance upon the capacities of the federal system became greater over time.

Clearly, with India as much as with China, 'the actual process of decentralization has gone far beyond its original intent'.[91] And in both cases it has been strengthened by the increased power of the political actors who have championed economic reform at the state/provincial and local level. By creating a 'cellular polity', the prospects for reversing either reform or decentralisation are limited.[92] That a number of the further political implications of decentralisation in China were unexpected outcomes emerges clearly in a study of rural enterprise reform in China by Zhou and White.[93] The authors quote Deng Xiaoping's view of this process: 'Generally speaking, our rural reforms have proceeded very fast, and farmers have been enthusiastic. What took us by surprise completely was the development of township and village industries . . . This is not the achievement of our central government'.[94]

The other side of this story of interest to our examination of the Indian case is the 'quiet' way in which authorities at the provincial and local levels went about implementing the reforms which produced the results that so impressed Deng. These reformers found it politically expedient not to trumpet their intentions. When pressed by higher authorities or powerful interests, they often obfuscated. It is not difficult to appreciate the wisdom of restraint in either democratic India (where vocal interests outside the state can make life difficult for reformers within government)

[91] Jia Hao and Lin Zhimin, 'Introduction', in Jia Hao and Lin Zhimin (eds.), *Changing Central-Local Relations in China: Reform and State Capacity* (Boulder, Colo.: Westview Press, 1994), p. 3.   [92] Ibid., p. 11.

[93] Kate Xiao Zhou and Lynne T. White III, 'Quiet Politics and Rural Enterprise Reform in China', *Journal of Developing Areas*, vol. 29 (July 1995), pp. 461–90.

[94] Ibid., p. 461.

or authoritarian China (where interests within the one-party regime can effectively thwart the efforts of those outside the state or operating at its peripheries). Zhou and White go on to highlight the complex nature of ends-means calculations which makes rational-choice explanations for political behaviour so very difficult, arguing that 'people often have an interest in making sure their ideals remain *ambiguous*, not choosing among preferences until the net benefits of doing so are clear'.[95] This conceptualisation finds direct parallels in the Indian experience with economic reform, where the actions (and even the awareness) of political actors 'can simply be fuzzier than a strict rational-action accounting of preferences suggests'.[96]

In summary, we find that in both China and India the incentives thrown up by economic reform can result in unpredictable political realignments. To the extent that these result in activity at lower levels of the political system, they may benefit the political sustainability of reform by generating responses that are: (a) couched in 'quiet' and 'ambiguous' terms that forestall political resistance; (b) based upon an unclear set of preferences, which may themselves assist plausible denials of reformist ambitions among the actors involved; and (c) useful in reducing the interest-group pressure facing reformers at the apex of the political system.

Before moving on to the other main country case – Mexico – it is worth taking a brief detour to Ghana, where Jeffrey Herbst's research furnishes similar lessons concerning the relationship between national and subnational political arenas in contributing to the sustainability of reform.[97] One of the difficulties facing Jerry Rawlings' government, according to Herbst, was its seeming inability to generate a new pro-reform constituency despite what were seen to be extremely positive economic-performance indicators. Here was a case where reform was actually working, and yet a widespread support base for the government was not coalescing. Part of this had to do with 'the ethnic split between the [ruling] PNDC and the majority of the rural population'.[98] The most promising remedy, according to party and government sources cited by Herbst, was the creation of decentralised representative institutions. This conclusion arose primarily from their assessment of neighbouring countries:

senior Ghanaian officials are critical of efforts at democratization, such as Nigeria's, that focus on creating national organizations (e.g., two major political parties) rather than a local base for democracy. In particular, they feel that such efforts are incompatible with economic reform.[99]

---

[95] Ibid., p. 482 (emphasis added).   [96] Ibid., pp. 481–2.
[97] Jeffrey Herbst, *The Politics of Reform in Ghana, 1982–1991* (Berkeley: University of California Press, 1993).   [98] Ibid., p. 86.   [99] Ibid., p. 89.

The district assemblies that did ultimately emerge were not equal to the task of 'providing the PNDC with the kind of institutional conduits needed to have a true rural constituency'.[100] The lack of such institutions meant that opposition to reform, mobilised in some cases around local-ised ethnic identity, had no subnational channels through which it could be accommodated. Consequently, it engulfed the apex of the political system, overwhelming the capacity of the national leadership to respond with sophisticated tactics of political management.[101] The over-central-ised approach to the early phase of reform – macroeconomic stabilisation – was deemed necessary in order to cope with political dissent. By the time the limits of this approach for a further deepening of the reforms became apparent, it was too late for corresponding alterations to the institutional context. The political die had been cast. As Herbst sum-marised it, 'the very approach to stabilization that the Rawlings govern-ment took makes winning political support during structural adjustment extremely difficult'.[102]

While the Indian reform programme announced in 1991 was also crafted and promulgated by a small coterie of advisers in the prime minister's inner circle, the depth of India's institutional structure, pen-etrating down to the state level and below, was already in place. This made possible a smoother transition to more broad-based political par-ticipation in the reform process – even when some of the actors involved in the later phase, such as state-level politicians, were 'participating' under duress. India's political institutions – formal and informal – may have been in an advanced state of decay following twenty or more years of assault from both within and outside the political system.[103] But they preserved the requisite degree of malleability, and are responding to the challenge. The nature of this adaptability is the subject of Chapter 5, while the interplay between ethnic/caste politics and issues arising during the course of implementing adjustment at the state level is discussed in the latter portion of Chapter 6.

This consistent focus on tactics of manipulation and obfuscation is not intended simply to point out the existence of such devious means. Inves-tigating the ways in which they are employed helps to highlight the

[100] Ibid., p. 91.
[101] The prevalence of this phenomenon in a range of policy areas has been noted in Richard Crook and James Manor, 'Democratic Decentralisation and Institutional Performance: Four Asian and African Experiences Compared', *Journal of Commonwealth and Compara-tive Politics*, vol. 33, no. 3 (Nov. 1995), pp. 309–34.
[102] Herbst, *The Politics of Reform in Ghana*, p. 86.
[103] For a good review of the many dimensions of political decay, see Paul R. Brass, *The New Cambridge History of India, IV-1: The Politics of India Since Independence*, 2nd ed. (Cambridge: Cambridge University Press, 1994).

foundations of 'actually existing democracy' as it is practised in both the developing south and the developed north. This is not an attack on democracy, an attempt to reveal its class biases or inherent conservatism. The analysis set forth in this book seeks to defend democracy from the charge of inflexibility, of sclerosis-inducing tendencies. As Eric Nordlinger argued persuasively almost two decades ago, governments operating within democratic political environments have a great deal of autonomy in their dealings with organised interests.[104] But the ability to avail of this luxury is often the result of a painstaking process of building networks of lasting relationships between political actors within and outside government. In other words, it rests upon a curious paradox: governmental autonomy from powerful interests can be seen to emerge, in large part, from the creation of institutions that appear to be based on collusion between government and powerful interests. The reason why is that the history of consultation, negotiation, and accommodation instils a sense of trust in the state on the part of organised interests. It is this legacy of trust which reformers have been able to exploit by pursuing a gradual programme of reform that cloaks change in the garb of continuity.

This phenomenon is found in countries other than India. Blanca Heredia's study of the political sustainability of economic policy reform in Mexico reveals that the Mexican government, faced with political dilemmas which in many ways resembled those encountered by their counterparts in India, pursued a similar course of action.[105] Though Mexico can be considered, at best, a quasi-democracy, reformers within the government clearly had to contend with the influence of powerful interests. And while many of the specifics of the two country cases diverge considerably, one of Heredia's main findings is strikingly similar to the one advanced in this book:

this chapter suggests that the relative causal weight of economic cleavages in the process of economic policy making, rather than being constant across space and time, is itself determined by the nature of the formal and informal institutions through which political power is generated and reproduced in different periods and national settings.[106]

Though Heredia connects this argument with other claims less relevant to the purposes of the present study, its implications are of direct relevance.

---

[104] Eric A. Nordlinger, *On the Autonomy of the Democratic State* (Cambridge, Mass.: Harvard University Press, 1981).

[105] Blanca Heredia, 'Making Economic Reform Politically Viable: The Mexican Experience', in William C. Smith, Carlos H. Acuna, and Eduardo A. Gamarra (eds.), *Democracy, Markets, and Structural Reform in Latin America: Argentina, Bolivia, Brazil, Chile, and Mexico* (New Brunswick, NJ: Transaction Publishers/North-South Center, University of Miami, 1993), pp. 265–91.

[106] Ibid., p. 266.

In particular, we must stress the analytical importance of the notion that institutions, rather than merely creating alternative patterns through which economically defined groups define and pursue their objectives, can actually help to determine whether conflict between economic interests becomes all-consuming.

Heredia provides an impressive array of evidence which demonstrates the capacity of formal and informal political institutions in Mexico to undermine the capacity of economic interests to thwart the reformist ambitions of governing elites. As we will see in Chapter 5, which examines how India's dense network of formal and informal political institutions defuses potentially crippling resistance to reform measures, there are very clear parallels in the Indian case. The formal institution of a federal division of political power, for instance, was crucial in both countries.[107] As Heredia summarises the Mexican situation, '*the highly differential regional impact* of crisis and adjustment expanded the government's room for maneuver by dispersing costs and, thus, dividing losers'.[108]

This book's discussion of the Indian case takes this logic one step further: while emphasising the refractory effects of federal politics, we also pay particular attention to the role which, in India's democratic setting, regional governments themselves have played in managing political conflicts that arise within their jurisdictions. That is, without the additional 'advantage' of a Mexican-style quasi-authoritarian setting, the political sustainability of India's reform programme relied to a much greater extent on spreading the burden of managing its political consequences among authorities operating at lower levels of the political system. Moreover, state-level politicians in India often cope with the interest-group pressures generated by economic reform by strategically shifting into the idiom of identity politics, which is far better suited to the

[107] This is also an important theme in analyses of reform in other federal countries. On Russia, see Peter Kirkow, *Russia's Provinces: Authoritarian Transformation versus Local Autonomy* (Basingstoke: Macmillan, 1998). For a contrary view, see Darell Slider, 'Russian Economic Reform: Regional Policies and Market-Distorting Federalism', paper presented at the Annual Meeting of the American Political Science Association, 28–31 August 1997, Washington, DC.

[108] Heredia, 'Making Economic Reform Politically Viable', p. 279 (emphasis added). On this point, see also, Blanca Heredia, 'The Political Economy of the Mexican Crisis', in Dharam Ghai (ed.), *The IMF and the South* (London: Zed Books/United Nations Research Institute for Social Development, 1991), pp. 117–38. For an account which stresses the importance of political centralisation (through an analysis of the Mexican government's Solidarity programme), see Wayne A. Cornelius, Ann L. Craig, and Jonathan Fox, 'Mexico's National Solidarity Program: An Overview', in Wayne A. Cornelius, Ann L. Craig, and Jonathan Fox (eds.), *Transforming State-Society Relations in Mexico: The Solidarity Strategy* (San Diego: Center for US-Mexican Studies, University of California, 1994), p. 12.

regional level. This question is dealt with in Chapter 6's discussion of 'political skills', in which we will find a close connection between the strategies pursued by India's (sometimes reluctant) reformers and Heredia's argument concerning the potential for political institutions actually to decrease the political salience of conventional economic cleavages, rather than simply to manage the contradictions more effectively.[109]

In approaching the empirical material on India, we have followed a broad conception of political institutions that also finds expression in Heredia's analysis of the Mexican case. While Heredia examines the impact of specific features of governmental organisation – such as federalism (mentioned above) and the fixed one-term presidency – she also treats institutions in a way that allows her to give adequate explanatory weight to political variables that in many studies of the politics of adjustment are marginalised because of their seemingly random occurrence. She thus expands the notion of institutions to include relationships that: (1) embody patterns of behaviour; (2) influence the expectations of a diverse set of actors; and (3) derive their legitimacy from their time-tested adaptability. In particular, Heredia's approach to institutions assigns a key role to interaction amongst economic, social, and governing elites. The capacity of these relationships to lengthen the time horizons of elites that might otherwise have fiercely resisted policy reform – 'by', in her words, 'increasing tolerance to what are perceived as short-term rather than permanent costs'[110] – is what allows them to play a role other than the sort of change-resistant function assigned to them by theories which advocate 'insulation' of policy-makers from representatives of sectoral interests.

Indeed, Heredia argues that in Mexico '[n]etworks of reciprocity that connect workers, labor elites, and government officials operate on the basis of long-term relations', a phenomenon which in India, as we shall see, has given both central and state governments considerable medium-term flexibility. This, in turn, has been used to chip away at the basis of organised labour's political power. This room for manoeuvre stems from individual governing elites' accumulated fund of goodwill, and the general belief that, '[r]ather than being dependent on the outcome of any given round of the game, relations between unions and the government are *premised upon the longevity of the game itself*'.[111] It is also worth noting

---

[109] Not all accounts of the Mexican case grasp the contribution that federalism can make to sustainable reform by pitting provincial politicians against one another. An editorial in the *Economist*, for instance, argued that 'granting more power to the states might strengthen reactionary PRI [Institutional Revolutionary Party] provincial bosses with whom Mr Salinas has clashed'. See 'The Clash in Mexico', *Economist*, 22 January 1994, pp. 13–14.   [110] Heredia, 'Making Economic Reform Politically Viable', p. 274.
[111] Ibid., p. 277 (emphasis added).

that Heredia considers this logic to contain other, less transparent, aspects: 'transactions involved in the relationship comprise much more than wages', she argues. 'They include both legal and illicit economic and political benefits for union elites as well as various compensations for the rank and file'.[112]

All of these dynamics find close parallels in the Indian experience of managing the politics of liberalisation. While the Mexican president may have at his disposal an 'array of both legal and informal' powers augmented by 'extensive systems of control developed over decades' that exceed those possessed by Indian prime ministers or chief ministers, the uses to which these are put in times of change bear a striking resemblance to what one finds in India. 'Discretionary executive power', Heredia argues, 'was extremely crucial, for instance, in recuperating or maintaining the support of key social groups through particularistic negotiations and concessions'[113] – a statement which is certainly as true of India. One reason why this technique proved so effective relates to the nature and extent of competitive pluralism in both polities. According to Heredia, '[t]he highly fragmented quality of political relations and traditional power-sharing arrangements that had long provided cooperation at the intra-elite level proved vital in allowing the political system to cope with the acute tensions associated with crisis and adjustment'.[114] It is this nexus of 'traditional power-sharing arrangements', elite 'cooperation', and a system of 'political relations' that constitutes one of the most important types of informal institutions that political leaders can possess – provided they conform to the three qualifications outlined above.

By explaining the political sustainability of economic reform from a perspective which considers elites as operating within a set of perception- and behaviour-conditioning relationships, Heredia is able to turn the 'collective action' dilemma on its head, shifting the question of why it is impossible for diverse economic interests to unite behind a policy of economic reform (which may ultimately be crucial to the revitalisation of the economic system on which they all rely), to the question of why it may be difficult for economic interests to mount a coordinated campaign of resistance to a reform programme which threatens each individually:

Potential allies were pitted against one another in their desperate pursuit of particular benefits [dangled during negotiations by governing elites] . . . In the case of industrialists, for example, collective action against the government proved extremely difficult to organize and sustain because government policy tended to exacerbate – intentionally or not – differences that naturally exist among private firms due to size and sectoral or regional location. *A long history of particularistic*

---

[112] Ibid.   [113] Ibid., p. 276.   [114] Ibid., p. 275.

negotiations with the state apparatus and a set of interest-based, private sector organizations – along with the crosscutting and often contradictory effects of different economic policy measures – further limited the ability of badly hurt economic sectors or politically active business elites to forge opposition coalitions and alliances.[115]

As in the Indian case, the history of government-interest relations – not merely privileged status in terms of outcomes, but the expectation of continued access and an ongoing relationship involving consultation, bargaining, and accommodation – was aided by a set of crucial assumptions among economic elites. Chief among these was a belief that, while economic reform might be based upon an assortment of policy guidelines, the government was pursuing these in its own 'flexible' fashion. This implied strategies that were open to change in response to shifting circumstances, thus permitting the possibility of accommodating the concerns of a wide array of interests. Interest groups in both Mexico and India, in other words, were aware that in the absence of a clear-cut recipe for adjustment, various governmental entities were improvising, and that while much of this improvising made possible manipulations designed to increase the government's negotiating leverage, it was still worth remaining engaged in order to maintain influence and benefit from new opportunities as they might arise. This logic has clearly been in effect in India, and gives ample grounds for us to concur with Heredia's conclusion: 'Discretionary executive power and hopes of preferential treatment were critical because they made individual negotiation the most reasonable course of action for private economic elites'.[116]

The important point is that it is not merely the executive's powers, but also the institutional context, that invested them with the capacity to help sustain economic reform. By this, we mean the set of complex, longstanding, and deeply embedded relationships within which influence was exerted in the process of negotiating political bargains. The very nature of economic policy-making renders coercive authority necessary though not sufficient to the task at hand. In their quest to manage the politics of economic policy reform, governing elites are seeking an economic response from the same agents whose political influence they are simultaneously trying to subvert. A stance which too vigorously exercises state authority to pursue the latter might succeed by sacrificing any hope of achieving the former. And from the larger perspective of political survival, most politicians – especially those in 'fragmented polities' – recognise that power flows from the ability to broker agreements. This requires, in addition to a credible threat of exclusion, a continued willingness of an

---

[115] Ibid., pp. 275–6 (emphasis added).   [116] Ibid., p. 276.

indefinable 'quorum' of elites to play the game. This will not be the case if the system fails to generate at least the appearance of a potential accommodation.

If, as we are arguing, institutions of this type are crucial to the relative capacity of political leaders effectively to pursue objectives, it is nevertheless the case that there are costs to maintaining the relationships which form the core of these institutions. Politicians who operate within such contexts – particularly, perhaps, those operating in systems in which the formal institutions of state are experiencing severe decay – are alert to both imperatives: the need to ensure that economic actors have an adequate incentive to remain economically engaged (and thus to assist in achieving the aims of policy reform) as well as politically incorporated (and thus willing to trust the state's capacity to, at a minimum, ensure their survival until the next round of negotiations). They are also aware of the constantly shifting relationship between the two. By building on Heredia's findings, this book will allow us to derive generalisable lessons that transcend the variable of regime type: for, in both semi-authoritarian Mexico and democratic India, 'the elitist nature of the political system and the multidimensional and long-term character of elite-client relations were absolutely central in allowing policy reformers to manipulate the highly unequal costs of crisis and adjustment effectively'.[117]

Democratic theorists such as Linz and Huntington have stressed the importance of elites in consolidating democracy, particularly their role in allowing institutions to emerge through painful transitions.[118] Expanding on this logic, one of the central arguments of this book is that elites are just as vital to the process of consolidating the political foundations of economic reform. This emphasis is found throughout the literature on the politics of economic reform, and for good reason. This important point relates to how we can explain variability in outcomes that emerge from relatively similar reform programmes. As Thomas and Grindle put it:

The range of outcomes results from the fact that implementation is an interactive and ongoing process of decision making by policy elites (political and bureaucratic officials who have decision-making responsibilities and whose decisions become authoritative for society) and managers (implementors) in response to reformist initiatives . . . They are concerned about achieving politically, institutionally, and economically viable outcomes of efforts to introduce change. We

[117] Heredia, 'Making Economic Reform Politically Viable', p. 279.
[118] The emphasis democratic theorists place on the role of elites is highlighted in Doh Chull Shin, 'On the Third Wave of Democratization: A Synthesis and Evaluation of Recent Theory and Research', *World Politics*, vol. 47 (October 1994), p. 139.

view the process of policy change as one shaped significantly by the actions of individuals in strategic locations to influence particular change. While change may take unexpected directions, it is a process that can be influenced by policy elites and managers and is not determined by impersonal forces.[119]

Focusing on the incentives facing Indian elites, and their skill in using and moulding institutions in reacting to them, allows us to assign to the process of change a locus of agency. Without ignoring important structural parameters, this mode of analysis avoids the determinism found in many earlier depictions of Indian political economy. It puts the state at centre stage, but does not impose a script on its leading players. Like Gramsci's conception of politics, it places primacy upon improvisation.

This book devotes separate chapters to incentives, institutions, and skills, though there is an explicit recognition that the three features interact. The literature on the new institutionalism works under the assumption that the shape of political institutions influences the type of incentives facing state elites.[120] In the context of capacity-building reforms in Latin America, Barbara Geddes, for instance, argues that in 'analyzing the institutionally determined incentives facing political leaders, one can explain state actions that might be unexpected from the perspective of more traditional approaches'.[121] While Geddes uses a more comprehensive rational-actor model, and focuses on schematic features of the institutional setting such as electoral and party systems, the basic thrust of her approach is adopted in this book's analysis of Indian adjustment. In particular, there is a common effort to transcend the depressing choice 'between systematic structuralist arguments that lack plausible individual-level foundations and plausible individual-level explanations that lack theoretical reach'.[122]

It also seeks to elaborate a more realistic view of democracy. Schmitter, for instance, has argued that democracies often work in rather complex ways, acting more like a set of interlocking mechanisms than a unitary whole. Perhaps most importantly, his work demonstrates that many (if not most) long-established democracies, as well as those of more recent vintage, exhibit traits that violate the hallowed principles of accountability, participation, and unrestricted freedom of association. This can be seen quite clearly, though both development theorists and aid practi-

---

[119] John W. Thomas and Merilee S. Grindle, 'After the Decision: Implementing Policy Reforms in Developing Countries', *World Development*, vol. 18, no. 8 (1990), p. 1165.

[120] See James March and Johan P. Olsen, 'The New Institutionalism: Organizational Factors in Political Life', *American Political Science Review*, vol. 78 (1984), pp. 734–49.

[121] Barbara Geddes, *Politician's Dilemma: Building State Capacity in Latin America* (Berkeley: University of California Press, 1994), p. 12.   [122] Ibid., p. 6.

tioners fail conspicuously to do so, in his complex model of how democracies incorporate fragments of civil society.[123] Schmitter views modern democracy as an interlocking network of five 'partial regimes', rather than a unified system based upon clear lines of accountability. The nature of each regime is determined by the 'action situations' in which political actors are engaged. 'Electoral regimes' structure relations between legislatures and political parties, while 'concertation regimes' organise the political role of particularised interests, such as capital and labour. Yet, clearly some of these regimes can rely upon restrictions upon associational freedom. As Olson famously pointed out, the exit options of trade-union members are often limited by organisational rules sanctioned by law.[124] And the 'clientelist regime', centred on the personalistic networks constructed by local party bosses found in many democracies, is 'formed on the basis of exclusive instead of inclusive participation of relevant social actors, thereby violating a key constitutive principle of the national democratic regime'.[125]

In the next three chapters, the nature of these ambiguities will become clearer. By examining the sometimes arcane details of policy formulation and implementation we will begin to see the ways in which democratic politics in India was able to accommodate far-reaching changes that many had thought beyond its capacity. Rather than attempting simply to expose democracy's authoritarian underside, the aim is to highlight the extent to which exploiting the coalition-building potential of open competitive politics often requires the underhanded tactics and impure motivations which all politics breed, but only democracy can tame.

[123] Philippe C. Schmitter, 'The Consolidation of Democracy and Representation of Social Groups', *American Behavioral Scientist*, vol. 35 (1992), pp. 422–49.

[124] Mancur Olson, *The Logic of Collective Action* (Cambridge, Mass.: Harvard University Press, 1965).

[125] James R. Scaritt and Shaheen Mozaffar, 'Toward Sustainable Democracy in Africa: Can US Policy Make a Difference?', *Working Paper No. 171*, African Studies Centre, Boston University, 1993, p. 5.

4 Political incentives: elite perceptions and the calculus of survival

Why would India's governing elites be willing to continue with reforms which – because they emphasise decision-making by markets instead of politicians – should have them fearing the loss of their political *raison d'être*? Regardless of the motivation for initiating policy reorientation, what incentives inclined politicians ruling in central and state governments to concentrate, in the main, on managing the political transition which sustainable adjustment demands, rather than battling to halt the reform process itself? These are hugely important questions, since incentives are crucial to any understanding of how democracies are able to cope with the political uncertainties that can undermine the sustainability of economic reform. A prosecuting attorney's first job in a murder trial is to establish the defendant's motive. Similarly, any attempt to build a case for democracy's ability to promote a sustainable reorientation of development strategy must detail the reasons why governing elites are willing to continue reforming once the immediate threat of economic meltdown has subsided.

The objective of this chapter, then, is to advance an argument for the importance of two broad types of incentives. They both proceed from the perspective of governing elites, because it is they who ultimately take the decision of whether or not to abandon reform. Interest groups do not halt adjustment programmes; politicians do. This, of course, is only half of the story, since social groups have influence as well as interests. So, while we are primarily concerned with the incentives facing governing elites, the notion of incentives must be characterised dialectically, because one of the primary forces shaping the actions of governing elites is their appreciation of how socio-economic interests themselves will respond to the new incentives created by the evolving policy environment.

The first incentive to continue reform (or at least not actively to oppose it) is that a move towards a more liberal policy framework need not spell the end of governing elites' ability to derive illegal income, or to use policy instruments to oblige important political constituencies. Creative politicians have been able to identify new sources of funds to maintain their political careers, while preserving or adapting some of the more established means of cultivating political support.[1] It should be emphasised, however, that while subverting public office for personal profit is clearly illegal, not all patronage can be considered 'corruption'. Patronage politics can make governments 'responsive', thus enhancing their democratic credentials according to various measures.

The sense of security engendered by knowing that old-style politics is not necessarily threatened with extinction, combined with the fluidity of the interest-group structure, provides Indian politicians with a second incentive to continue reforming. This is that they can be relatively confident that by exercising the tactical skill that experience in democratic politics has honed in them, and by relying on the resilience of formal and informal institutions to contain the conflicts that can undermine broad-based coalitions of support, they will be in a position gradually to forge new sorts of alliances from among the diversity of interests which prevail in India's vibrant civil society, and which policy alterations tend continuously to reshuffle. Governing elites, in this sense, have immense faith in the capacity of socio-economic interests to respond creatively, rather than intransigently, to new policies, and to do so in ways that will provide fresh material for political coalition building.

It is important to appreciate that these two incentives do not come ready-made from a packet. They depend on the supreme self-assurance one finds among India's veteran politicians regarding their capacity to adapt to change – a not unjustifiable attitude given their experience of managing the wrenching social, economic, and political transformations that have occurred in the fifty years since independence. Politicians with little exposure to constant change are less inclined to believe they can weather its vicissitudes. The capacity to respond to the types of incentives thrown up by Indian democracy, in other words, is largely a function of system longevity: survivors often begin to think of themselves as survivors, and so have less fear of change.

The argument advanced in this chapter is not that governing elites' political self-confidence is in itself sufficient to ensure the sustainability of economic adjustment. This would amount to an assertion that Indian politicians are particularly fearless, feel impervious to political pressure, and routinely take tough decisions without care for the consequences. Their record of populism and their increasing inability to get re-elected at all levels of government clearly do not support such conclusions. The argument, instead, is that: (a) this confidence, and the political peace of

[1] A similar dynamic has been noted in Peru. See Kenneth M. Roberts, 'Neoliberalism and the Transformation of Populism in Latin America: The Peruvian Case', *World Politics*, vol. 48, no. 1 (October 1995), pp. 82–116.

mind it breeds, inclines governing elites to take limited political risks on gradual reform because of the existence of two important political incentives thrown up by the combination of liberal democracy and economic reform; and (b) the successful response to these incentives reinforces the self-confidence among a broad range of political elites by demonstrating that these risks do not necessarily imperil political survival.

In addition to providing a revealing glimpse into some of the less wholesome reasons why democratic political systems are more open to change than many models of political economy acknowledge, the arguments advanced here also help to highlight three themes that are central to the arguments this book seeks to advance. First, each of the two incentives for governing elites to continue with reform demonstrates the key contribution of gradualism. The gradual nature of the reform process allows politicians to write the rules of the transition as they go along, providing ample scope for self-serving decision-making. This, in turn, can be used to augment resources, reward collaborators, and divide opponents of reform. It also removes some of the pressure which can lead positions on policy matters to become hardened by the apprehensions that often accompany dizzyingly rapid change.

Second, the combination of the two incentives also demonstrates the delicate balance between transparency and obscurity. The ability of opportunistic politicians to devise new methods of obtaining illegal income in a liberalising economy relies upon the exploitation of decision-making structures that are obscured from the public gaze. Many examples of self-serving, secretive decision-making are ultimately cloaked in the rhetoric of promoting public welfare. On the other hand, the belief that established interests are not immutable – that they are susceptible to negotiation, manipulation, and the threat of being abandoned in favour of emergent interests – depends crucially on the openness and transparency of India's liberal political system. This is because politicians' assessments of when to bargain, when to gamble on the support of a nascent interest, when to deploy scarce political capital by offering limited concessions, when to employ divisive tactics – all depend on their ability to gauge the strength and cohesiveness of interest groups. This is far more difficult in a polity characterised by impeded information-flow and barriers to free association.

Third, and finally, the emphasis placed on the scope for inducing change in the interest-group basis of political support demonstrates the importance of a diversified civil society. Interest groups in India are not merely divided, compensated, and coopted by politicians pursuing policy aims. They are not simply passive. They are capable of perceiving new ways of achieving goals and reorienting their attitudes accordingly. This is because the sheer diversity of interests in India leaves their constituent members many options. There is not one national business organisation, but at least four influential 'apex chambers'. This, naturally, leaves business open to 'divide-and-rule' tactics by various government agencies. But it also provides an opportunity for individual actors to evaluate the relative worth of alternative adaptive strategies. Other manifestations of a functioning civil society – such as a free and vibrant press, discussion fora which regularly and informally bring together policy-makers and representatives of diverse interests, and even organisations based on caste and communal affiliation – infuse public life with a fluidity profoundly lacking in countries where representatives of 'front organisations', led by individuals with few alternative career paths, are either cowed by government repression or take unrealistically intractable positions.

With these thoughts in mind, let us examine each of the two incentives.

Profiteering and patronage amidst economic reform

The first incentive to continue reform is that reform does not deny politicians the ability to profiteer personally or to build networks of patronage by steering benefits to political supporters. In most cases the ability to profiteer and to oblige supporters amount to the same thing, political 'brokerage commissions' being the clearest example. Sometimes, however, politicians exchange favours not for money, but for vague promises which can be encashed subsequently for political services such as delivering votes, staging demonstrations, and even engaging in political violence. Since the line separating profiteering from patronage is rather blurred, these two types of transactions will be discussed together in this section, with distinctions highlighted only when they are relevant to the specific events under consideration.

To make proper sense of the dynamics of profiteering and patronage in an economy undergoing a transition, it is essential to understand that Indian politicians are concerned not only with the amount of political funding they can raise, but above all with the fate of their political careers. Those who compete for power in democratic political systems must win elections, and thus crave popularity. Consequently, they fear the loss of the means by which they can influence individual segments of a diverse electorate. One of the most important means of influence at their disposal is money. By manipulating the levers of policy and abusing positions of power, Indian politicians have been able to build substantial personal fortunes and immense political war chests. The two are often indistinguishable. As we will see, the process by which economic reform has been introduced in India has allowed the perpetuation of many existing sources of patronage. It has also opened up entirely new avenues of deriving corrupt income and obliging particular segments among powerful interest groups. This, combined with other elements of the political framework in which politicians operate, has generated a tangible sense of optimism that they can weather the political storms that change carries in its wake.

Furthermore, a democratic political system furnishes three features which facilitate the successful operation of this system of incentives. First, electoral accountability provides a built-in mechanism that keeps a check on the avarice of the political class, preventing an upsurge of popular revulsion that could undermine the sustainability of economic reform. Second, the tactical skill that prolonged experience with democratic politics has inculcated in Indian politicians has allowed them to judge which types of compensatory actions will most effectively mask their self-serving decisions. (This is elaborated further in Chapter 6, on political skills.) And, third, the existence of well-integrated political parties as a means of sharing the illicit spoils of reform tends to decrease the sense of resentment among political elites who do not hold the key decision-making positions that they are not getting their fair share. (This forms a large part of the discussion on informal political institutions in Chapter 5.) As one analyst put it, 'this is the honour-among-thieves factor . . . Even if we find it sickening, it keeps cropping up in Indian democracy'.[2]

It is of course true that many successful and widespread methods for skimming from public funds have been swept away by policy reforms. One of the most lucrative was the system of industrial licensing, under which business plans had to be approved for the establishment, expansion, relocation, or diversification of an industrial venture. This has been almost entirely dismantled, as has the hugely corrupt and inefficient Directorate General of Technical Development, which issued mandatory clearances in a variety of industries. The vast bureaucracy charged with enforcing the various anti-trust provisions of the Monopolies and Restrictive Trade Practices (MRTP) Act has also been a victim of industrial-policy reform. Abolishing the office of Controller of Capital Issues and the discontinuation of the finance ministry's practice of making *ad hoc* changes in customs and excise duties has also weakened corrupt relations between businessmen and high-level bureaucrats and ministers in New Delhi. Also a large blow to the political fundraising business has been foreign-exchange liberalisation and relaxation of import regulations on gold and silver that had sustained a complex network of black-market

---

[2] Interview with Kumar Ketkar, associate editor, *Maharashtra Times*, 20 January 1994, Bombay.

operators in need of political patrons to protect them from the enforcement machinery.[3]

Preservation of existing methods

But while it is impossible to measure with any precision how much these and other reforms have affected the political fundraising prospects for politicians at various levels of the political system, it is important to recognise that many proven sources continue to fill the coffers of political parties. As one commentator noted, '[d]elicensing has not ended bribery in the sphere of economic activity. There are hundreds of thousands of things that need to be done in the course of conducting a business or running an industry'.[4] Supporting this conclusion was a survey of business executives conducted almost three years after the initiation of economic reform which found that bribery was still considered essential to obtain those clearances necessary for proceeding with industrial projects, particularly at the state level, and especially in states outside the western region.[5]

Reports of the Comptroller and Auditor General of India are filled with damning indictments of state-government actions which it would be difficult to attribute entirely to administrative failures.[6] At a very basic level, politicians continue to be needed as fixers. In early 1994, for instance, Glaxo India Ltd. successfully avoided an order by the Maharashtra Food and Drug Administration to close down its factory in Bombay following the intervention of a high-ranking member of the Bombay regional unit of the Congress Party whose brother was a major supplier to GIL.[7] Facilitating the process of obtaining a water or electricity connection is still a mainstay of 'constituency service', offered to those willing to pay a price, or in some cases to urban slum communities in exchange for *en bloc* voting. And there is also no plausible end in sight for the common system of dividing the standard 10 per cent 'commission' on public works and supply contracts in a ratio of 7:2:1 among those officials and politi-

[3] Vivek Bharati, 'Corruption and Reforms: Cutting the Unholy Links', *Times of India*, 16 July 1993. I am grateful to Vivek Bharati for pointing out to me the larger implications of the points he makes in his article. Interview, 12 October 1993, New Delhi.
[4] R. Vijayaraghavan, 'Corruption is a Cost of Production', *The Hindu*, 5 July 1993.
[5] National Council of Applied Economic Research, *Ninth Survey on Business Attitudes* (New Delhi, March 1994).
[6] A report on Maharashtra, for instance, discussed in detail the case of a polyester-yarn unit in Raigad district which avoided taxes of Rs. 191 million because of 'incorrect' interest charges. To make matters worse, the firm was allowed to repay arrears in instalments, and subsequent government demands were dropped in the absence of exact targets. Government of India, Office of the Comptroller and Auditor General, *State Report – Maharashtra* (New Delhi: Government Printing Office, April 1993).
[7] Interview with a management consultant who has worked for the Maharashtra state government, and has had direct contact with the cabinet, 4 March 1994, Bombay.

cians who sign the order, push the file, and fix the deal, respectively.[8]

Also providing a 'security blanket'[9] for reluctant reformers is the fact that even decisions not consistent with liberalisation continue to be effected since there is no non-negotiable injunction to prevent ministers taking actions they deem appropriate. Shortly after being appointed minister of chemicals and petrochemicals, Ram Lakhan Singh Yadav initiated a move to shift monoethyl glycol (MEG) to the 'negative list' of imports, thereby imposing quantitative restrictions on foreign purchases of this critical raw material for the polyester industry. The largest domestic producer of MEG, Reliance Industries Ltd., whose chairman has been considered close to the Congress Party since the days of Rajiv Gandhi, was expected to be the largest beneficiary of this move. Reports that notings on the administrative file relating to this issue underwent an inexplicable change in tenor in the weeks prior to the announcement at the very least raise strong suspicions about intent.[10]

Control over government jobs also remains an important source of patronage for politicians, one which shows little sign of giving way in a liberalised economy. Given the unequal social relations in legislative constituencies, the power of elected representatives to arrange appointments and transfers of employees in government educational, administrative, and police services not only raises resources, but is also a perquisite valued highly by legislators.[11] There are also scores of posts to which chief ministers, often at the recommendation of loyal legislators, can appoint sympathetic supporters. In an effort to consolidate his political position, in May 1994 Rajasthan chief minister Bhairon Singh Shekhawat began the process of nominating political appointees to more than forty quasi-government bodies, including sports organisations, cultural boards, business facilitation councils, 'urban improvement trusts', and commissions set up to aid minorities and other groups defined on the basis of social identity.[12]

Also reducing the trauma of transition is the ability of state-level

---

[8] This system, revealed by a civil servant from Tamil Nadu to journalist Sunil Sethi (*Mid-Day*, 26 March 1994), was also followed in Rajasthan and Maharashtra, according to industrialists in both states (interviews, 16 December 1993, Jaipur; and 22 February 1994, Bombay); and interviews with a middle-ranking bureaucrat in the Rajasthan department of medicine and health (15 December 1993, Jaipur) and a senior IAS officer in a Maharashtra government industrial agency (8 February 1994, Bombay).

[9] An IAS officer in a department which audits accounts of major spending ministries used this term to describe the way that politicians regarded those money-generating activities that liberalisation would not alter. Interview, 12 October 1993, New Delhi.

[10] *Indian Express*, 4 March 1994.

[11] According to a long-time observer of local politics in Karnataka, the ability to control appointments to these posts in a local constituency is the primary concern of the average MLA. Interview, E. Raghavan, Resident Editor, *Times of India*, 21 March 1994, Bangalore. Raghavan is currently finalising a book that develops this argument in detail.

[12] *The Hindu*, 29 May 1994.

politicians to continue providing political protection for leaders of local criminal organisations. This provides politicians with both 'money and muscle power', two of the assets considered crucial to the maintenance of a political machine in contemporary Indian politics. While former Maharashtra chief minister Sharad Pawar's connections with powerful underworld figures controlling elaborate international smuggling operations is an extreme example, ruling parties in most states forge links with small-time local mafias. Manufacturers of liquor are commonly allied to members of state governments, receiving assistance in evading excise taxes and securing lucrative vending concessions that involve substantial kickbacks. In early 1994, the Congress chief minister of Madhya Pradesh, for instance, was criticised by members of his own party for being too close to members of the local 'liquor mafia'.[13] In 1994 and 1995, the Rajasthan government effected seemingly benign reforms to the system of vending rights in order to benefit certain segments of the state's liquor lobby.[14] These and other unsavoury 'interest groups', such as operators of protection rackets, cultivate ties with state-level politicians,[15] and increasingly stand for office themselves.

Reform-minded politicians at the centre and in the states have also been careful to allay fears that control over local 'development' patronage by individual legislators will become a casualty of liberalisation. In December 1993, responding to pressures from within his own and other parties, the prime minister himself approved the creation of the Local Area Development Scheme, under which each MP is permitted to sanction projects worth Rs. 10 million per year within his or her own constituency.[16] As a result, almost 10 per cent of the Integrated Rural Development Programme (IRDP) budget of Rs. 70 billion for 1994–95 was to be spent according to the recommendations of India's nearly 700 MPs.[17] To the extent that such projects become associated directly with the elected representative, they are of immense political value. The BJP state government in Delhi subsequently initiated a similar scheme for MLAs, while in the 1994–95 Maharashtra budget the funding for the state's longstanding legislators' scheme was increased by 25 per cent.[18]

The state import canalising agencies, such as the State Trading Corporation, remain attractive to politicians in search of kick-

[13] *Economic Times*, 20 March 1994.
[14] Interview with the local correspondent of a national daily, 2 May 1995, Jaipur.
[15] This phenomenon was termed a 'protection racket within a protection racket', and was considered to be on the increase, by a retired IAS officer in Karnataka who has held extremely senior posts. Interview, 21 April 1994, Bangalore.
[16] *The Week*, 23 January 1994, pp. 28–35.
[17] *India Today*, 31 January 1994, p. 16. This number includes members of India's upper house, the Rajya Sabha.   [18] *Times of India*, 30 March 1994.

backs,[19] as do positions capable of influencing decisions on the import of high-tech engineering equipment[20] and weapons systems.[21] By the mid-1980s, it became difficult not to suspect that the type of high-level, big-payoff corruption associated with import kickbacks constituted a qualitative shift in the composition of corrupt income. Stanley Kochanek, an authority on business–government links in South Asia, argued that '[t]he extension of the permit-license-quota Raj to civilian and defense contracts clearly represents a whole new dimension to the problem'.[22] His conclusion was that the 'impact on Indian business is largely negative' because, among other things, it 'sharply reduces the leverage that political contributions have provided to Indian business'.[23]

One implication of this is that politicians have begun to enjoy a greater measure of autonomy from one of the interests that has been seen to have constrained any movement towards a more liberal economy. Relative increases in the autonomy of governing elites must be considered an important incentive to promote change. How reformers in the 1990s have built on this new-found autonomy to defuse the potency of business resistance to economic reform will be discussed later in this chapter, in the section on the fluidity of the interest-group structure. A second, related, implication of this relative shift in the composition of corrupt income is that it provided reformers an object lesson in the potential for finding alternative sources of profiteering and patronage – a potential they have further developed during the process of liberalisation. Some of the alternative sources are largely new to the Indian scene, while others are modifications to existing practices that were made more attractive in the context of a liberalising economy.

The emergence of new methods

Rhetorical justifications   That 'liberalisation' provides a convenient excuse for justifying a range of actions is an important point too often

---

[19] These were reportedly abused in the sugar import scandal of mid-1994, ultimately leading to the resignation of food minister, Kalpnath Rai, who later became a member of the anti-Narasimha Rao dissidence movement led by former cabinet minister Arjun Singh.

[20] Examples of kickback scandals include the purchase of drilling rigs allegedly involving top officials in the state-owned Mineral Exploration Corporation Ltd. (*Indian Express*, 10 December 1993), and a $19 million electric-locomotive deal approved by the railways minister against the advice of the Asian Development Bank and a Parliamentary Railway Convention Committee (*Sunday*, 8–14 August 1993, p. 36).

[21] The most well-known defence-related scandal involved the purchase of artillery guns from the Swedish firm Bofors, which played an important part in undermining the 'Mr Clean' image of former primer minister Rajiv Gandhi.

[22] Stanley Kochanek, 'Briefcase Politics in India: The Congress Party and the Business Elite', *Asian Survey*, vol. 27, no. 12 (December 1987), p. 1301.   [23] Ibid.

overlooked by analysts of the politics of economic adjustment.[24] The prevailing ethos of liberalisation, for instance, offers a means by which parties that head state governments can defend politically motivated actions designed to aid their core constituencies.

In May 1995 the newly elected BJP government in Gujarat seized the edible oil stocks of the parastatal National Dairy Development Board (NDDB) in what was seen as an effort to undermine its market-intervention operations, which over the previous six years had caused great damage to the fortunes of the state's private traders, a mainstay of the BJP's support base.[25] BJP politicians justified their actions by invoking the need to rectify the 'market-distortions' of the NDDB's operations, claiming that excessive warehousing had led to prices rising out of control.[26] Naturally, private traders were not averse to high prices in the short term, but weakening the NDDB was of great strategic interest. The significance of this episode is that the state government could use market-friendly rhetoric, legitimated by the environment of liberalisation, to take action on behalf of a clearly defined constituency (private traders) against a powerful enemy (the NDDB) by blaming it for prohibiting the free operation of the market and thereby failing to meet its stated objective of keeping prices in check. The validity of the government's economic logic is less important than its political implications.

The concept of liberalisation can also be invoked to justify tax changes – whether increases or decreases. Tax increases necessary to finance spending on the patronage-ridden state bureaucracies are often characterised as 'additional resource mobilisation' to reduce budget deficits, a major aim of liberalisation.[27] Tax cuts, often designed to benefit very narrowly defined constituencies, are often defended as removing barriers on private-sector business activity. The Maharashtra finance minister, for instance, justified the 1994–95 budget's reduction in sales tax for studded diamonds from 12 per cent to 2 per cent on the basis of the vital role this sector could play in the state's economic growth in the context of a liberalising economy, ridiculing the opposition's allegations that the ruling party had received kickbacks to the tune of Rs. 50 million.[28]

---

[24] For an exceptional account which has not ignored this dimension, but has in fact highlighted the way in which it responds to and reinforces ideological prejudices, see Narendar Pani, *Redefining Conservatism: An Essay on the Bias of India's Economic Reform* (New Delhi: Sage Publications, 1994).

[25] Russell Foulds, 'NDDB's Loss Could be Oil Lobby's Gain', *Deccan Herald*, 17 April 1995.   [26] *Economic Times*, 10 April 1995.

[27] See, for instance, the discussion relating to sales tax in: Government of Rajasthan, 'Budget Speech of Rajasthan Chief Minister Bhairon Singh Shekhawat for Fiscal Year 1993–94' (Jaipur: Government Publications Office, March 1993).

[28] *Times of India*, 30 March 1995.

The current emphasis in government policy statements on export-led growth also affords abundant scope for actions to benefit specific industry associations. In early 1994, for instance, the union commerce ministry announced its decision to set up an export promotion council for rice. This had been suggested by the All-India Rice Exporters' Association. The resources the council's political-appointee chairman would command were expected to help compensate for some of the opportunities for profiteering and patronage lost when the government abolished the export quota for non-basmati rice varieties.[29] The commerce ministry also obliged rice traders by removing the minimum export price (MEP) for basmati rice and beginning a phased reduction in the MEP for non-basmati varieties.

Despite liberalisation's association with dogmatic economism, Indian politicians have proven themselves capable of using the ideologically plastic environment it furnishes to continue favouring well-endowed lobbies – whether at the local, state, or central levels of the political system. Ironically, this is a characteristic it shares with socialism.

Privatisation and disinvestment Public-sector enterprises (PSEs) owned by state and central governments have been widely used for the personal benefit of politicians.[30] Politicians placed in charge of PSEs control access to employment opportunities within their firms, and in some cases have influenced hiring decisions in private-sector subcontractors. Non-management jobs are awarded largely on the basis of services rendered during election campaigns. Obtaining a management position often involves the payment of a 'commission', the amount of which is related to the percentage of the rents the manager is likely to receive from colluding with the MP, MLA, or non-elected party functionary in charge of the enterprise to subvert the firm's interest to their own. The means of profiteering include undercharging business buyers for the firm's products, receiving kickbacks for supply contracts, informally leasing out the firm's land or machinery to private firms, and diverting subsidised raw materials.[31] Since centrally owned PSEs in industries deemed 'strategic' faced little or no competition from licensed private-sector firms, politicians who controlled them could avoid even the trouble of under-invoicing clients, relying instead on the product or commodity's scarcity to generate illegal rents.

In addition to the apprehension that dismissing large numbers of

---

[29] *Financial Times* (London), 17 June 1994.
[30] See Baldev Raj Nayar, *India's Public Sector* (New Delhi: Popular Prakashan, 1990).
[31] Interview with an IAS officer in a Maharashtra state government industrial agency, 9 February 1994, Bombay.

workers will generate widespread discontent among the unionised working class generally, state and central governments are reluctant to shut down or sell off PSEs because of their importance as building blocks of political machines. Even committed reformers are hesitant to take action, or even to signal their intention to take action, for fear it may catalyse a revolt among their party colleagues. The prime minister and chief ministers are able to maintain support in their parties largely as a result of their ability to distribute posts which allow their occupants to cultivate their own political bases. Constantly plagued by intriguing dissidents from within their legislature parties, governments already find the existing number of posts insufficient to placate insurgents.[32] The idea of reducing this number through sell-offs and closures would seem to be anathema.

But the pecuniary gains from privatisation are potentially very attractive and can, in some circumstances, act as an incentive to politicians wary of losing a source of illegal income, but perhaps convinced that India's fiscal position is too precarious to sustain its bloated public sector much longer. By this logic, it makes sense to beat one's successors to whatever financial gain might be available. The ability of politicians both to profit directly and to oblige supporters in the business community (some would say that since assistance to supporters comes at a price this amounts to the same thing) has been a driving force behind efforts to divest at least a percentage of government holdings in PSEs.[33]

Evidence that privatisation could serve more than just a limited technical policy objective came fairly soon after the Narasimha Rao government announced its liberalisation programme. In early 1992, the Uttar Pradesh (UP) government's procedure for divesting a substantial stake in Uptron Colour Picture Tubes Ltd. faced serious allegations of corruption. The state government held 40 per cent of Uptron, the other major shareholders being national government financial institutions (35 per cent), and the Japanese firms Toshiba and Mitsubishi (a combined 16 per cent). Two resource constraints associated with adjustment made the divestment plan necessary. First, the UP government corporation that had invested in Uptron could not come up with the additional Rs. 140 million working capital needed by the company to continue production. Second, the national financial institutions, under pressure due to adjustment-related reductions in government budgetary support, needed to raise cash. The result of these pressures was that the UP government agreed to

---

[32] Arjun Singh, a rival of Narasimha Rao's for the Congress leadership until his expulsion from the party in late 1994, was notorious during his chief ministership of Madhya Pradesh for doling out chairmanships of public-sector firms to MLAs who could not be accommodated with cabinet berths. *India Today*, 28 February 1993, p. 30.

[33] Interview with a Congress MP, 1 April 1994, Bombay.

sell its 'rights shares', which would dilute its 40 per cent holding to 21 per cent. In addition to this 19 per cent, any new investor would have an immediate option to purchase the stakes held by the financial institutions, which had indicated their willingness to sell.

A combination of three irregularities in the UP government's method of selling its rights shares raised serious suspicions that the process was rigged to suit just one potential buyer – private-sector television manufac-turer Videocon – and that kickbacks were going to politicians.[34] First, the government was entering into private negotiations with individual firms instead of offering the shares to the public. Second, the offer was 'restrict-ive', meaning that only consumer electronics corporations with a turn-over of roughly Rs. 2 billion could bid for the shares. (Videocon's turn-over was the closest to this figure.) And, third, not all relevant information was provided to the firms interested in investing.[35]

Two main arguments are commonly invoked to counter the notion that privatisation (or partial disinvestment) may provide a new source of corrupt income for politicians. The first is that PSEs have been so poorly managed and burdened with such high levels of debt that potential private-sector buyers would not be interested in investing. The second is that any firms that might see an advantage to investing would be deterred by the prospect of managerial partnership with an inefficient and corrupt government organ – especially one that was already asking for bribes up front. The Uptron case helps to illustrate why these arguments, though in many instances valid, are not always so. The most compelling reason why a loss-making firm such as Uptron, which was Rs. 620 million in the red as of 1992, would make a good acquisition for a buyer such as Videocon was that it could provide vertical integration in a sector that had suffered from production bottlenecks. Uptron would provide Videocon's televi-sion-manufacturing plants with an assured supply of picture tubes, while at the same time serving as a captive buyer of the glass shells (a key input in picture tubes) produced by its newly created joint-venture in this sector. It is not unreasonable to assume that this kind of motivation might exist with respect to potential investors in other loss-making PSEs.[36]

The details of the Uptron example also help to undermine the conten-

---

[34] *Business World*, 26 February–10 March 1992, pp. 34–5.
[35] *Indian Express*, 25 February 1992.
[36] A study of the TVS group of companies found that the liberalisation programme of the early and mid-1980s led to increased vertical integration, allowing the conglomerate to 'further perpetuate' its dominance in the market for automotive ancillaries and compo-nents. This suggests another reason why business interests can be less opposed to economic reform that many theories might suggest. Padmini Swaminathan, 'Liberalisa-tion, Market Concentration and Prospects for Growth: A Study of the TVS Group of Companies', *Economic and Political Weekly*, 14 May 1988, pp. 1026–31.

tion that the continued involvement of a bribe-taking government as both shareholder and regulator would put off potential investors in PSEs. In fact, partnership with a state government would offer Videocon many advantages, including privileged access to vitally important publicly provided infrastructure inputs. In addition, an export agreement signed by Uptron during the period when a controlling interest was held by the UP government, could be transferred to Videocon. These and any other such advantages might come at a price – included either in any initial kickback that may have been involved, or at rates to be determined subsequently – but to argue that these costs would necessarily deter private investors from buying shares in PSEs, particularly if it involved paying a bribe, is to ignore the larger logic at work. Indeed, the scope for subsequent rent-seeking might be an added incentive for state-level politicians.

There are two crucial lessons from this story. First, there are ample reasons to believe that politicians have recognised that liberalisation need not spell the end of their influence over key decisions. And, second, that the process of implementing these decisions – because it is characterised by improvisation, which can mask corruption – is a vital contextual feature. Viewed in this light, it is no surprise that in late 1993 the newly elected UP government headed by a coalition of backward caste parties, began to develop variations on this theme. For example, to recover bad debts, it put up for sale the assets of fifteen private-sector loss-making units that had fallen, through defaults, into the hands of the state's industrial investment corporation.[37]

Though most state governments were slow to join the privatisation bandwagon initially, activity quickly picked up in many regions. The Karnataka government began the process of selling equity in the National Government Electrical Factory, and two high-level officials involved in the preparation of privatisation plans were of the opinion that before the end of the decade an elected state government would find it expedient to privatise at least half of the public-sector firms that a high-powered committee has suggested be sold off.[38] The Gujarat government has identified 41 units for privatisation or disinvestment, and the Gujarat Industrial and Investment Corporation Ltd. has already significantly reduced its stake in seven companies, including the Gujarat Lease Finance Corporation and Gujarat Lyka Organic. The state government has also begun the process of selling a 20 per cent equity stake in the GIIC itself. In Madhya Pradesh, Tata Exports was in early 1994 negotiating the takeover of a government-owned sericulture unit. In a novel experiment that has the potential to avoid some of the more politically unpleasant

[37] *Business World*, 15–28 December 1993, pp. 44–5.
[38] Interviews, 20 and 21 April 1995, Bangalore.

aspects of direct privatisation, the Orissa government has handed over two state-owned sugar cooperatives to private firms on long-term management contracts. The Orissa State Mining Corporation signed an agreement with De Beers Ltd. for mining and international marketing of diamonds.[39] The Tamil Nadu government announced plans to reduce its stake in all joint ventures to 11 per cent. In addition, Tamil Nadu Industrial Explosives and Tamil Nadu Cements have been converted into joint ventures, run by private firms.[40] In West Bengal, leading private-sector firms such as Siemens, Nicco, and Peerless have been offered stakes in state-owned units.[41] The Maharashtra government divested a portion of its stake in the State Industrial Corporation of Maharashtra, while drawing up a list of other units that could be sold without engendering too large a political crisis.[42]

The central government's disinvestment programme is for much higher stakes. And due to the vast potential for trading on insider information, manipulating prices on the secondary market, and holding shares in the names of family members and business associates, the prospects of abuse are that much greater.[43] The massive controversy surrounding the central government's first round of disinvestment in 1991–92 fuels suspicion that politicians regard privatisation as a money-spinner. As usual, the question is whether irregularities were due to corruption or administrative bungling – whether the decision-makers involved were knaves or fools. The report of the Comptroller and Auditor General (CAG) of India, tabled in parliament in July 1993, was highly critical of the department of public enterprises, estimating the loss to the exchequer at Rs. 30.44 billion. Even opposition politicians friendly to the prime minister accused his aides of abetting the abuse of the process in order to fill the party's coffers.[44]

One particularly egregious irregularity was that, contrary to a previous government directive, shares of public-sector units listed on the stock exchange, such as Cochin Refineries and Andrew Yule, were included in

[39] *India Today*, 15 September 1995, p. 69.
[40] The Gujarat, Madhya Pradesh, and Tamil Nadu examples are drawn from *Business Today*, 22 February–6 March 1994, p. 87.
[41] An IAS officer closely involved in these negotiations stated that chief minister Jyoti Basu's personal knowledge of trade unions in the public sector had given him more autonomy on privatisation than practically any other chief minister. While some members of the ruling party were keen to profit from the transactions, the chief minister himself was not interested in bribe-taking in this instance. Interview, 25 April 1995, Calcutta.
[42] The continuity between the Congress and BJP–Shiv Sena governments in their thinking on this issue has been noted by both a prominent labour activist and a senior IAS officer. Interviews, 10 and 12 April 1995, Bombay.
[43] *Business World*, 28 July–10 August 1993, pp. 26–31.
[44] *Frontline*, 30 July 1993, p. 116.

the bundled share offerings assembled by the government. Also raising suspicions of foul play was the fact that in 'forward trading' deals, some banks and mutual funds offloaded PSE shares to brokers, in violation of the official decision that shares be sold only after they were listed.[45] Charges of corruption have also been levelled at subsequent privatisation efforts. In August 1995, the government was subjected to a fierce on-slaught in parliament over its decision to compel the National Mineral Development Corporation to sell an iron-ore mine to Calcutta-based Nippon-Denro Ispat Ltd. for what was considered an artificially low price. This took place despite opposition from the finance ministry.[46] Such decisions were made possible because of ambiguities in the Mineral Concession Rules of 1960. As one news report stated: 'In the absence of clear guidelines, any interpretation can be made. Nor are there any rules on captive mining: who is to be given them and under what condition – is all left at the discretion of the executive'.[47]

Given what the New Political Economy tends to regard as the pathol-ogy of corruption – in which discretionary decision-making is assumed axiomatically to give rise to disproportionate levels of corruption – it is hard not to believe that at least some illicit income was generated by privatisation and disinvestment transactions at the centre and in the states, and that even more resources will flow to decision-makers as the process gains further momentum.

Dereservation of core infrastructure sectors   This area of reform is distinct from privatisation and disinvestment in that it denotes not the selling of PSEs, but the opening up to private-sector investors of econ-omic activities previously reserved for government departments or PSEs. The very nature of this activity makes it susceptible to bribery and favouritism. Since no existing 'assets' are being transferred, as they would be when a PSE is sold, and there are no clear rules on how to proceed (such as stock-market regulations in the case of disinvestment), there are even fewer obvious grounds on which government–industry arrange-ments can be effectively exposed as corrupt. The sheer ambiguity of this process provides ample scope for politicians to engineer the transition in ways beneficial to themselves and their associates. Members of both central and state governments have been active in scouting out innovative opportunities in this area. The keen interest expressed in infrastructure

---

[45] Government of India, Office of the Comptroller and Auditor General, *Report on the Disinvestment of Public-Sector Enterprises, 1991–92* (New Delhi: Government Printing Office, 1993). Variations on this practice were involved in the massive 'securities scam', unearthed in April 1992, which was said to have cost the government and other investors more than $2 billion.   [46] *India Today*, 15 September 1995, pp. 48–51.
[47] Ibid.

industries by well-funded multinational corporations, and the possibility of diverting illicit income to difficult-to-trace foreign currency bank accounts, have made dereservation one of the most important new sources of political funding. As one commentator has argued, 'rent-seeking – relentlessly objected to in the past in respect of the political-bureaucratic nexus of decision-makers by renowned expatriate Indian economists – is now practised more vigorously, more openly, with greater assurance (verging on arrogance) by private foreign capital in India'.[48]

At the national level, allowing the private sector into strategic industries is often a very selective process. Emphasising the need for caution when dealing with core infrastructural sectors – out of a declared concern for national security – cabinet ministers are able to secure for themselves a great deal of discretion in important decisions. The case of opening up the state-run telecommunications sector to private competition is one prominent example. The frequent changes in the tendering guidelines for potential investors in cellular and basic telephone services were widely believed to represent more than indecision on purely technical matters.[49] In at least one documented case, a foreign firm was found to have been permitted by officials (on an *ad hoc* basis) to exceed the stipulated ownership stake in its joint venture with a local partner. An investigative news report cited the case of previously little-known entrepreneur, Sunil Mittal, and his firm, Beetel Telecom, concluding that '[i]n the telecom sector "fixing" is still the order of the day'.[50] After leaving office, the former minister for telecommunications, Sukh Ram, was charged with 'amassing assets disproportionate to his known sources of income', the standard formulation of corruption charges in India. Cash and other financial instruments worth Rs. 30 million were discovered in a police raid on his New Delhi ministerial residence.[51]

The opening up of the petroleum sector has also been the subject of much speculation. Indian and foreign private-sector firms have been slowly and selectively permitted to enter a range of business activities, including exploration, production on both new and existing oil fields, refining, and marketing of petroleum-based products. Claims that MNCs were swooping in to reap the rewards of long-term government investment in this field were rife. The liberalisation of shipping and ports is yet another infrastructural area which can be abused for the private profit of governing elites. Action in this sector proceeded almost immediately,

[48] Arun Ghosh, '"Rent-Seeking" and Economic Reform', *Economic and Political Weekly*, 1–8 January 1994, p. 13.
[49] Interview with a political risk consultant whose clients include large multinationals involved in the Indian telecommunications bidding process, 25 March 1995, London.
[50] *Sunday*, 8–14 August 1993.   [51] *Business India*, 9–22 September 1996, pp. 62–6.

with Union Minister for Surface Transport Jagdish Tytler announcing important reforms at the beginning of 1992. Significantly, he did not move actually to sell off port facilities, for fear of reaction among powerful dockworkers' unions.[52] (In exchange for assurances on this issue, Tytler was able to sign accords with the Bombay dockworkers' unions in which a 10 per cent wage reduction was agreed.) Instead the emphasis was on 'modernisation', in which private investors would be charged a fee to build and operate berths and jetties. The tendering process for setting up dry-dock repair facilities was also under way within months of the Rao government taking office. The scope was expanded in early 1994 when investment was invited for larger projects, such as container-handling facilities.[53] The potential for bid-rigging and sweetheart deals was considered enormous.[54]

Subcontracting   The phenomenon of new forms of rent-seeking emerging to replace those that have been abolished or are on the wane is found in many other areas of public policy. Government financial corporations, for instance, have been 'adjusting to adjustment'.[55] As rules governing the activities of private finance companies have been relaxed, state and central financial institutions have had to face increased competition. Coupled with corresponding liberalisation of rules governing their own operation, this has led many institutions to offer a broader array of banking services. The Rajasthan Industrial Development and Investment Corporation (RIICO), like many others, has entered the merchant banking field with great vigour. RIICO officials are said routinely to make approvals for working capital and term loans contingent on the applicant agreeing to a package deal in which the merchant banking services are also provided. Not possessing great capacity in merchant banking, RIICO in many cases then subcontracts the business to a private finance company, with an undocumented 'commission' payable to RIICO officials.[56] This source of money helps to compensate bank officials and their political patrons for the loss of other sources of corrupt income that have been curtailed by policy reforms. For instance, with fewer resources available from the state government, there has been pressure on RIICO to be less forgiving in allowing loan-repayment schedules to slip. This is reflected in the corporation's improved repayment rate.[57]

[52] Interview, *Business World*, 11–24 March 1992, pp. 30–1.
[53] *Asian Age*, 12 April 1994.
[54] Interview with a business consultant specialising in infrastructure projects, 11 February 1994, Bombay.
[55] This term was used by an official of RIICO. Interview, 20 April 1994, Jaipur.
[56] Interview with a private investment banker, 4 May 1995, Jaipur.
[57] RIICO Annual Reports, 1991–92, 1992–93, 1993–94.

Accusations of corruption do not constitute proof, nor does the existence of unresolved litigation initiated by unsuccessful bidders. Yet hard evidence is similarly lacking for profiteering and patronage under the licence-permit Raj, though these are widely considered established facts by Indian and foreign economists. Given such acknowledged patterns of behaviour it would be unreasonable to expect the new business activities to be sanctioned without substantial payoffs. The number of irregularities raises enough suspicions that it is fair to regard privatisation and the dereservation of core infrastructure sectors as an important contributor to the replenishment of income lost through other deregulatory reforms.

The modification of previous methods

Liberalisation also has the potential to augment the value of many of the time-honoured means by which politicians raise political funds. Narendar Pani has called this 'the modernisation of corruption'.[58] Manipulation of limited-company share issues and sales, for instance, are nothing new to India, and looking the other way when securities regulations are broken has yielded cash for those politicians willing and able to protect the violators. But the amounts involved in share transactions increased so rapidly during the late 1980s, and even more so in the 1990s, that politicians have increasingly got into the act directly. A popular method, one of the many employed in the securities 'scam' that hit the headlines in April 1992, was for politicians to arrange the 'parking' of funds from public bodies under their control with selected brokers. In exchange for the temporary use of the funds, brokers passed on lucrative 'rights issues' (stock options) to the politician's family members and business associates, according to reports by the Central Bureau of Investigation (CBI) and the Joint Parliamentary Committee (JPC) constituted to examine the matter.[59]

Another dimension to this phenomenon is that liberalisation in one aspect of a particular sector can increase the attractiveness of placing discretionary controls (with their accompanying potential for corruption) on another aspect of policy in the same sector. The case of private health care is a good example. The relaxation by many state governments of regulations governing the establishment of private hospitals, nursing homes, and diagnostic centres has led to a proliferation of such facilities. It has also added substantially to the demand for imported medical equipment, such as CT scanners, incubators for premature infants, and magnetic resonance imaging devices. Recognising this, the former Union

[58] Narendar Pani, 'The Modernisation of Corruption in Karnataka' (mimeo, n.d.).
[59] *India Today*, 31 March 1995, p. 26.

Minister for Health, in a move characterised as 'a step back from de-bureaucratisation', took upon himself the responsibility of personally clearing cases relating to customs-duty exemption for imported medical technology.[60] Previously, this task was the responsibility of the Director General of Health Services.

There is also no shortage of examples from the state level. A number of Maharashtra's politicians, mostly leaders of powerful sugar cooperatives, have built fortunes through the creation of private educational institutions, earning for themselves the derisive title of 'education barons'. Many also control access to 'free' government-quota seats in private institutions (as they do in other states as well). The creation of the education business in Maharashtra over the past fifteen years was itself an example of political adaptation among opportunistic elites: 'The law of diminishing returns meant that many sugar barons began to look for alternative sources of income as cooperative capitalism degenerated into monopolistic corruption'.[61] And with liberalisation generating additional pressures, another round of adaptation is underway. As the resource constraints associated with fiscal adjustment have further exacerbated the already inadequate financial positions of public institutions of higher and professional education – particularly in engineering and business management – the scope for profiting in private institutions is said to have increased accordingly.[62] This is in addition to recent supreme and state court rulings – relying on arguments relating to liberalisation – which 'practically provide for charging fees much above Rs. 1 lakh [Rs. 100,000] per student per year from half the students in each private institution'.[63]

From 'land-grabbing' to 'facilitating investment'   The most noteworthy example of liberalisation increasing the potential of an established method of deriving illegal funding is the case of land transactions. Over the years, politicians in various states have developed a variety of illegal means for profiting from land speculation. The registering of cooperative housing societies in the names of friends and relatives, for example, has provided privileged access to an extremely rare resource. Politicians have also employed criminal gangs to intimidate residents into abandoning their rights under heavily pro-tenant legislation, allowing them to obtain

---

[60] *Times of India*, 26 February 1994.
[61] Rajdeep Sardesai, 'Machiavellian Politics: Maharashtra Congress in a Bad Way', *Times of India*, 4 March 1993.
[62] Interview with an influential figure in a major diversified cooperative in western Maharashtra, 4 April 1994, Bombay.
[63] Jandhyala B. G. Tilak, 'The Pests are Here to Stay: Capitation Fee in Disguise', *Economic and Political Weekly*, 12 February 1994, p. 348.

possession of and sell prime land in city centres. Special exemptions from local land-ceiling acts are another means by which real-estate developers with political connections can derive lucrative economic rents from projects such as suburban shopping centres.[64]

These practices continue today,[65] as do others with an even longer tradition, such as tampering with village land records.[66] But they are considered relatively small-time by those who have witnessed the scramble to manipulate the process of acquiring land for private-sector industrial and infrastructure projects. Indeed, this area has emerged as one of the primary avenues through which state-level politicians have been able to benefit financially from the process of liberalisation.[67] As we will see in the next chapter, the political fragmentation inherent in India's federal structure provides enormous leverage to reformers in New Delhi by, among other things, undermining the potential for concerted resistance to liberalisation among political elites from different regions. But just as important as such mechanisms of restraint is the increasing perception among state-level ruling parties that it is not only ministers in New Delhi that can use liberalisation to profiteer and build networks of patronage.

The standard practice by which state-level politicians benefit from land transactions for infrastructure projects is to use official land-acquisition procedures, which commonly involve a tribunal consisting of state legislators, local politicians, and district bureaucrats.[68] The tribunal offers landowners either nominal compensation, or if they are worried about electoral implications in that constituency, prices above the market rate, with

---

[64] The 'Baldev Plaza affair' in Rajasthan, dating from the early 1980s but still a source of lingering controversy, involved such a mechanism, allegedly benefiting the son of prominent Congress MP Ram Niwas Mirdha. *Frontline*, 9 October 1992, p. 133.

[65] An investigatory committee in Madhya Pradesh, for instance, identified several anomalies in land deals in Mandsaur district which allegedly benefited the brother of former BJP chief minister Sunderlal Patwa. *Asian Age*, 27 February 1995.

[66] For instance, several cases involving the nephew of Rajasthan's BJP chief minister have been documented by opposition politicians and have figured prominently in assembly debates. These cases are cited in page three of a letter from Surendra Vyas, MLA, to Home Minister S. B. Chavan, dated October 1992, requesting the Government of India to withhold its assent to the Rajasthan Tenancy (2nd Amendment) Bill 1992, passed by the Rajasthan Legislature on 26 September 1992. See also *Observer of Business and Politics*, 18 March 1994.

[67] Interviews with a senior IAS officer in the West Bengal government, 27 April 1995, Calcutta; a member of the Rajasthan BJP, 9 December 1993, Jaipur; an opposition MLA from Karnataka, 23 March 1994, Bangalore; and a dissident member of the Maharashtra cabinet, 5 April 1994, Bombay.

[68] This process was described to the author in interviews with a middle-ranking bureaucrat in the Rajasthan land-revenue bureaucracy, 19 November 1993, Jaipur; the president of an agro-processing firm in Rajasthan, 12 November 1993, Jaipur; an expert on agro-processing business practices for a major Indian consulting firm, 4 February 1994, Bombay; and by a Congress MLA from Rajasthan, 22 April 1994, Jaipur.

a 'commission' then going to one or more local politicians and bureau-crats. Often, the senior politicians involved arrange for friends or relatives to buy back the land from the state at a later stage when the project finds that it has 'surplus' land.[69] Bought for the same price at which it was sold, this land is then more valuable because of the commercial potential stemming from its proximity to the venture in question.

An example is the process by which the proposed Bangalore Interna-tional Airport is being developed. This is the first airport in India to be financed, owned, and operated by the private sector. Yet the allotment of land requires action by the Karnataka state government, which operates under very advantageous land-acquisition legislation. According to an opposition MLA, the government has gone about acquiring far more land than the project actually requires.[70] This will enable the government eventually to 'denotify' the land and sell it to private development com-panies in which ruling-party politicians (through friends, relatives, and associates) hold substantial stakes. This investment will take time to mature, however. As if to support the contention that Indian politicians have longer time horizons than generally thought, one local journalist stated that 'the proceeds will fund the 1999 assembly election'.[71]

The decision to allow the private sector into developing private toll roads on a build-operate-transfer basis is also likely to open the door to large-scale profiteering from land deals. As an analyst in a major manage-ment consultancy firm involved in this process commented, 'it's not a percentage of the tolls that the politicians are really interested in, it's the fact that private money means more roads, and more roads means more roadside land development. Who do you think is going to have a fat stake in that land?'[72] Some states have already begun the process of building private toll roads. The first in India was in Madhya Pradesh, connecting Indore and the industrial estate at Pithampur.[73] In March 1994, the Maharashtra government announced its intention to sign a memoran-dum of understanding with private-sector Infrastructure and Finance Leasing Services.[74] In April 1994, the Renong Group, a Malaysian engin-eering firm, agreed to pay for acquiring land for a toll road in Andhra Pradesh.[75]

With public funds scarce, the private sector is able to contribute to the building of India's public infrastructure, as neo-liberal economists have advocated. But more importantly, private-sector investment also pro-

[69] For a discussion of some noteworthy cases, see Lynus Paul Misquitta, *Pressure Groups and Democracy in India* (New Delhi: Sterling, 1991), pp. 184–6.

[70] *Sunday*, 9–15 April 1995, p. 14.   [71] Interview, 17 April 1995, Bangalore.

[72] Interview, 12 February 1995, Bombay.

[73] *Business India*, 14–27 February 1994, p. 22.

[74] *Economic Times*, 21 March 1994.   [75] *Dateline Business*, 27 April–3 May 1995.

vides the opportunity for the type of mega-projects that would have been unthinkable given the resource constraints facing a country like India – projects from which India's entrepreneurial politicians can profit. This is an incentive that, surprisingly, political economists working from a rational-choice framework routinely ignore when attempting to understand why politicians might find economic reform an attractive proposition. One Indian venture capitalist argued that what is required for road projects to pick up 'is the political will to deal with land acquisition'.[76] What this chapter is attempting to argue is that the existence of proper arrangements for politicians to profit is likely to be the handmaiden of such 'political will'.

While public–private finance partnerships are important, it is the power that the legal system gives elected officials to deliver land to promoters of private industrial projects that politicians regard as the biggest benefit of liberalisation. Delicensing and dereservation have led to a large increase in the number of project proposals. A particularly high-profile example is Reliance Petroleum's use of 'dubious means and underhanded tactics', with the alleged help of political patrons, to acquire 4,000 acres of land in Gujarat for a refinery project.[77] But virtually any firm contemplating a new facility requires the assistance of the relevant state government.

Subsequent to the announcement of the state's New Industrial Policy in 1993, the Maharashtra Industrial Development Corporation (MIDC) acquired more than 30,000 hectares of land, with plans to acquire an additional 28,000 hectares over the next three years.[78] This was in anticipation of investment flows, and in response to more liberal guidelines. In the name of promoting market-led industrialisation, MIDC has been allowed to acquire land for purposes other than setting up its own government-operated industrial estates.[79] As a 'facilitator' in the process of providing the necessary inputs for investors, it has been permitted to acquire land for private entrepreneurs. In at least four cases, the entrepreneurs involved had ties to the Congress Party. Their intention, not to mention capacity, to establish functioning business ventures was questionable at best.[80] Also officially justified by the need to provide infrastructure for private investment has been the acquisition of land to build a network of airstrips throughout the state. Among the first to be built, according to the plan, was to be located in then chief minister Sharad

[76] *Business Today*, 22 March–6 April 1995, p. 50.   [77] *Indian Express*, 8 October 1993.
[78] *Observer of Business and Politics*, 25 March 1994.
[79] The land acquisition process, especially the issue of compensation to farmers, has been the subject of much discussion in the state legislature. See, for instance, *Observer of Business and Politics*, 31 March 1994.
[80] Interviews with two local journalists with intimate knowledge of Congress politics, 31 March 1994 and 11 April 1995, Bombay.

Pawar's home town of Baramati. To prepare the site, Rs. 6,837,000 was distributed among sixty-eight landowners.[81] The lucrative possibilities continued to increase as various arms of the Maharashtra government became more active in land-related activities.[82]

Significantly, the ethos of liberalisation – and its attendant rhetoric of necessity – has created the climate in which such actions have become politically justifiable, even if their subversion for private profit remains at least nominally obscured. For politicians who have had to collude with criminal gangs to take possession of urban and rural property, in a process popularly known as 'land-grabbing', the opportunity to become 'facilitators of investment' – an option made possible by the hybridised policy environment that has emerged – would seem to present a relatively efficient and attractive alternative. In the lingo of 1930s gangster films, they could 'go legit'. It is for this reason that state-level ruling parties representing a variety of ideological hues have found it attractive to 'streamline' the process of obtaining land for industrial purposes. In 1994, then chief minister of Uttar Pradesh Mulayam Singh Yadav, a professed 'socialist', said that under the state's new industrial policy, 'a clearance from the Divisional Commissioner shall be sufficient for obtaining land above 12.5 acres'.[83] And the 1994 'new industrial policy' of the BJP government in Rajasthan highlighted 'simplified' land acquisition and land conversion procedures.[84]

Transparency, policy feedback, and interest-group fluidity

Having argued that despite liberalisation – in some cases *because* of it – governing elites find themselves with a wide variety of old, new, and modified methods for building political machines, we now turn to the second incentive to avoid actively opposing the general direction of policy reorientation. This is the reasonable assumption that India's democratic political system would prove flexible enough to reconstitute new political coalitions amidst currents of profound change. This calculation rests upon a belief in the fundamental flexibility of interest groups and the

[81] *Observer of Business and Politics*, 24 March 1994.
[82] For instance, the Development Commissioner (Industries) announced in early April 1994 the acquisition of 250 hectares for each of three export processing zones in Pune, Aurangabad, and Nagpur; 500 hectares for a software technology park in Pune; and 350 hectares for a hotel-convention centre in Bombay. *Observer of Business and Politics*, 6 April 1994.
[83] This was stated during a three-day investment promotion visit to Bombay, in which he also declared: 'I would like to clarify that our being a socialist government does not imply that we are opposed to industry or industrialists'. *Asian Age*, 8 July 1994.
[84] Sandeep Bhargava, 'Industrial Liberalisation in India: Policy Issues at the State Level', *IDS Working Paper* (Jaipur: Institute of Development Studies, January 1995), p. 11.

interest-group structure in India. The existence of a liberal political order, in which groups are free to organise and influence politicians directly through lobbying, and indirectly through the mobilisation of disaffected voters, is essential to this conviction. This second incentive is closely related to the first in so far as the preservation of substantial powers of discretion, as well as the emergence of new sources of patronage, provide additional resources with which to *manage* the process of interest-group realignment.

Most conceptions of democracy portray interests as either benign (as a counterweight to an overweening state) or malignant (as 'special interests' which exert a 'stranglehold' over policy). The latter view, whether of the Marxian 'ruling class' or neo-liberal 'rent-seeking interest' variety, tends to overstate the power of interest groups over policy-making by governing elites. The crucial misapprehension here is the underlying assumption that interest groups are intractable in their demands, which is itself based upon a belief that interest groups and interest-group coalitions are monolithic and immutable. The evidence presented in the following discussion, as well as in subsequent chapters, will illustrate why this need not always be the case.

Indian politicians have first-hand experience of the malleability of interest groups. The predominant view among governing elites is that neither the economic profile nor political stance of interest groups hostile (or potentially hostile) to liberalisation are carved in stone. Indeed, the orientations and structural configurations of interest groups in the pre-reform era were the result of the statist policy environment and political ideology of national self-reliance. Consequently, reforming politicians are able to calculate that the open-ended and gradual nature of the reform process, *as managed by politicians themselves*, will produce intermediate political perceptions and economic effects that cause some interests opposed to liberalisation to lose political influence, and others to adapt, economically and politically, to liberalisation in ways likely to result in support of the policy direction and the government itself. This involves playing interests off against one another and introducing first-generation reforms by stealth to disarm potential opponents (two processes detailed at length in Chapter 6's discussion of 'political skills'). It will also rely upon the burden-sharing capacity of India's formal and informal political institutions (discussed in Chapter 5). The confidence that interests can be dealt with, and that the means to do so have not evaporated, makes politicians operating within India's democratic polity significantly less risk-averse than many theories suggest.

One of the premises of ostensibly practical models for successfully managing the political consequences of adjustment is that governing elites can construct coalitions from among 'winners' of specific reforms,

and that these will substitute for the loss of political backing from er-
stwhile supporters, who may 'lose' from the same or other reforms. The
main difficulty with effecting this strategy, according to the comparative
literature, is in overcoming the temporary differentials in power among
these two constituencies. The problem is the time lag between when
winners win and losers lose. Potential losers, after all, have been nourish-
ed by the status quo they are aiming to preserve. It has provided them
with organisations, resources, and influence, and has instilled in them the
urgency that comes with knowing the certainty of loss. Potential winners,
until the benefits of a new policy dispensation begin to flow, have only the
promise of future prosperity. They, therefore, have few political resources
(such as organisational infrastructure or funds) to offer governing elites
wary of rocking even a sinking boat.

In non-democratic systems, any potential solution to bridging this
resource differential among winners and losers runs headlong into a
systemic shortcoming: the lack of conviction that substituting support
bases can be effected. This crisis of confidence stems not from obduracy,
or a lack of 'political will' or 'vision', but from a very reasonable assessment by governing elites of the types of change their experience has
prepared them to manage successfully. They might, in such systems,
rationally expect that losers will mount immediate and powerful resistance to economic reform – perceiving their loss of perquisites as irre-
coverable. Politicians in democratic systems, on the other hand, are
well-versed in the art of constructing flexible coalitions.

Politicians' decisions on whether to press ahead with reform depend on
assessments of the ability of losing interest groups to deploy political
resources in ways likely to deprive them of power. A credible threat from
business groups to withhold vital election finance, for instance, could
persuade reforming elites to reverse direction in one or more policy areas.
The iterative nature of India's adjustment programme, and the opportunity to write the rules of the transition as they go along, makes its governing
elites less vulnerable to such threats. The most important implication of
the gradualism inherent in the reform process is that even modest changes
in policy at one stage in the adjustment process can significantly affect the
inclination or capacity of interest groups to oppose later reforms. In the
theoretical literature, these are referred to as 'policy feedback' effects,
processes in which the impact of one set of policy initiatives on the
structure of interests becomes a determining factor in the decision of
policy-makers to press on with subsequent reforms.[85] To the extent that
politicians understand this declining capacity among certain groups as

---

[85] For a useful review of the literature which outlines the various forms policy feedback can
take, see Paul Pierson, 'When Effect Becomes Cause: Policy Feedback and Political
Change', *World Politics*, vol. 45, no. 3 (July 1993), pp. 595–628.

well as the causal role of incremental reform in bringing it about, they can become emboldened to initiate further reforms. The net effect is that politicians operating within a liberal democracy become willing to take limited gambles, with avenues for profiteering and patronage acting as a sort of insurance policy.

One way to reduce an interest group's capacity to oppose reform measures is to exploit divisions within its ranks.[86] This is most deadly when it happens slowly over an extended period of time. Incremental reforms are often potent catalysts. The way in which early reforms to the banking sector were handled meant that some groups of employees received better terms and conditions of employment than others. This led to a division within union ranks on the issue of privatisation and the closure of loss-making branches of nationalised banks. In early 1994, the All-India Bank Employees' Association (AIBEA) was reluctant to join the agitational activities organised by the Joint Action Committee, an umbrella group of all the unions in the banking sector. The AIBEA's reluctance was due to its October 1993 agreement with the Indian Banks' Association on an improved pension scheme for its members. The threat of immediate redundancies had given the union's president 'no choice but to make a deal for my people'.[87] Other unions were angered, and their belief that the AIBEA had 'sold out' was complete when in late 1993 it signed a memorandum of understanding with the employers' association on computerisation in exchange for certain compensatory payments.[88]

Small-scale industry policy is another good example. A former adviser to the industry ministry, Rakesh Mohan, has argued that the policy of reserving certain product categories for production solely by small-scale enterprises is no longer justified on the basis of techno-economic criteria, but on political grounds: 'if you have 500 politicians, maybe 100 will know 200 big industrialists, and 400 will know 5,000 small ones. Which do you think will be the stronger lobby?'[89] The way this political obstacle is being overcome is through what amounts to a gradual process of 'policy feedback' – what Mohan calls 'glacial progress'. For instance, in the garment-manufacturing sector, which is reserved for small enterprises, the definition of 'small' for new factories was raised to Rs. 30 million

---

[86] It should be noted that this is a two-way street: business lobbies, for instance, have been able to exploit intra-bureaucratic rivalries and thereby play one government agency off against another with great success. For instance, exporters welcomed the creation of a new Export Promotion Board, headed by the cabinet secretary, because it allowed them an alternate channel of influence when decisions of the Directorate General of Foreign Trade were not to their liking, as was the case when rules for the export of electronic items were changed in late 1997. See 'Exporting, Cabinet Secretary Style' (editorial), *Economic Times*, 2 November 1997.

[87] Interview with a high-ranking AIBEA official, 4 March 1994, Bombay.

[88] *Indian Express*, 23 January 1994.

[89] 'India Survey', *Economist*, 21 January 1995, p. 19.

worth of investment, provided that 50 per cent of the product was exported. This provision helps some firms (the big among the small), thereby leading to fragmentation among the 'garment lobby'.[90] A first step down a slippery political slope has thus been taken, making dereservation of this sector far more politically palatable in the future. Mohan argues that reform to the small-scale sector is not an isolated case: 'The same thing happened with the industrial licensing system. We chopped away at the edges, and finally the whole thing was abolished'.[91]

Indeed, chopping away at the edges is a good way to describe the Indian government's approach to a whole range of reform issues. But its strategic value depends upon ruling elites' confidence in their ability to use carrots and sticks to restructure interest groups gradually, as well as sequencing tactics to avoid direct confrontation until the most propitious moment. Significantly, however, its efficacy also depends heavily on the flexibility displayed by interest groups themselves. Were the elites who represent interests intractable rather than pragmatic, reformers would have little incentive to gamble on the prospect of future realignments. The argument here is that liberal democracy provides the political space for groups not only to defend their interests, but also to redefine and reinterpret them based on, among other things, the content and direction of government policy initiatives and the strategic behaviour of their rivals for political influence. Interest groups in India, like ruling elites, display such flexibility because operating within a competitive system has provided them abundant experience of doing so.

Demanding parity: the chain reaction effect

One manifestation of this flexibility is the way in which democratic systems with well-elaborated interest-group structures sometimes also produce a chain reaction for more reform. That is, when certain groups are perceived to have obtained benefits from reforms, other groups demand 'consistency' in government treatment. This can result in mobilisation which swells the ranks of those pressing for reform. Witnessing the huge gains of the cotton textile industry from such basic reforms as rupee

[90] In fact, expanding the definition of the small-scale sector has had an even greater fragmentary impact, since even the larger firms which now qualify as small-scale producers find their fortunes diverging: while all such firms benefit from the shrinking (though still substantial) benefits associated with membership in the small-scale sector, a subset of these (those with acute financial problems) find the advantages more than cancelled out by the fact that, as small-scale industries, they no longer qualify for relief from the Bureau for Industrial and Financial Reconstruction (BIFR) under the provisions of the Sick Industrial Companies (Special Provisions) Act of 1985. The sheer complexity of the regulatory environment, in short, tends systematically to undermine the coherence of particular 'lobbies'.   [91] 'India Survey', *Economist*, 21 January 1995, p. 19.

devaluation, some farmers' leaders began to mobilise cotton farmers around demands to abolish Maharashtra's Monopoly Procurement Scheme (MPS) for cotton, under which it is illegal for cultivators to sell their crop in neighbouring states where market prices are often higher. Sharad Joshi is one such 'political entrepreneur',[92] a pro-liberalisation IAS officer-turned-farmers'-advocate who has derided India's bureaucrats as 'black Englishmen'.[93] Joshi claims that this issue breathed new life into his Shetkari Sanghathana, an organisation established in the early 1980s to demand remunerative pricing for a range of agricultural commodities, but which has developed an expanded agenda that includes allowing farmers to benefit from export opportunities.[94]

Though Joshi's party fared poorly in the state assembly elections of 1995, his organisation's prolonged campaigning on the MPS forced a response among the major parties during the campaign. The previous Congress government, in its customarily ambiguous manner, had begun to show signs of softening on this issue as early as the end of 1993. Despite the chief minister's announcement that the state government had not decided to permit the sale of Maharashtra-grown cotton across state borders, the industries minister, Jawaharlal Darda, made repeated public statements that the government would allow this on an *ad hoc* basis. He had even informed the collector of his native Yavatmal district to permit cotton movement outside the state, though this was officially illegal.[95] According to a senior bureaucrat closely involved with the issue, there is more pressure from within the Shiv Sena–BJP coalition government that took power in March 1995 to have the scheme scrapped, though change is likely to be gradual.[96]

The openness of the democratic political system made this incremental step possible in three ways. First, it provided space for a political entrepreneur like Joshi, from outside the leading parties, to mobilise disaffected farmers. Second, the electoral process acted as a signalling mechanism, allowing both the old and new governments to judge the strength of cotton farmers, particularly in the northern and eastern parts of the state. Third, it added another piece of experiential evidence with which India's reluctant reformers could appreciate the salutary contribution of

[92] For our purposes, these are defined as political actors who attempt to anticipate or react to incipient changes in the policy environment by mobilising resources in the form of finance or votes. On the varied roles of political entrepreneurs and the circumstances under which they are able to assist the problem of overcoming barriers to collective action, see Terry M. Moe, *The Organization of Interests: Incentives and the Internal Dynamics of Political Interest Groups* (Chicago: University of Chicago Press, 1980).

[93] *The Hindu*, 1 November 1993.

[94] Interview, 25 February 1995, Amethan, Pune District.

[95] *Times of India*, 24 November 1993.   [96] Interview, 12 April 1995, Bombay.

'policy feedback' – in this case in the form of a chain-reaction effect that could serve as a stronger foundation for future reforms.

Another example of a group demanding parity in respect of liberalisation is the National Dairy Development Board (NDDB). Not long after the new thrust in economic policy got under way, the chairman of the NDDB, Mr V. Kurien, began a series of actions to demand that the cooperative sector be given the 'chance to compete on a level playing field' with Indian business. As a result of legislation allowing private-sector investment in the milk and milk-products sector, the profitability of NDDB's widely hailed dairy operations came under pressure. By resisting intense lobbying by Kurien's formidable political patrons to reverse the reforms in this sector, the government was in effect gambling that the NDDB, with a grassroots following in village-level dairy cooperatives throughout the country, would not prove intractable, but would adapt.

That is precisely what happened. Before long, Kurien began advocating amendments to legislation which gives state-level bureaucrats wide-ranging powers, such as the authority to issue permits for new cooperatives and to replace the elected directors of existing cooperatives with government administrators. Kurien later proposed to change this through a 'cooperative companies act'. An additional benefit of such legislation, from his perspective, was that cooperatives would be able to raise funds from private investors more easily. The NDDB also started to turn its guns on a different constituency, the already beleaguered small-scale sector. Ice cream, a high value-added dairy product, is one of 836 items reserved for small enterprises, and Kurien wanted his member cooperatives to get a slice of this growing market. He was able to see a specific potential benefit from reform and was in a position to persuade his loyal followers.[97] The point of all this is that a powerful interest group adapted its strategic goals in response to the pressures generated by first-generation reforms. Though pursuing its interests, as a liberal political-economy model would predict, the NDDB's leader was not intractable. Kurien's response, in fact, provided another voice to the chorus demanding liberalisation of policy relating to the small-scale sector. Reformers depend on this type of response to produce chain-reaction effects. Democratic space makes it possible.

A similar dynamic was at work in the steel industry, which was burdened by a varying per-tonne levy that contributed to an Engineering Goods Exports Assistance Fund. The purpose of this fund was to finance the 'international price reimbursement scheme' for engineering exports. Public-sector steel companies began lobbying strenuously for its abolition in early 1994, arguing that in a deregulated market, with no budgetary

[97] As of early 1994, four plants – in Delhi, Bangalore, Patna, and Chandigarh – were awaiting dereservation. *Business Today*, 22 February–6 March 1994, pp. 118–19.

support for public-sector plants, such as the Steel Authority of India Ltd. or Rashtriya Ispat Nigam Ltd., it was unfair to impose compulsory levies, especially as export industries had benefited from a devalued rupee and corrections to the anomalous duty structure.[98] The Chelliah Committee, constituted to recommend changes to India's tax system, stated in its report that 'we don't find any justification for making the domestic producers bear a levy to support the export of engineering goods'.[99] When the finance ministry ultimately supported this position, after receiving a recommendation from the steel secretary, it was clear that the chain-reaction effect which an open polity fosters had again made an impact.

Interest adaptation: the transformation of big business

The most noteworthy case of an interest group redefining its agenda in a way that aids the political sustainability of economic reform is that of big business. As we saw in Chapter 2, the determined opposition of highly protected, import-substituting industrialists was viewed as one of the main factors which thwarted Rajiv Gandhi's efforts to liberalise the Indian economy in the mid-1980s. And yet 'big business' was considered to be among the main supporters backing the economic reform programme of the early 1990s. What accounts for the shift from recalcitrant to cheerleader?

The answer is that the question is based on a false premise: 'big business' as a coherent lobby does not exist. According to Sanjaya Baru, some segments of business did in fact back Rajiv Gandhi's reform programme.[100] Chief among these was the emergent 'regional business class' from outside the traditionally dominant business houses of west and northwest India.[101] These firms had been largely shut out of the national spoils system during most of the period since independence, and began to emerge strongly during the 1980s under the patronage of regional leaders

---

[98] *The Hindu – Business Line*, 18 April 1994.

[99] Government of India, *National Report on Tax Reform* (New Delhi: Government Printing Office, 1993).

[100] Sanjaya Baru, 'Continuity and Change in Indian Industrial Policy', paper presented at the conference, 'Terms of Political Discourse in India', York University (September 1990).

[101] While many observers concede the importance of prominent business people from particular regions, there is great reluctance to accede to the notion of region-specific classes. There are, however, indications that capitalists within regions do act in ways that resemble class-like behaviour. When the Andhra Pradesh-based Raasi Cements was threatened with a hostile takeover by an out-of-state competitor, one prominent businessman in the state said: 'We're not going to let an outsider take away the company'. *Business Today*, 22 March 1998, p. 47. Further support for the political importance of the 'regional bourgeoisie' can be found in Mahendra Prasad Singh, 'Political Parties and Political Economy of Federalism: A Paradigm Shift in Indian Politics', *Indian Journal of Social Science*, vol. 7, no. 2 (1994), p. 160.

like Andhra Pradesh chief minister N. T. Rama Rao, of the regional
Telugu Desam Party, whose winning election campaigns in the early
1980s were funded by local industrialists. As Baru argues, 'it was only
natural that these groups should clamor for the end of a system that
denied them its benefits'.[102] Attempting to address this concern, Indira
Gandhi took actions to placate select members of this group, and her
strategy was followed by her son and successor, Rajiv.

It is true that many large business houses and the associations that
represent them opposed import liberalisation during the early and mid-
1980s. But when a new, more far-reaching round of economic reform was
initiated by the Rao government in the summer of 1991 – reportedly with
little consultation outside a handful of advisers[103] – traditional big business houses were faced with the prospect of the emergent business
groups, whose clout had grown during the 1980s, eclipsing them in
political influence.[104] The wise strategy, the one that was predominantly
followed, was for traditional big business to support the government's
policy line, while lobbying hard for special treatment for their firms and
industries. This is the type of political adaptation on which reformers in a
genuine liberal democracy such as India rely. Indeed, leaders of organised
interests can sometimes shepherd their flocks in ways that help reformers.[105] At other times, when an irreconcilable multiplicity of interests
exists, competition among the associations that represent them can work
to the benefit of governing elites. Of crucial importance is the fact that
political influence remains extremely important during the transition to
an economy based, to a much larger degree, upon market forces. This is
especially true when reformers are devising a customised recipe for economic restructuring as they go along. The discussion of profiteering and
patronage earlier in this chapter is testimony to this.

The benefits that can accrue to industrialists who maintain their politi-

---

[102] Baru, 'Continuity and Change in Indian Industrial Policy', p. 7.
[103] This commonly recounted version of events was corroborated in interviews conducted
by James Manor on 8–10 February 1992 with various members of the prime minister's
staff. For further insights into the thinking of those at the top, see James Manor, 'The
Political Sustainability of Economic Liberalization', in Robert Cassen and Vijay Joshi
(eds.), *India: The Future of Economic Reform* (Delhi: Oxford University Press, 1995).
[104] Evidence that conflicts between the 'traditional' and 'emergent' business groups for
political influence continued during the period of liberalisation was set forth in 'The
North-South Business Divide', *Tycoon*, August 1996, pp. 18–25.
[105] That proclaiming support for reform required some associations to silence rather than
amplify certain voices among their membership is consistent with the pattern of
surreptitious political manoeuvring detailed in this book. As one executive put it: 'I must
confess that CII was doing a good turn to liberalisation by muffling the anti-reforms
sentiment among many members and drumming up a fervour for liberalisation. The
limited reforms in the country have been implemented by the government with support
from industry'. Reported in Kingshuk Nag, 'CII's Dilemma: To Speak or Not to Speak',
Times of India, 21 April 1996.

cal influence during the liberalisation process are many. By using political contacts to get compliant 'nominee directors' from national financial institutions placed on their boards, many large companies are able to violate regulations of the Securities and Exchange Board of India regarding mandatory levels of promoters' equity and the transfer of funds between divisions within a company.[106] As one report argued, '[a]ll businessmen have a plethora of small investment companies for putting through their insider deals'.[107] The abuse of the Value-Based Advanced Licensing Scheme, designed to reward exporters with vouchers for duty-free imports, was so widespread that the scheme had to be scrapped.[108] Political representation at the highest levels is still sought by industrialists in 'pre-budget consultations', with lobbying by individual MPs on very specific issues not uncommon.[109] At the state level, major industrial firms continue to see the value of patronage. Reliance Industries was considered to have attained benefits by bankrolling the 1993 election campaign of chief minister Digvijay Singh.[110] These included diamond-mining concessions[111] and even a place for one of its executives on the state planning board,[112] a position of direct influence that would have been unthinkable before the advent of economic liberalisation, and which still rankles with many observers.

Aside from such direct patronage, business groups have also been able to influence policy in ways that make their support for the general thrust of liberalisation seem like a gamble that paid off. One issue that concerns many of the traditional family-dominated business houses is loss of management control.[113] In order to raise resources to modernise and face up to foreign competition, these firms must go to the market. This means diluting the shareholdings of India's business elite – the predominantly family-run managements of the largest business houses. The fear of losing control led in 1993 to a strategy meeting among senior representatives of

---

[106] The widespread use of these tactics by businesses in collusion with national financial institutions was commented upon by a high-level executive from a diversified industrial business house. Interview, 24 February 1994, Pune. See also Sucheta Dalal, 'Why Aren't the Institutions Accountable?', *Times of India*, 6 July 1995, which details many cases of abuse, concluding that 'the Indian corporate sector reads deregulation as a synonym for no regulation, and it has never had it so good'.

[107] *Business Today*, 22 December 1992, p. 28.

[108] *Business World*, 23 February–8 March 1994, p. 45.

[109] Several MPs were reported to have 'bombarded' the finance minister and prime minister with letters arguing for the imposition of *ad valorem* duty on cigarettes, which would benefit the tobacco firm GTC. *India Today*, 15 July 1995.

[110] *Asian Age*, 3 September 1994.   [111] *Financial Times* (London), 12 July 1994.

[112] *Indian Express*, 4 April 1994.

[113] According to one businessman, '[i]nheritance of the CEO's job' is by far the most important issue to the traditionally family-run business houses, who over the years were able to retain disproportionate control through the acquiescence of government financial institutions which held large stakes but did not insist on management oversight. Gaurav Dalmia, 'Reforms and Indian Businessmen', *Economic Times*, 10 November 1993.

prominent business houses which came to be known as 'the Bombay Club'. The main complaint was the lack of a 'level playing field' *vis-à-vis* foreign investors on corporate finance issues such as 'preferential share allotments' (a financial mechanism for retaining management control) and the consolidation of corporate accounts.[114] The government ultimately conceded to some of their demands,[115] but as usual was able to rely on divisions within the business elite to blunt the edge of political opposition to opening up the Indian economy to the outside world. The Indian vice-chairman of foreign joint venture DCM-Toyota, for instance, asked: 'What, then, are they complaining about? It's basically the guys who've exploited the licensing system who are worried'.[116] The old insider–outsider split was at work again.[117]

The other reason why supporting liberalisation made sense for large segments of the business community was the prospect of influencing decisions that would determine which groups would bear the costs of the transition. One of the main targets was the small-scale sector, which had enjoyed substantial concessions under the old policy regime. When decisions on specific industries are made, according to an officeholder of one of the major national business chambers, 'it is the small scale sector that is invariably squeezed – and this is no accident'.[118] The small-scale steel industry, for instance, felt victimised by a failure to abolish import duties on its main input, steel scrap.[119] Smaller petrochemical companies have similarly felt the pinch of liberalisation, even as industry giants benefited.[120] Small-scale units in a variety of sectors have been encouraged to forge stronger links with large firms, and through a variety of indirect methods the government has reduced their leverage with larger firms. The emergence of a government 'takeover code' stoked fears that big

[114] *Financial Express*, 11 October 1993.
[115] A number were found in the 1994–95 budget. For an analysis of the pre-budget negotiations, see *Dateline Business*, 27 January–2 February 1994.
[116] *Business World*, 20 October–2 November 1993, p. 25.
[117] There are countless other examples of divisions within the business community: divisions between producers of raw materials and downstream users, a conflict the CII president has been at pains to bridge (*Business Standard*, 27 April 1994); differences between the CII and FICCI over the desired level of protection (*Indian Express*, 9 October 1993); resentment among existing Export-oriented Units (EoUs) in Maharashtra towards newly established EoUs, which were receiving advantageous tax breaks (*Economic Times*, 21 March 1994); and divisions between one product segment and the leadership of a business association, as was the case when cold-rolled steel units felt dissatisfied with the representation of their cause by the CII and decided to join with other disaffected groups in a new industry association (*Business Standard*, 10 March 1994). The last point, concerning the divergence of interests between leadership and membership, is highlighted in Mick Moore and Ladi Hamalai, 'Economic Liberalisation, Political Pluralism and Business Associations in Developing Countries', *Discussion Paper 318* (Brighton: Institute of Development Studies, 1993).
[118] Interview, 15 February 1994, Bombay.   [119] *Economic Times*, 7 February 1994.
[120] See 'Small is not Beautiful', *Business India*, 20 May–2 June 1996, pp. 88–97.

business's apprehensions about foreign competition would be assuaged by making it easier for them to gobble up smaller players. We have already had a taste of the tactics used to undermine the lobbying power of the small-scale sector in our discussion of how the government is 'chopping away at the edges' of this constituency. The significant point is that big business was able to calculate that retaining influence over the process of reform was more rational than outright opposition.

Of course, there is every chance that numerous businesses which supported liberalisation in an effort to retain influence over the transition made serious errors in judgement. Many business leaders have voiced this view openly. Referring to the traditional business houses, Great Eastern Shipping Director Ravi Sheth stated: 'Let's face it. In their heart of hearts nobody wanted liberalisation. It sounded nice, so everyone cheered. Now that it begins pinching you, you cry foul'.[121] Another leading industrialist confessed, 'I am afraid many of us, who were for liberalization, did not understand the full ramifications'.[122] L. M. Thapar, chairman of the Ballarpur Group, admitted, '[w]e did not realise (in 1991) how quickly we would need funds to face the competition that was round the corner'.[123] And Ravi N. Ruia, Essar Gujarat's managing director: 'I think the true implications of liberalisation are only now gripping people, and they are realising the problems'.[124] Similar statements from disillusioned business leaders could be heard once the first wave of joint ventures with multinational corporations began to go sour in mid-1996.[125]

This does not make their initial strategy irrational. Groups such as the Federation of Indian Chambers of Commerce and Industry (FICCI) that were originally more vocal in their opposition to liberalisation have found their ability to produce results for their members on the wane. Rivalry for political influence among competing associations – representing different interest-group fragments – is an important benefit that ruling elites who initiate and carry through economic reform are able to count upon.[126] Its value becomes increasingly apparent as the programme unfolds. If

---

[121] *Business World*, 20 October–2 November 1993, p. 25.
[122] *The Statesman*, 11 October 1993.
[123] *Business India*, 22 November–5 December 1993, p. 54.
[124] *Business World*, 20 October–2 November 1993, p. 24.
[125] See, 'Lows after the Early Highs', *India Today*, 15 August 1996, pp. 87–9.
[126] There is abundant evidence that cleavages within Indian business grew substantially during the 1980s, and again during the 1990s. The case for this is made convincingly in Marcus Lindemann, 'The Licence-Raj Revisited: The Political Economy of Changing State-Business Relations', unpublished MA dissertation, Department of Government, University of Essex, September 1995. The differing reactions of the Federation of Indian Export Organisations (anti) and the Confederation of Indian Industry (pro) to the government's decision to introduce the Minimum Alternative Tax was a classic example. *Observer of Business and Politics*, 9 September 1996. Regarding the different approaches by FICCI and CII to courting central government support, see 'Inter-Chamber Rivalry Comes to the Fore', *Financial Express*, 11 September 1996.

some groups miscalculated, and later felt cheated, it is above all a tribute to Indian democracy's capacity to effect an impressive 'confidence trick'. Indian politicians have ample reason to believe in the democratic system's ability to instil a perception among a larger set of groups than can possibly benefit that they will manage to be among the lucky survivors, whether by adapting, wielding influence, or a combination of the two. The reasonably good chance of successfully pursuing strategies of this type provides a strong incentive for skilled politicians to continue reforming.

Though they have been of immense value, the incentives outlined in this chapter are insufficient to sustain adjustment politically. The same confidence that permits politicians to take risks must also apply to their faith in the capacity of India's diverse array of formal and informal political institutions to absorb some of the political shocks associated with adjustment, and thereby to avoid overloading the apex of the political system. The complex ways in which both formal and informal political institutions contribute to the sustainability of adjustment forms the subject of the next chapter.

5   Political institutions: federalism, informal networks, and the management of dissent

If we assume a hypothetical level of political strain at which apex re-formers will reverse the direction of policy change – which, even in the absence of the means of measurement, we must – it is reasonable also to assume that a political system's capacity to reduce this strain will contribute to the sustainability of reform. This chapter attempts to demonstrate the contribution of India's political institutions to this process. It does so by examining the ways in which institutions act as a sort of scaffolding, distributing the 'force' of political resistance across a wider network of pressure points than is found in more centralised political systems with less fully elaborated institutions.

The argument, to use a different metaphor, is that the abandonment of reform by the apex elites who have initiated it is less likely when there exist additional circuits through which currents of political discontent can be channelled. Institutions thus serve, in a crude sense, as voltage trans-formers, or substations dispersing energies throughout a national power grid. The central theme in this chapter is that of burden-sharing – how it combines with the incentives outlined in the last chapter, and how this dynamic enhances the need for, and effective exercise of, advanced political skills, which is the topic of the next.

This chapter is divided into three sections. The first is a brief introduction to the way in which institutions will be treated in the discussion of the empirical material. In the second section the practical utility of India's *formal* institutions of state is illustrated through an examination of the implications of the federal political system for the capacity of both governing and socio-economic elites to organise resistance to economic reform. Of particular concern is the way in which both tend to become drawn into the preoccupations of state-level politics. While it is impossible conceptually to separate the federal system from the many other formal institutions which make up the structure of Indian government, we will attempt to highlight the mechanisms through which the federal ordering of state power helps to reduce the political pressures facing reformers at the apex of the political system. The final section of this chapter will examine the role of *informal* institutions in managing the conflicts that arise in the course of implementing new policies and in arriving at politically expedient solutions. The emphasis here will be on the tendency of Indian parties to be constructed around individual leaders whose networks of influence: (1) blur the boundaries between party and non-party structures; (2) are relatively easily detachable from particular parties; and (3) comprise a diverse enough range of interests to allow governing elites to broker the political transactions that complex policy reform requires.

The nature of political institutions

The emergence and consolidation of political institutions is what transforms the activity known as politics into a functioning political system. Institutions, therefore, are part of any political system – democratic or authoritarian. Guillermo O'Donnell, states that

Institutions are regularized patterns of interaction that are known, practiced, and regularly accepted (if not normatively approved) by social agents who expect to continue interacting under the rules and norms formally or informally embodied in those patterns. Sometimes, but not necessarily, institutions become formal organizations: they materialize in buildings, seals, rituals, and persons in roles that authorize them to 'speak for' the organization.[1]

In attempting to delimit the subset of *political* institutions, O'Donnell identifies six 'characteristics of a functional institutional setting'. The last of these – that '[i]nstitutions lengthen the time-horizons of actors' – is of concern to our study of how Indian politicians assess the risks and opportunities thrown up by economic liberalisation:

The stabilization of agents and expectations entails a time dimension: institutionalized interactions are expected to continue into the future among the same (or a slowly and rather predictably changing) set of agents. This, together with a high level of aggregation of representation and of control of their constituencies, is the foundation for the 'competitive cooperation' that characterizes institutionalized democracies: *one-shot prisoner's dilemmas can be overcome, bargaining (including logrolling) is facilitated, various trade-offs over time become feasible, and sequential attention to issues makes it possible to accommodate an otherwise unmanageable agenda.*[2]

It is this tendency to promote longer time horizons and to arrange bargains between competing groups that has made India's political institutions so useful in neutralizing resistance to economic reform. Also of

---

[1] Guillermo O'Donnell, 'Delegative Democracy', *Journal of Democracy*, vol. 5, no. 1 (January 1994), p. 57.   [2] Ibid., p. 59 (emphasis added).

crucial importance has been the extent to which institutions have proven adaptable, integrated, and capable of containing and redirecting political energies of powerful interests in ways suited to a variety of circumstances.

While this book lays much emphasis upon the role of institutions, it must also be acknowledged that they are an exceedingly slippery concept. In particular, there is great controversy in determining what constitutes an informal political institution. As suggested in Chapter 3, a full explanation for why the redirection of economic policy has been sustained despite seemingly inauspicious circumstances requires a broad conception of political institutions. Yet there is a qualitative difference between the formal institutions of state – including constitutional provisions for a federal political system – and those which have arisen in response to political exigencies, but which have not been formally codified. The latter are piecemeal, the sorts of norms and conventions that evolve to fill the interstices between state and society. Such institutions link socio-economic elites with each other, and with governing elites, in ways that provide greater flexibility for all concerned, though not necessarily always for the common good.

Making a distinction between formal and informal institutions permits a more focused examination of the relations between state and society. Gordon White has argued that

democracies differ not merely in the character of their political institutions, but also in the ways these interact with society. The organization of state–society relations has two basic dimensions: first, the constitutionally defined realm of formal political, administrative and legal entities which set the institutional framework of a democratic regime and, second, the informal and formal organizations and channels which connect politicians, officials, and agencies with social constituencies in 'civil society'. These could be called the 'exterior' and 'interior' worlds of democratic politics.[3]

This is a useful distinction, particularly as the terms 'exterior' and 'interior' hint at the lack of transparency that accompanies democratic politics. But there is, of course, no clear boundary between the formal and the informal. Institutions overlap with one another, and each resides somewhere along a continuum between the formal and the informal.

Political parties are a key institution, but they are neither formal nor informal. In the case of parties, much of the ambiguity stems from the fact that, as alluded to above, there are two important dimensions to consider

[3] Gordon White, 'Towards a Democratic Developmental State', *IDS Bulletin*, vol. 26, no. 4 (April 1995), p. 32. For an analysis of the value of informal institutions in reducing ethnicity-based political conflicts among elites, see Donald Rothchild and Michael W. Foley, 'African States and the Politics of Inclusive Coalitions', in Donald Rothchild and Naomi Chazan (eds.), *The Precarious Balance: State and Society in Africa* (Boulder, Colo.: Westview, 1988), pp. 233–64.

when assessing a political institution's degree of formality: its degree of 'stateness', and its degree of codification. Unlike legislatures and courts, Indian parties are not state organs, though they aspire to state power and are governed by specific electoral laws. They also possess rule-bound procedures, but these are routinely subordinated to considerations of power. So while parties may be considered formal in respect of their degree of organisational elaboration, and yet informal because they are non-state entities, their status is rather unclear on each of these criteria.

Even if we were to approach parties on the basis of their most clearly articulated axis of formality, their codification, we would fail to capture their vital role in India's democratic setting. For to focus on parties *per se* – their ideological positions, operational roles, formal organisational structures, and relations with other parties – would be to neglect the many ways in which they provide channels through which individual leaders are able to construct sustained relationships among a great diversity of social groups. And it is this feature which stands out in India. These relationships occur both within and outside parties, and often result in mutual understandings between representatives of socio-economic interests and party elites in their personal capacities, rather than in their institutional roles – that is, as individual factional leaders, not as holders of a specified office.[4] In this sense, a party is not only an institution itself, but also a device through which other, decidedly more informal institutions ('regularised patterns of interaction') are created, nurtured, and pressed into service on occasions when more formal institutions on their own (including parties *qua* parties) prove incapable of effecting policy objectives.

This is an exceedingly complex business, one that defies cut-and-dried classification. The important point, however, is that under certain circumstances, such as prevail in India, the organisational resources of parties can combine with their fuzzy boundaries to permit a greater quantity and diversity of political transactions to take place between holders of state power and independently constituted economic interests than would otherwise be possible. By contributing to the maintenance of

---

[4] There are many different conceptualisations of faction and party. Most have a tendency to portray the relationship between them in zero-sum terms. Thus, political groups 'can most usefully be thought of as on a continuum, with faction-like groupings at one polar extreme and political party type at the other'. Janet Bujra, 'The Dynamics of Political Action: A New Look at Factionalism', *American Anthropologist*, vol. 75 (1973), p. 133. In India, the two are not only intertwined, but in the process of *governance* they tend to be less important than loosely defined support bases which span party and non-party organisations. For the purposes of our discussion, the notion of a network of influence is more informative, as it captures this reality more succinctly, while possessing none of the intellectual baggage associated with either party or faction. See also René Lemarchand, 'The Dynamics of Factionalism in Contemporary Africa', in Zaki Ergas (ed.), *The African State in Transition* (Basingstoke: Macmillan, 1987), pp. 149–65.

a wider sphere of influence within which trade-offs can be arranged, these expectation-shaping relationships (centred within, though not contained by, political parties) provide far more flexibility for governing elites embedded within them than much theorising about democratic states might lead one to believe.

Grasping the implications of this situation also allows us to avoid the undue reverence for civil society found in much of the good-government literature. Civil society is, in itself, neither virtuous nor pernicious: freely associating groups can check the power of states or enter into unholy alliances with them. Groups operating in civil society are also capable of producing healthy or dysfunctional economic outcomes by either reinforcing market competition or sharing the spoils of a protected economy among themselves. Appreciating the varied role played by party elites in creating broader networks among representatives of associational entities in India provides a clearer understanding of how a polity in which civil society flourishes could generate, first, an economic malaise symbolised by 'the Hindu rate of growth',[5] and then a policy reversal that has surprised and delighted neo-liberals. The mere existence of civil society accounts for nothing. However, the way in which its constituent parts relate with Indian political elites, who are members of parties but operate clearinghouse-style networks of influence that spread far beyond party organisations (including into the decidedly *un*-civil society of the criminal underworld), accounts for a great deal of the variation between a state-dominated policy dispensation and one in which the relative salience of markets is much greater. When political elites have sufficient incentives to initiate economic reform, they are often able to rely upon the pre-existing set of relationships fostered by, though not contained within, their membership in a political party in order to help bring about its implementation.

Parties, then, are bridging institutions between state and society, and between the world of rule and the realm of informal, often interpersonal, arrangements and understandings. Under certain circumstances they make possible diverse relationships, while possessing the means, when in power, to reorder the nature of these relationships. In India, key members within ruling parties are able to rely upon the organisational resources of their political networks to assess the implications of drastic 'reorderings', such as severing a relationship with a once-close ally. More often, they are able to act as brokers between groups in civil society. All of this takes place within a democratic setting – which institutions influence and are influenced by – but is not synonymous with democracy. It must be stressed

[5] Deepak Lal, *The Hindu Equilibrium* (Oxford: Clarendon Press, 1988).

that what we are discussing in this book is Indian democracy, not democracy in the abstract. While we cannot generalise from one particular case, revealing the details of one case *does* allow us to take issue with *existing* generalisations. In so doing, we can also identify features which may have a bearing on other cases.

This book has no pretensions to grand theorising about the evolutionary paths of institutions in democratic settings. It may, however, be worth mentioning one relevant insight which has emerged in the international relations literature on informal institutions. In the early 1970s, as the more formal international institutions, particularly those created at the Bretton Woods conference, became inadequate to meet the needs of a more interdependent world, the importance of less formalised institutions grew commensurately. These 'regimes' were related to particular issues and were created to meet the requirements of specific political contexts. Robert Keohane has argued that such relatively informal solutions became attractive to both states and non-governmental actors because, in comparison to formal institutions, they minimised transaction costs, lessened inequalities of access to information among the participants, and provided greater grounds for assigning a party's liability.[6] As one commentary on the regime literature put it: in a context in which formal institutions are declining in capacity, informal institutions 'pave the way for greater volumes of mutually advantageous transactions than would transpire in their absence'.[7]

Clearly, there are limits to any comparison of international relations theory with the practice of domestic politics in India. Yet, these observations about the changing nature of international relations can enhance our understanding of the practical utility of democracy. While India's formal institutions of state suffered severe decay for two decades before the initiation of economic reform in 1991, its informal political institutions continued to thrive. They resemble international regimes in so far as the latter incorporate substantive norms, influence principles of behaviour, and result in mutually comprehensible decisional processes. The capacity of India's informal institutions to augment the interest-articulation and conflict-mediation functions of its formal federal system, and thereby to smooth the path for the types of political transactions which a sustainable process of reform requires, has been very substantial. Let us now turn to some of the detailed empirical evidence for these claims.

[6] Robert Keohane, *After Hegemony: Cooperation and Discord in the World Political Economy* (Princeton: Princeton University Press, 1984), Chapter 6.
[7] Neil R. Richardson, 'International Trade as a Force for Peace', in Charles W. Kegley, Jr. (ed.), *Controversies in International Relations Theory: Realism and the Neoliberal Challenge* (New York: St. Martin's Press, 1995), p. 285.

Formal institutions: federalism, economic reform, and the division of political labour

Federalism – enshrined in the Indian constitution in the form of electoral rules and a division of political powers – is a classic formal institution. It is both codified and constitutive of the state. A federal system is, moreover, well suited to a country of India's striking diversity. The frequency with which identity-based politics asserts itself at the regional level invests Indian federalism with a substance not found in many putatively federal political systems, and provides an important decentralising tendency that runs like a thread through politics since independence.[8] The federal political structure, which encompasses a range of institutions such as state and national legislatures, national finance and planning commissions, and inter-state coordinating bodies, is a defining feature of Indian democracy – one which is a clear response to the regional diversity of Indian civilisation. Federalism reflects an adjustment through which once-alien institutions have been adapted to social reality and political practice.

The division of political labour between the centre and the states in independent India has been the subject of much political debate and almost as much academic theorising. As the Congress Party slowly lost its dominant position in Indian politics, a process which began as far back as the 1967 general election, tensions between national and provincial political forces took on an increasingly partisan character. Efforts to reverse this trend, such as the increasing abuse of the constitutional provision known as President's Rule to supersede state governments, have not been successful, and have arguably accelerated the deterioration in federal relations. It is also generally accepted that attempts by Congress prime ministers over the past twenty-five years to undercut up-and-coming Congress state chief ministers have, paradoxically, diminished the national party's ability to influence events in the states where Congress held power.[9] In recent years, the Congress has been reduced to a marginal electoral force in India's two most populous states, Uttar Pradesh and Bihar. During 1991–96, when it held power in New Delhi under Narasimha Rao, it was usually out of power in more states than it controlled.

---

[8] See, for instance, Paul Brass, 'Pluralism, Regionalism and Decentralising Tendencies in Contemporary Indian Politics', in A. Jeyaratnam Wilson and Denis Dalton (eds.), *The States of South Asia: Problems of National Integration* (London: Hurst and Co., 1982).

[9] See James Manor, 'The Electoral Process amid Awakening and Decay', in Peter Lyon and James Manor (eds.), *Transfer and Transformation: Political Institutions in the New Commonwealth* (Leicester: Leicester University Press, 1983), pp. 87–116; and 'Indira and After: The Decay of Party Organisation in India', *The Round Table* (Oct. 1978), pp. 315–24.

In the context of liberalisation, one political observer has argued that

> If the post-Nehruvian order is to strike roots, the Congress may find itself having to reach some kind of an understanding with regional outfits based on a division of political articulation. Under such an arrangement, the Congress can continue to promote itself as a protector of national unity, guarantor of security against external threats, overseer of at least a minimal level of law and order throughout the country, *and as a facilitator of globalisation of the Indian economy*. In return its allies and adversaries will be free to . . . cater to regional and sub-regional aspirations and frustrations. This kind of division has become inevitable because the Congress has lost the capacity to co-opt new forces.[10]

While underplaying a number of complicating factors, such as the role of the Hindu nationalist BJP, this analysis highlights two important features of the current political terrain. First, though economic reform was initiated (and its most visible elements largely orchestrated) by national elites in New Delhi, state-level politicians and political systems have a key role to play in managing its implications, and contributing to its sustainability. They absorb much of the political burden.

Second, the politics of economic reform will be intimately bound up with any solution to India's worsening centre–state political disequilibrium that may emerge. As we saw in the last chapter, new means of profiteering and patronage have emerged at the national level as an accompaniment to economic liberalisation. In particular, the new sources of corrupt income provided by foreign capital have, as Pranab Bardhan had speculated in the mid-1980s, reduced the reliance of national elites on domestic business interests for funding political activities.[11] This has also allowed national politicians to relax investment policies in ways which give state governments new responsibilities, in the process providing the politicians that run them access to new resources. Many of these money-spinning activities had, in a different form, been the exclusive preserve of national political elites.

There have also been parallel moves by central reformers to buy peace with state-level political elites by directly passing responsibilities to the state level. In 1992, for example, the petroleum ministry decentralised the process of selecting retailers for petroleum products and cooking gas. The Rajasthan Oil Selection Board thus came into being in January 1993, and it was not long before it was embroiled in charges of corruption.[12] As we will see in the next section, these new opportunities have been a mixed

---

[10] Harish Khare, 'Beyond Congress Infighting: Dilemma of Sustaining the New Order', *Times of India*, 12 January 1994 (emphasis added).

[11] Pranab Bardhan, 'Dominant Proprietary Classes and India's Democracy', in Atul Kohli (ed.), *India's Democracy: An Analysis of Changing State-Society Relations* (Princeton: Princeton University Press, 1988), p. 224, fn 9.   [12] *Asian Age*, 25 February 1995.

blessing for state governments, which as a result must now take difficult political decisions affecting sectoral interests that have supported them in the past.

None of this is without political risk for the state-level politicians involved. But they have little choice but to play the game. Indeed, they have been doing so for some time. The critical role played by state governments in managing the politics of economic change was apparent even during the 1980s. Walter Neale argued that '[t]wo important aspects of the relationship between state governments and the Indian economy have been, firstly, their role as agents of regional interest groups and, secondly, as inaugurators of new political alliances and as accommodating initiators in the process of incremental reforms'.[13] The importance of state governments has also been noted by analysts of conditionality-based lending by multilateral financial institutions and bilateral donors.[14]

Often, state governments are viewed, by both Indians and foreign observers, as an obstacle to coherent and effective implementation of policy reforms. It is undoubtedly true that the existence of multiple levels within the political system introduces the potential for linkage problems to emerge. Policy directives formulated in New Delhi can become hopelessly distorted by the time they reach a state capital, let alone a district or sub-district headquarters. Public resources – whether for productive activity or poverty alleviation – are vulnerable to illegal appropriation at the many decision points along the chain of political and bureaucratic command. The inefficiency inherent in this system was one of the stated reasons for reforming the economy by divesting the public sector of some of its responsibilities. As a result of reform, however, there have been many alterations to the over-centralisation of economic decision-making. Indeed,

[o]ne of the most important changes taking place in India is the gradual diffusion of power to the states after the centralised, statist years of the Nehru-Gandhi family. It is happening for good reasons (political pluralism and the workings of the market) and bad ones (weak leadership at the centre and the growth of parochial, sectarian political parties).[15]

Despite the complications and uncertainties it introduces, the existence of a federal political system has been an extremely important ingredient in

[13] Walter Neale, 'Congress Presiding Over Progress and Change: State Governments and the Indian Economy', in Mike Shepperdson and Colin Simmons (eds.), *The Indian National Congress and the Political Economy of India, 1885–1985* (Aldershot: Gower Publishing Co., 1988), p. 293.
[14] See J. D. Pederson, 'Complexity of Conditionality: The Case of India', *European Journal of Development Research*, vol. 5, no. 1 (June 1993), p. 105.
[15] Economist Intelligence Unit, *Country Report – India*, 2nd Quarter, 1995 (London, 1995), p. 14.

helping to make India's economic reform programme politically sustainable – that is, in reducing the pressure on political decision-makers in the central government to abandon reform. In addition to unloading thankless political burdens on to state governments, in the guise of devolving decision-making authority in certain areas[16] (a tactic to be analysed further in Chapter 6), there are three main ways in which this process operates, each of which stems from the impact of economic reform on the incentives facing political actors. We will discuss each of these in turn.

Inter-state disparities, inter-state rivalries

The first, and most basic, advantage to reformers at the centre is that the impact of economic reform varies from state to state. Some states derive significant benefits, while others do not. Politicians from states that benefit have little motivation to oppose reform. Those from states that suffer relative declines in economic performance (or autonomy in determining economic policy) have both less clout and fewer allies with which to mount a serious challenge to liberalisation. Even among states that can be considered *net* losers, there is often little commonality in the nature of their grievances, since almost all states have gained in at least some areas. Since these small compensations tend to be jealously guarded, efforts to mount coordinated resistance to reform from this crucial tier of the Indian political elite have faltered.

A good illustration of this problem was the reaction of state governments to the central government's approach to the 'freight equalisation' scheme, a classic piece of statist industrial regulation which attempted to negate disparities in transport costs between India's regions. The scheme had long worked to the disadvantage of states in the eastern part of India. Successive chief ministers in the three main states in the eastern region – Bihar, West Bengal, and Orissa – had been decrying the unfairness of freight equalisation for years. When, as part of its efforts to marketise the economy, the Narasimha Rao government announced the abolition of the scheme, all three states were governed by non-Congress parties who were officially critical of efforts to dismantle the regulatory state. And yet, because of the popularity of the abandonment of the freight-equalisation scheme among interests within their states, three usually liberalisation-

---

[16] One example was the announcement in early 1998 by the central ministry for chemicals and fertilisers that it endorsed the plan to transfer authority over regulation of molasses (production, pricing, distribution) to state governments. This led to great pressure being exerted on chief ministers of sugar-cultivating states, such as Andhra Pradesh's Chandrababu Naidu, by manufacturers of rectified spirit and alcohol-based chemicals, both of which use (price-controlled) molasses as a key input. See *Economic Times*, 6 February 1998.

bashing chief ministers found themselves politically constrained from opposing it.[17] Their self-interested acceptance of this policy shift not only dulled the edge of their public fulminations against other aspects of the central government's reform programme; it sent a signal to political leaders in other regions that the prospects for a united front against liberalisation would be fruitless in the face of chief ministers willing to cave in on individual reform measures that suited their particular political circumstances.

This was not an isolated incident. For instance, politicians from states with significant mineral resources failed to voice opposition to liberalisation in the mining sector,[18] regardless of objections from their colleagues in non-mining states who claimed that such tacit approval lent further political credibility to the reform process as a whole. With each state holding a soft spot for liberalisation measures that worked to its advantage, coordinated resistance to the overall redirection of economic policy became extremely difficult. While discontent can be found among political elites in every state in India, there is no common *basis* for welding that discontent into a unified programme of opposition to reform. Making matters worse, from the perspective of potential collective action among state-level political elites, is the fact that it has been more difficult to predict reform's winners and losers than was originally anticipated. For instance, economists from the Delhi-based National Institute of Public Finance and Policy expressed surprise that Central Statistical Office data showed richer states like Haryana and Gujarat registering negative growth in terms of per capita net state domestic product.[19] The tendency for such variations – from sector to sector and from year to year – to translate into a divided lobby demonstrates that the nature of liberal representative politics can afflict political elites in the same way, if not with the same dire consequences, that it does dispersed marginal groups.

None of this is meant to deny that in some cases divisions among state governments can hamper the introduction of particular types of reforms. As Vito Tanzi's review of the international literature indicates, 'in several

---

[17] Buddhadeb Bhattacharjee, West Bengal's minister for information and cultural affairs, captured the dilemma facing state leaders when he stated: 'While we are opposed to the philosophy and approach of the Centre's New Economic Policy, we must take advantage of the withdrawal of the freight equalisation scheme and delicensing in regard to some major industries'. *Sunday*, 3–9 April 1994, p. 68.

[18] Among these states was Rajasthan. At a press conference announcing the state's 'New Mineral Policy 1994', BJP chief minister B. S. Shekhawat openly thanked the Congress prime minister for going out of his way to remove bottlenecks relating to environmental regulation so that Rajasthan could make the most of its natural resources. *The Hindu*, 17 August 1994. Further decentralisation of power in the mining sector was announced by the United Front coalition government in 1996. See *Hindu – Business Line*, 5 September 1996.   [19] *Economic Times*, 28 February 1998.

cases decentralization has made it harder for countries to eliminate their structural fiscal deficits' and implement other reform measures.[20] In the case of India, for instance, proposals to create a unified market for agricultural produce have been effectively stalled, because the prospect of decontrolling the price and movement of various commodities pits food-deficit states against those with food surpluses. Federalism also means that reformers in New Delhi are faced with the prospect of elections in at least one major state (and usually more) every year, rather than every five, with all the temptations to indulge in populist gestures this implies.[21]

Therefore, rather than casting federalism as an unalloyed boon to reformers, the more limited argument advanced here is that in many cases where political resistance has been attenuated, or overcome completely, jealousies between political elites in different states have been at least partly responsible. Policy decisions by central authorities have been deliberately designed to exploit these divisions. For instance, when increasing the administered price for petroleum products in 1997, the United Front government's policy statement contained a provision which meant that consumers in some states would pay higher prices than those in others, based on the logic that some states were raising resources through taxation on petroleum-processing activities within their borders, and that these resources could be used to cushion the blow of price rises. The centre had effectively seized the assets of *some* state governments, or at the very least placed enormous pressure on individual states to take up the political slack generated when the central government decided to arrogate to itself the high moral ground of fiscal rectitude.[22] Little sympathy was forthcoming from leaders of states in which there were no processing activities to tax.

Even in the one area in which virtually all states have fared poorly – the devolution of resources from the central government – the specific sources of forgone income have varied from state to state. While much of the commentary on public expenditure highlights the continued profligacy of India's states,[23] another view of this phenomenon is that it has been caused (or at least accelerated) by 'step-motherly treatment' at the hands of the central government. Due to complicated tax-sharing formulas and

[20] Vito Tanzi, 'Fiscal Federalism and Decentralization: A Review of Some Efficiency and Macroeconomic Aspects', *Proceedings of the Annual World Bank Conference on Development Economics*, 1995, p. 295.

[21] For details of one case – the Andhra Pradesh assembly elections of 1994 – see Sudha Pai, 'Elections and Fiscal Reform', *Economic and Political Weekly*, 13–20 January 1996, pp. 142–7.

[22] See Sukumar Muralidharan, 'Paying the Price', *Frontline*, 3 October 1997, p. 37.

[23] For instance, 'State Finances Spin Out of Control', *Business World*, 29 May–11 June 1996, pp. 48–50.

the difficulty of tracing the downstream effects of non-tax policy reforms (such as the partial freeing of interest rates), estimates of adjustment's impact on the fiscal position of state governments are uncertain at best. It is generally believed, however, that almost all states have experienced a decline in the level of fiscal transfers from the central government. But, again, both the level and nature of the reductions have varied between states.[24] Increases in central-government loans to some state governments have been offset by reductions in grants, with the interest-payment consequences negatively affecting financial manoeuvrability.[25] For the most part, state governments have resorted to market borrowing. As a consequence, the average interest rate on state debt increased from 9.2 per cent in 1990–91 to 12.7 per cent in 1997–98, while combined state revenue deficits almost tripled – from Rs. 53 million in 1990–91 to Rs. 150 million in 1997–98.[26]

One economist asked whether even the moderate degree of fiscal discipline the central government has been able to impose during the reform era has been at the cost of state governments.[27] To the extent that this is the case, it represents a politically expedient means by which reformers in the central government are able to take advantage of the existence of a federal system.[28] There are substantial grounds for this claim. Net transfers to the states as a percentage of the central government's total receipts, including borrowing, fell from 31 per cent in 1990–91 to 26 per cent in 1994–95.[29] Central transfers to the states as a percentage of GDP fell from 5 per cent of GDP in 1990–91 to 3.4 per cent in 1997–98.[30] During the 1980s, aggregate transfers from the central government to the states grew at an annual rate of 17 per cent in net terms – that is, when payments from the states to the centre are taken into account. During 1990–95, however, the annual growth rate averaged

[24] This view was expressed by Rathin Roy at a seminar organised by a major British multinational firm to assess the investment climate in India, 4 September 1995, London.

[25] And while most states have received increased levels of loans from the central government, by 1995–96 some among them had found that annual debt repayments to the central government outweighed new loan finance. See *Business World*, 29 May–11 June 1996, p. 50.

[26] *Business World*, 22 March 1998, p. 45.

[27] Madanmohan Ghosh, 'Fiscal Management at the Cost of the States?', *Mainstream*, 14 May 1994, pp. 17–18.

[28] Similar claims could be made about other federal systems undergoing reform programmes. For a taste of the battle between Venezuela's central and regional governments over who is to bear the costs of fiscal adjustment – and the extent to which regions should be able to respond to their predicament by increasing taxes – see *Financial Times*, 4 November 1997 and 17 February 1998.   [29] Ibid., p. 18.

[30] World Bank, *India: Sustaining Rapid Economic Growth* (Washington, DC: The World Bank, 1997), Table 4, p. 40. The 1997–98 figures are government 'budget estimates'. Central transfers comprise both grants and gross loans to the state governments.

only 7 per cent.[31] The first five years of reform (1990–91 to 1994–95) witnessed a reduction in the proportion of state government spending covered by central transfers: from 43.59 per cent to 39.49 per cent.[32] Because it places central funding levels in the context of the increasing commitments facing state government – many of which resulted from the central government devolving responsibilities – this is perhaps the best indicator of both the increased autonomy and increased insecurity facing state governments, which must fend for themselves in an increasingly difficult world.

To summarise: from a situation in which year-to-year increases in central funding exceeded inflation, the states have had to cope with central-funding levels which have not even kept pace with inflation. Since many central funds are tied to specific programmes over which states have little or no control, and which have generated demands which far outstrip the available funding, even the notion of 'grants' is often more illusory than real. Most importantly, since some states are much better equipped than others to regain a part of the lost revenue by adapting to other aspects of the central government's liberalisation policies, this further divides political elites from different states.

Individual reforms taken by the central government can, for instance, allow some states the opportunity to increase certain tax revenues. Again, the argument is not that the net effect on states' revenue is positive. On any given reform, only one or two states might benefit. One example is the Government of India's gradual reform of the coffee marketing system. In 1992, coffee growers were for the first time permitted to sell 30 per cent of their crop in the open market, having previously been required to sell to the government-controlled Coffee Board at what were considered below-market rates. In 1993 the Free Sale Quota was increased to 50 per cent. In April 1995, in a long-anticipated move, all obligations to the Coffee Board were removed for 'small growers' (those with land holdings of less than ten hectares). In need of new sources of revenue, states with substantial coffee-growing operations began to cast an avaricious eye towards coffee growers who had received 'windfall' profits. The Karnataka government, for instance, was able to raise resources in this way, justifying the new tax by saying that the coffee growers who had benefited should be prepared to contribute resources for the welfare of the poor.[33] These

---

[31] Ghosh, 'Fiscal Management at the Cost of the States?', p. 17.

[32] Pinaki Chakraborty, 'Growing Imbalances in Federal Fiscal Relationship', *Economic and Political Weekly*, 14 February 1998, p. 351.

[33] *The Hindu*, 18 April 1995. This tax increase was just one part of a complex political understanding, arranged through the informal networks of leaders from three different parties, which included unofficial permission for large-scale coffee growers to encroach on

adaptations further delink states' economic fates from one another – contributing to the pattern of provincial Darwinism that, we have argued, has reduced the effectiveness of resistance among state-level political elites.[34]

Other examples reinforce this perception. In March 1995, the Communist chief minister of West Bengal, Jyoti Basu, agreed to his finance minister's suggestion to introduce a State Value-Added Tax on iron and steel.[35] This type of measure is not available to all chief ministers. When an opposition leader of Basu's stature took such an action he sent a message to other non-Congress chief ministers that each state must look out for its own interests, rather than join forces to oppose the underlying direction of the central government's policy reforms. Previously, Basu had headed a committee of chief ministers reviewing alternatives to the state-level goods-transport taxes within and between states. The committee was an attempt to provide a united front among state governments, and thus avoid debilitating competition. In the committee, Basu steadfastly opposed an agreement to scrap these transport taxes, arguing that the states were already being hard hit financially by other central government decisions. By 1995, however, Basu had reversed course, abolishing West Bengal's tax on intra-state goods transport known as *octroi*.[36] This further entrenched the every-state-for-itself logic – good news for reformers in New Delhi who could more easily manage dissent from a divided state-level political elite.

As of early 1999, the effectiveness of economic reform in reducing the prospects for collective action among anti-reform politicians from different states showed no signs of waning. For instance, the prospect that the Reserve Bank of India might permit better-managed states to borrow funds at lower rates of interest than others was sure to cause bad blood between leaders of 'advanced' and 'backward' states.[37] An analysis by the Finance Secretary of the Andhra Pradesh government concluded that the central government's response to the report of the Tenth Finance Commission would 'freeze the proportion of taxes to be devolved to the states and thus extinguish the one issue that united the states against the

lands nominally designated for scheduled-caste groups. Interview with one of the party leaders involved in this process, 19 April 1995, Bangalore.

[34] There have been some moves to counter this trend, including the creation of multi-state economic cooperation zones, particularly in the south. *Deccan Herald*, 17 April 1995. At a CII summit in January 1995, West Bengal chief minister Jyoti Basu strongly emphasised the need to end the inter-state 'taxation war and incentive war to woo investors' because it would ultimately be of 'zero gain to the states and result in loss of revenue'. *Asian Age*, 6 January 1995.   [35] *Business Standard*, 25 March 1995.   [36] Ibid.

[37] Reserve Bank of India, *Bulletin*, Supplement: 'Finances of State Governments – 1997–98' (February 1998).

centre'.[38] Moreover, '[t]he ability of central transfers to neutralise the fiscal disadvantages of backward states will also diminish as advanced states are unlikely to acquiesce in an open ended obligation of cross-subsidising the poorer ones'.[39] All this, the author argued, was a natural culmination of trends, fuelled by liberalisation, which had led to division among states and state-level political elites:

> Because of the fragmentation of markets by different sales tax regimes, the more advanced states, being net exporters of manufactures, are also able to export their tax burden. Willy nilly these states are taxing consumers outside their states and appropriating the benefits.[40]

That the tax bases of industrially advanced states provide greater scope for adapting to lower levels of central financing is reflected in RBI data. It was only in such states – such as Maharashtra, Gujarat, Punjab, and Tamil Nadu – that average annual growth in tax revenue during the first five years of reform (1990–91 to 1994–95) was higher than in the five years prior to reform (1985–86 to 1998–90).[41] Roughly the same pattern holds if states' tax revenue is measured as a proportion of their revenue expenditure.[42]

The most overtly divisive area of reform has been liberalisation of industrial policy. Under the licence-permit Raj, business location decisions were effectively taken by central planners in New Delhi. With the abolition of this system, both Indian and foreign capital have been freed to seek locations offering the best returns. This has set off an intense competition among state governments to attract investment, resulting in a proliferation of tax-incentive schemes and promises of speedy administrative procedures, expedited land acquisition for new industrial projects, and efforts to maintain a 'conducive' industrial-relations climate. (The tax-holiday elements of some of these schemes have actually further worsened state financial positions.) Chief ministers have courted business leaders at conferences, investment seminars, trade fairs, and in one-on-one consultations throughout India. Many chief ministers have gone on foreign tours to convince sceptical investors of the merits of his or her state. The arrival of Maharashtra chief minister Sharad Pawar in Calcutta to woo business leaders from West Bengal struck many observers, particularly among Calcutta's elite, as the epitome of all that was wrong with the new competitive climate.[43] The competition between the govern-

[38] Duvuuri Subbarao, 'Inter-state Disparities and Reform', *Economic Times*, 6 February 1998. [39] Ibid. [40] Ibid.

[41] Reserve Bank of India, *Bulletin*, Supplement: 'Finances of State Governments – 1996–97' (February 1997), p. 65. [42] Ibid., p. 41.

[43] A former high-level official in the West Bengal Industrial Development Corporation referred to Pawar's operation, which was run from a suite in the posh Park Hotel, as 'a

ments of Tamil Nadu and Maharashtra to win a proposed Ford Fiesta assembly plant – which eventually went to Tamil Nadu in early 1996 – was particularly fierce.[44]

The curtailment of the central government's vast discretionary powers over industrial licensing means that state governments have become the crucial point of contact for entrepreneurs. State government agencies are where industrialists must go if they want environmental and labour clearances, water and electricity connections, land and zoning permits, and so on. If competition among states in a climate of fiscal retrenchment represented the 'stick' imposed by the new policy dispensation, then the prospect of enhanced opportunities for corruption was the 'carrot'. Given the investment boom, and the new-found demand for their 'investment-facilitation services', leaders of state governments suddenly found their earnings potential enormously increased. Indeed, political 'fundraising' increasingly takes place at the state level.[45] The opportunities this offers for generating illegal income were discussed in Chapter 4. But there was also an aspect of inter-party rivalry in the response of state-level leaders. As Harish Khare has argued, many

non-Congress [state] governments . . . moved with considerable finesse to seek terms of mutual collaboration with regional business interests . . . before these [were] appropriated by a businessman-friendly regime in New Delhi. The new regional leadership saw no reason why . . . Congress leaders at the centre should be allowed to co-opt business communities from their backyards.[46]

The point that needs emphasising here is that *centre-state* conflict has been at least partially displaced by *inter-state* competition for inward investment. There is, however, a systemic check on the ability of ministers in state governments to derive illegal income from their suddenly pivotal positions: the competition to create an investor-friendly climate, which in theory should penalise states that impose heavy 'corruption taxes' on businesses. In reality, inter-state competition for inward investment has driven a wedge between political elites in states capable of offering a conducive business environment (while *still* being able to extract significant levels of illicit rents) and elites from states that are constrained in this

---

disgusting display'. Interview, 25 April 1996, Calcutta.

[44] The sales-tax concessions alone were estimated at Rs. 2.9 billion. There have also been complaints regarding the lack of transparency in the state-government's handling of the negotiations. *Frontline*, 20 September 1996, pp. 82–8.

[45] This view was expressed by office bearers of influential business associations in Maharashtra, Karnataka, and Rajasthan. Interviews: 31 January 1994, Bombay; 23 March 1994, Bangalore; and 19 November 1993, Jaipur.

[46] Harish Khare, 'Ten Headlines in Search of a Regime', *Seminar*, no. 437 (January 1996), p. 28.

regard.[47] This lack of unity has helped to take some of the sting out of anti-reform dissidence among state-level political leaders.[48]

Recognising the divisive impact of the liberalised environment, one Congress leader from Rajasthan went so far as to caution states against demanding more autonomy from the central government, which had been a standard rallying cry among state-level politicians from practically all parties since independence. In the assembly debate on the 1994–95 state budget, Chandan Mal Baid argued that it was in the interest of 'backward' states like Rajasthan that the centre remained strong enough to dictate terms to more prosperous and powerful states.[49]

His fears were not far-fetched. The divisive impact of liberalisation goes beyond the efforts of state governments to outdo one another with packages of incentives for private-sector investors. The Himachal Pradesh Congress government which took power in late 1993, for example, soon realised that it had inherited a financial mess from its BJP predecessor. It wasted little time in informing the neighbouring (Congress-ruled) states of Haryana and Punjab that it would need to call in the Rs. 11 billion they owed it for power supplied by the Himachal Pradesh electricity grid. This inter-state conflict supplanted the centre-state conflict over electricity debts that had preoccupied the previous BJP state government.[50] One of the main reasons for the Himachal Pradesh government's need to call in its neighbours' debts was that it was being squeezed by the central government's fiscal policies, including its failure to pay its own debts. Thus, even governing elites from adjacent Congress-ruled states found it difficult to make common cause against specific provisions of the new economic policy dispensation on which they had similar grounds for complaint. In this case, differences in the nature of their fiscal relations with the central government led to the eruption of an inter-state conflict that had been masked previously by central government institutions responsible for arranging cross-subsidies.

---

[47] Some states, such as the industrial powerhouses of Maharashtra and Gujarat, began the race for investment pre-eminence with such an advantage in terms of human and physical infrastructure that threats by entrepreneurs to take their projects elsewhere were usually empty. This headstart may narrow over time, but in the early stages of reform, when the perceptions of state-level elites were crucial to its political sustainability, this was not the case.

[48] This was particularly true of Congress chief ministers during the early Narasimha Rao years, when the discontent among state leaders was reportedly vented regularly at meetings between state-level party presidents and the prime minister – for instance on 23 October 1992. A potential revolt by state-level leaders was considered a major threat to the political sustainability of the reform process. *Sunday*, 8–14 November 1992, pp. 14–15.   [49] *The Hindu*, 10 March 1994.   [50] *Hindustan Times*, 15 April 1994.

The federal prism: fragmenting interest-group resistance

The second aspect of federalism which assists the sustainability of economic reform is its tendency to disperse the political energies of economic interests, as opposed to political elites, by forcing them to battle in twenty-six states rather than in just one unitary political authority at the national level. The result is a significant fragmentation among certain interests along regional lines. This often reduces their political potency. Quarantined within individual states, where they are often less effective to begin with, many socio-economic interests find it difficult effectively to influence policy. The issues that concern them tend to get bound up with the day-to-day political mudslinging of state politics, further reducing their potency, and making the maintenance of a coordinated national lobbying effort even more difficult.

As early as the 1960s, Clifford Geertz recognised a similar dynamic at work in the realm of cultural change, arguing that the reorganisation of states along linguistic lines in 1956 provided India's 'pattern of civil hub and primordial rim its official institutionalization'.[51] This was part 'of the general approach of attempting to insulate parapolitical forces from national concerns by sequestering them in local contexts'.[52] In a slightly different context Subrata Mitra likened the divisions between states to 'tidal barriers'. When the role played by state-level political elites declined in the 1970s and 1980s, he argued, 'local and regional conflicts tended to spread from one region to another'.[53] But on the whole this has not happened with the social and political conflicts arising from economic reform. Arguably, this has been due to the decentralising tendencies associated with liberalisation itself. For this reason, Myron Weiner's conception of state-level 'quarantine' is more relevant to the issues under discussion here.

Weiner has pointed out that India's regional diversity, mirrored institutionally in its federal political system, has kept explosive issues from engulfing the apex of the political system.[54] His argument was concerned with violent social conflict, rather than the milder sphere of interest-group responses to economic policy. But it is still of relevance to the political sustainability of economic reform in so far as the case-study evidence that will be discussed in the latter portion of Chapter 6 illus-

---

[51] Clifford Geertz, 'The Integrative Revolution: Primordial Sentiments and Civil Politics in the New States', in Clifford Geertz, *The Interpretation of Cultures: Selected Essays* (New York: Basic Books, 1973), p. 290.   [52] Ibid., pp. 290–1.

[53] Subrata Kumar Mitra, 'Crisis and Resilience in Indian Democracy', *International Social Science Journal*, no. 129 (August 1991), p. 564.

[54] Myron Weiner, 'The Indian Paradox: Violent Social Conflict and Democratic Politics', in Myron Weiner (ed.), *The Indian Paradox: Essays in Indian Politics* (New Delhi: Sage Publications, 1989), p. 36.

trates the capacity of state-level political systems to subsume issues of concern to economic interests into the matrix of identity politics – that is, assertions based on caste, language, and religion. For this reason, Weiner's basic argument – that the combination of social diversity among regions and a functioning federal polity helps to 'quarantine' conflict within the boundaries of state-level political systems – has a direct bearing on how we understand the impacts of federalism on the political sustainability of economic reform.

What needs to be emphasised is that the tendency for central government policy reforms to have different impacts in different states has affected not only the incentives and collective-action prospects facing state-level politicians, but also the way in which socio-economic interests respond to economic reform. Responses to the same reform can vary from state to state. This happens for two main reasons. The first has to do with the initial conditions which prevail in various states: both the economies and political complexions of different states vary considerably, affecting the relative costs and benefits of individual reforms, as well as the capacity of interests to influence state-level responses. The second reason why interest-group responses vary from state to state is that state-level governing elites pursue different strategies for coping with the changed policy environment wrought by central government reforms. This encompasses economic policy as well as tactics of political management, both of which are affected by the differences in initial conditions mentioned above.

Moreover, liberalisation is increasingly implemented in the form of successive micro-reforms in different states, at different times, and under different political circumstances. This combination means that the political impact of economic reform is refracted through the prism of federal India. This results in a slower pace than many proponents of reform would prefer. But it also helps to blunt the edge of opposition. Efforts to mount coordinated political resistance to one or another reform tend to become severely dissipated in such a fragmented environment, especially when governing elites at the state level are able to bring their formidable political skills and wide-ranging networks of influence to bear on groups operating within their jurisdictions.

Indeed, one of the main assets of the Indian political system on which reformers in the central government rely is the political-management capacity of state-level governments. The existence of functional competitive arenas at various levels of the political system helps to spread the burden of conflict resolution over a broader institutional base. Though the impetus for reform came from a relatively small circle of advisers around the finance minister and the prime minister, state governments are forced to cope with its varied consequences. S. Guhan has argued that, compared to the central government,

> States are much closer to the electorate and also much more vulnerable to instability . . . The States are responsible for much that affects the daily lives of people: law and order, land administration, power supply, irrigation, agricultural services, public road transport, education, health, urban development and water supply. By the same token, these several activities that lie at the cutting edge of administration expose State governments more intimately and continually to popular demands, conflicting pressures, and diverse local grievances. Pushing through reforms that are likely to affect one interest group or another and carrying varying burdens and benefits to different groups will, in these circumstances, require considerable political education and commitment.[55]

State governments, in short, must face the fallout from the central government's reforms. This happens in a variety of ways, some of which have been hinted at in the discussion of centre-state finances. Others are more subtle, and less easily quantifiable, such as the nationwide truck-drivers' strike in July 1993, in which commercial road transport was brought to a virtual standstill. The drivers' main gripe concerned state-level border taxes, the collectors of which routinely demanded exorbitant bribes. However, as this had been a long-simmering source of discontent, the timing of the strike was odd, as nothing had changed in regard to this issue. According to many commentators, the reason why it boiled over just then was that the central government had recently raised petrol prices as part of an effort to reduce the subsidy bill. State governments, because they are seen as more responsive than the central government to interest-group pressure, had to bear the truck drivers' ire.[56]

Ironically, state governments also come under pressure when the central government takes *il*liberal policy decisions. In June 1998, the Gujarat Chamber of Commerce and Industry demanded that the state government reduce by 4 per cent the sales tax on textile product categories in which foreign competitors would not face the central government's newly announced special additional import duty.[57] Their argument, in effect, was that the state should forgo revenue from sectors which had not managed to benefit from the centre's sudden bout of protectionism. Even when the centre becomes *less* liberal, state-level interest groups demand that states become *more* liberal, in this case by reducing taxes to offset the ill-effects.

In the light of these examples, we can extend Guhan's point by arguing that the political pressure facing reformers at the apex of the political

---

[55] S. Guhan, 'Centre and States in the Reform Process', in Robert Cassen and Vijay Joshi (eds.), *India: The Future of Economic Reform* (Delhi: Oxford University Press, 1995), p. 101.

[56] See C. P. Bhambhri, 'The Politics of Manmohanomics', *Financial Express*, 23 July 1993.

[57] *Economic Times*, 30 June 1998.

system is reduced in proportion to the capacity of state governments, acting as the first line of political defence,[58] to outmanoeuvre and/or reach agreements with interests which might be aggrieved by either central- or state-level policy reforms.

The example of the trade union response to economic reform provides a useful illustration of the way in which the actions of state governments help to sap the political potency of interest groups. With state governments, in the words of one labour activist, 'doing the centre's dirty work', the resources of trade unions have been spread thin.[59] They have been unable to respond to the many trespasses upon labour's collective interests that have occurred in isolated incidents in different states.

These have taken many forms. Invoking the Industrial Disputes Act of 1947, the Maharashtra government declared the products of four companies essential public-utility items, thus making them immune to strike action.[60] Chief minister Sharad Pawar also worked assiduously to effect splits in various powerful unions.[61] Even in communist-ruled West Bengal, the state government has attempted to de-register unions which do not comply with a narrow definition of the Trade Union Act. Some 8,783 unions were served with 'cancellation notices' during 1994 and 1995.[62]

Moreover, despite laws forbidding firms from dismissing workers, many chronically loss-making companies have simply locked their factory gates as elected state governments looked the other way, preferring to let

[58] The classic example of this phenomenon is the response of an economic sector concentrated in just one or two states when it is adversely affected by import liberalisation. The fall in rubber prices – from Rs. 51 per kilo in February 1996 to Rs. 29 per kilo in February 1998 – was driven by foreign competition; that is, it resulted from national trade policy reforms. But because rubber is produced almost exclusively in Kerala, it was the state government that faced the ire of farmers during the 1998 general election campaign. *Economic Times*, 6 February 1998.

[59] Interview with a labour activist and writer, 11 September 1996, Bombay. The involvement of state governments in this process, rather than the central government acting alone, was considered politically effective because it was 'like the police interrogating suspects individually, and working them over one at a time'.

[60] *India Today*, 15 April 1994, p. 97.

[61] Pawar's role was most significant in the textile industry. In late 1993, he played a major role in the exit of five senior members from the Maharashtra General Kamgar Union, controlled by independent trade unionist Datta Samant, as well as the earlier departure of T. S. Bhokade, once Samant's trusted lieutenant. Interview with Datta Samant, 26 March 1994, Bombay, and with an independent labour activist, 29 January 1994. See also *Business India*, 27 September–10 October 1993, p. 23. Pawar was also known to have backed the ascendancy of crime-syndicate bosses to leadership positions in the main Maharashtra textile union, in the hope that they could intimidate rank-and-file members into supporting deals that would work to the advantage of a coalition comprising company management, corrupt union bosses, and their political patrons. See, for instance, Stephen Rego, 'Pall of Doom', *Humanscape*, May 1997, p. 15.

[62] Ernesto Noronha highlights a range of government abuses spanning the period since the railway strike of 1974 in his 'Trade Unionism: Changing Slogans', *Humanscape*, May 1997, p. 11.

this practice proceed quietly. By failing to pay water and electricity bills, employers who find their enterprises no longer profitable – or those who would like to establish a new business with a docile workforce made up of contract labourers – thus invite a 'de facto closure, obviating the necessary legal permission from the government under section 25 of the Industrial Disputes Act'.[63]

Labour disputes have also often been used as a pretext for effecting an 'indefinite lockout'. Representatives of a workers' rights organisation which held a rally in Bombay in January 1994 stated that more than 20,000 workers had lost jobs in the Bombay area alone due to the failure of the Maharashtra government to prevent the closing of factories.[64] Union leaders argue that while they have shown flexibility by toning down labour stridency, 'management militancy' has been on the rise, abetted by state governments. This is borne out by the statistics: while the number of person-days lost because of strikes decreased almost by half, from 12.43 million in 1991 to 6.6 million in 1994, the number lost due to management lockouts actually increased over the same period.[65] Over the twenty years from 1978–97, the ratio of strikes to lockouts (in terms of total man days lost as a result of industrial disputes) fell from 54:46 to 19:81.[66]

While de facto alterations to previous norms have been the primary means used by state governments to create more favourable conditions for employers, there have been several instances in which state governments have taken pro-active steps in the form of regulatory action or compromises offered to settle disputes. The Andhra Pradesh government, for instance, prepared a Government Order designed to 'rationalise' the system of factory inspections.[67] While this step may indeed reduce the extortionate role of labour inspectors, its ancillary effect, no doubt, will be to further relax the pressures facing the private sector to adhere to existing labour legislation.[68] Chief ministers in a number of states have also been centrally involved in pushing through Voluntary Retirement

---

[63] Praful Bidwai, 'May Day! May Day!', Times of India, 1 May 1994.
[64] Interview with two organisers of the Bandh Karkhana Samgharsha Samiti, 24 January 1994, Bombay.   [65] Business World, 7–20 February 1996, p. 114.
[66] Mayank Bhatt, 'Clutching at Straws', Business India, 9–22 March 1998, p. 220.
[67] The Hindu, 14 August 1998.
[68] Amidst this pattern – of active regulatory change, duplicitous interventions in industrial disputes and permitting prohibited practices by firms – was another important passive non-decision: the minimum wage (which is set by state governments) has been allowed to fall far below subsistence levels. The daily rates of Rs. 8 in Maharashtra, Rs. 10 in Tamil Nadu, Rs. 11 in Andhra Pradesh, and Rs. 15 in Gujarat are nowhere near the necessary levels. The culpability of state governments in this regard, as well as with respect to conditions facing workers in the unorganised sector, was highlighted in the Background Papers (mimeo) distributed at the January 1998 Indian Labour Conference, an apex tripartite body that meets annually. See also Economic Times, 18 January 1998.

Schemes[69] – about which more in Chapter 6 – as 'compromises' between unions and managements. The great majority of labour leaders, however, consider VRSs a cave-in to corporate power – in fact, a shabby example of firms preying on workers' fears that they might end up with nothing if they decline whatever the VRS might offer. The litany of abuses detailed above, after all, might give any rational actor pause to consider whether he could rely on the state government to protect his statutory rights.

Because these sorts of episodes have occurred only sporadically – under diverse circumstances in different states – and because of the preoccupation of national trade union federations with national labour reform (the much-talked-about 'exit policy'), local unions have had fewer financial and organisational resources with which to oppose state government actions and inactions.[70] The result is that the trade union movement – already fragmented on the basis of party affiliation and the public–private sector divide – is becoming more regionally fragmented as well.[71] This is likely to impair its ability ultimately to oppose more thoroughgoing reform of national labour legislation, and is an example of the way in which the effect of even modest, incremental policy changes on the structure of an interest group can help to cause reformers to reduce their estimates of the potential political costs of subsequent reform.

Federalism's contribution to the gradual ebbing of trade union power is vividly illustrated by an incident that occurred in West Bengal. The failure of national trade unions to protect the interests of jute workers at the Kanoria Jute Mill in Howrah District led to a rank-and-file revolt among employees. After the state government did nothing to stop the company from closing the unit,[72] the workers found that their representa-

---

[69] In the tripartite talks convened to discuss the dispute between textile firm Binny Ltd. and union officials, Chief Minister M. Karunanidhi of Tamil Nadu himself proposed that workers take the VRS route. *Times of India*, 4 February 1998. It was widely speculated that certain politicians were angling for a share of the profits Binny would eventually realise from selling the prime real estate on which the ailing factory is sited. The sale could not be made until the labour question was resolved.

[70] For instance, the Orissa government's crushing of a strike among workers at the state electricity board, which was backed by the All-India Trade Union Congress. *Frontline*, 14 January 1994, p. 23, or allegations that the Maharashtra state police tortured striking workers at automotive manufacturer Mahindra and Mahindra. *The Independent*. Bombay, 8 September 1994.

[71] The involvement of state governments as brokers often results in workers in one state reaching agreement with employers, thus undercutting the union's representatives at a location of the same company in a different state. This happened in the case of Philips India. See *Observer of Business and Politics*, 3 September 1996.

[72] Indeed, the state government 'passively' allowed other jute manufacturers to close down their mills on the grounds that raw jute was in short supply. In typical fashion, it blamed the central government: by sacrificing the Jute Corporation of India at the altar of fiscal austerity, the central government had allegedly rendered it incapable of intervening to shore up procurement prices for raw jute – hence the shortages which caused the factories to close, and workers to lose their jobs. See *Hindustan Times*, 29 August 1996.

tives were both unable and unwilling to assist them. Leaders of the CPI-M affiliated union were at that time focused on national-level mobilisation campaigns, such as those against GATT and the proposed amendments to industrial relations legislation. Their exposure on so many fronts left them unprepared to counter the unofficial guerrilla war being waged by state-level authorities. The combination of ineffective union leadership and a complicit state government resulted in the establishment of an independent union, which hoped to run the mill as a workers' cooperative. The Kanoria episode demonstrates that worker resistance to the adverse effects of economic reform has not died. Rather, unions have been neither willing nor able to channel their demands.[73] The result, to use the Rudolphs' phrase (introduced in Chapter 2), has been more 'involution', of the type that pluralism in Indian conditions tends to promote.[74]

The ability of federalism to weaken interest groups by quarantining them within state-level political systems is of immense value to reformers in New Delhi, who would like to see the strength of the trade union movement reduced before embarking on major national legislative reform.[75] Governments in many, though not all, states possess the capacities needed to accomplish this task without fomenting levels of dissent that can threaten their own survival. The contribution of political skills in this process will be treated in Chapter 6.

National opposition, state-level accommodation

The third way in which federalism contributed to the political durability of reform stems from the fact that, during the first five years of reform, when Narasimha Rao's Congress Party ruled in New Delhi, many non-Congress state governments eventually 'fell into line with liberalisation'.[76] In large part this was a response to the general incentives outlined in the last chapter, as well as those which benefited particular types of states (discussed above). This complicity not only provided greater depth to the technical aspects of the reform agenda, it also reduces the effectiveness of political resistance. It does this in two main ways.

First, the reform measures enacted by non-Congress state govern-

---

[73] A number of new initiatives have sprung up to fill this gap. See, for instance, Mohan Mani, 'New Attempt at Workers' Resistance: National Centre for Labour', *Economic and Political Weekly*, 7 October 1995, pp. 2485–6.

[74] For an analysis of the state government's role, see 'Workers: New Hurdles', *Economic and Political Weekly*, 15 January 1994, p. 69.

[75] Interview with an ILO official who has held extensive consultations with members of government, industry, and labour, 6 September 1996, New Delhi.

[76] This expression is often used in India – for instance, with reference to the actions of the Janata Dal chief minister of Bihar (Laloo Prasad Yadav) and the Shiv Sena chief minister of Maharashtra (Manohar Joshi), *Financial Express*, 27 April 1995.

ments undermine the heated anti-reform rhetoric emanating from their parties' MPs in the national parliament.[77] While we have seen the demoralising effect of the West Bengal government's every-state-for-itself attitude on political elites in other states, its impact on national CPI-M representatives is perhaps even worse. Thus, finance minister Manmohan Singh was able to deflect opposition parties' criticism of the government's accession to the 1994 GATT agreement, including the creation of the World Trade Organization, by claiming that it was a decision around which consensus had formed in India:

Economic reforms are no more an object of contention among political parties. This is evident from their manifestos and speeches of various leaders, and more so from the recent industrial policy statement of the left-ruled West Bengal which is virtually an endorsement of the Centre's policy.[78]

A year later the West Bengal government's embrace of market-oriented reform was even more highly visible. The CPI-M's parliamentary leader, Somnath Chatterjee, was greeted with derisive laughter from all sides when he launched a broadside on the floor of the Lok Sabha against 'the government's total surrender to the IMF and World Bank'.[79] Parliamentary debates generally have little influence over policy, but when well-orchestrated they can help to frame public debates in advantageous ways for groups that are out of power. To the extent that discrepancies between national rhetoric and state-level reality undermine this, it is a blow to opposition efforts to reverse the direction of government policy.

Federalism provides political shelter for politicians operating at all levels of the political system. Reluctant reformers at the state level are able to claim that actions taken by the central government leave them no option but to liberalise.[80] The chief minister of Rajasthan stated in 1994 that the state's new mining policy, which was significantly more liberal towards the private sector, was a matter of necessity: 'the new economic policies being pursued by the centre had left the states to fend for

[77] A leaked memo from BJP national executive committee member and economic adviser Jay Dubashi to party president L. K. Advani admitted as much. The damage-control efforts of the party's spokeswoman only revealed further divisions within the party. *Economic Times*, 18 January 1994.   [78] *Economic Times*, 22 November 1994.
[79] *Hindustan Times*, 27 April 1995.
[80] Such 'counter-manifesto' policy decisions by lower-tier party representatives also happen regularly in advanced capitalist democracies, with similar consequences for the national party organisation. Britain's Labour Party had its official opposition to the Conservative government's 'technology college' scheme undermined when Labour-controlled councils transformed ten secondary schools into technology colleges. Though Labour had long opposed the idea of technology colleges as a threat to the system of comprehensive education, the Labour chairman of the Association of Metropolitan Authorities' education committee explained that funding constraints from the central government forced them 'to swallow the principle to get the money', *The Guardian*, 25 July 1995.

themselves'.[81] These and other liberalising moves were rejected as 'sheer hypocrisy' by the Rajasthan Congress president, Paras Ram Maderna: 'It is shocking that while the state BJP leadership charges the Centre with taking loans from world bodies, burdening the nation with debts, it is itself securing huge loans running into thousands of crores [tens of billions] from international agencies'. Maderna's words were picked up by Congress MPs from the state and used to blunt the edge of BJP criticism in the national parliament.[82]

Similarly, in April 1998 the power-sector reforms introduced by Andhra Pradesh chief minister Chandrababu Naidu, of the regional Telugu Desam Party, were criticised by state-level Congress leaders. He countered by pointing out the inconsistencies between these local voices of dissent and the views of the rest of the Congress organisation, which had of course initiated economic reform under Narasimha Rao. At a public meeting, Naidu read aloud a statement from the president of the Congress-affiliated trade union welcoming Andhra Pradesh's reforms as consistent with Congress policy. He then pointed out that the Congress government in Orissa had already implemented the sorts of reforms he was proposing. 'But here [in Andhra Pradesh] the Congress opposes it. What sort of a national party is this? Do they disown their own election manifesto for local advantage?' Anticipating potential complaints from BJP leaders in the state, Naidu mentioned that the BJP government in Rajasthan had also introduced similar power-sector reforms.[83] Exposing contradictions within parties at different levels assists, though of course does not guarantee, the political sustainability of economic reform.

Some of the support lent by non-Congress state governments to the central government's reform agenda resulted from direct arm-twisting, rather than the indirect effects of the reforms themselves. For instance, immediately following the 1993 Uttar Pradesh assembly elections, the newly elected chief minister, Mulayam Singh Yadav of the nominally socialist Samajwadi Party, 'found himself dependent on the Congress for the very survival of his Government'.[84] Like virtually every other party contesting the Uttar Pradesh elections – other than the Congress, which was saddled with the responsibility of holding power at the national level – the Samajwadi Party's manifesto contained a 'Dump Dunkel' clause, referring to the final draft text produced by the Uruguay round of the GATT negotiations. But after the elections, Mulayam defended India's

---

[81] *The Hindu*, 17 August 1994.   [82] *Rashtriya Sahara*, April 1994, p. 47.
[83] *The Hindu*, 8 April 1998.
[84] There was, at that time, a very real possibility that the Congress-ruled central government would recommend that the President dissolve the UP assembly and impose central rule. *Hindustan Times*, 15 May 1994.

signature to the GATT agreement, arguing that 'no one occupying the seat of Prime Minister could have avoided it'.[85] Mulayam's support, as well as that of parties in the northeast of India that relied on Congress backing, helped to rescue the Congress from its position of isolation on the GATT issue. The operation of competitive politics on many levels of the political system made this possible.

The second way in which the capitulation of states ruled by non-Congress parties to the central government's policy agenda helps to make reform politically sustainable stems from the 'federal learning effect'. This was mentioned in Chapter 3 in the discussion of federalism and economic reform in China. The central idea was that economically successful reforms in one province could become models for others. A variation on this theme is found in India, where *political* innovations in one state can be replicated in others. State governments, in this sense, serve as controlled laboratories within which political-management experiments can be carried out. The federal system allows states which successfully manage the politics of reform to act as models for parties which rule in other states. This often takes place in a rather diffuse and general manner: state-level governing elites may simply discover from studying their neighbours that, in principle, it is possible to retain a traditional electoral base despite ideological reversals. In some instances, however, rather more specific techniques are borrowed from other states.

The capacity for one state government to act as a model for reformers in another is illustrated by the plans to overhaul the state electricity board in West Bengal. Politically astute IAS officers in Calcutta hit upon the idea that dividing the transmission, generation, and maintenance functions of the West Bengal State Electricity Board (WBSEB) might be not only economically efficient, but also, if handled with finesse, politically shrewd.[86] The calculation was that the corrupt 'engineers' lobby' within the WBSEB, which has backing from powerful politicians, could be divided by offering inducements to those engineers associated with one or another function – most probably maintenance – while effectively privatising (or 'commercialising') the other two.[87] If effected gradually, and with proper sequencing, this might allow the much-needed reforms in the state's power sector to proceed without encountering crippling political resistance. This plan was put on hold, however, for other political reasons – namely, the fierce opposition among farming groups who understood that engineers and local managers from private-sector trans-

---

[85] Hindustan Times, 15 May 1994.
[86] There was also a related plan to decentralise the WBSEB by breaking it up into zonal power authorities. *Hindu Business Line*, 20 April 1994.
[87] Interview with a senior IAS officer, 27 April 1995, Calcutta.

mission firms would be less corruptible than the existing state employees. Their fear of higher electricity prices led to agitations which caused the state government to rethink its proposed restructuring.

But Orissa's Janata Dal chief minister, Biju Patnaik, appreciated the political advantages of the model West Bengal had felt compelled to shelve, and calculated that conditions in his state might be more amenable. In particular, Orissa's farmers would be less likely to oppose a gradual break-up of the state's electricity board because they had never coalesced as a forceful and articulate interest. One reason they had not, in fact, was that power tariffs had not been a serious issue in the rural sector. Orissa's plentiful surface-irrigation potential means that electric-powered lift irrigation is used to a much lesser degree than in other states. Just 7–8 per cent of the state's electricity consumption is accounted for by agricultural users. With a number of the state's main industrial customers themselves in the running to obtain private supply and transmission contracts, the public-sector engineers' unions were isolated, leaving them vulnerable to the divide-and-rule tactics envisaged first in West Bengal. Echoing views attributed to the chief minister, officials of the World Bank, which is helping to finance the reorganisation, argued that Orissa's 'homegrown' solution to the political dilemmas of reforming a state electricity board 'will become a kind of generic model', especially 'in terms of planning and sequencing'.[88] While other states may adopt a wait-and-see attitude before committing themselves to similar reforms, it is not likely that they will allow party-political rivalries to prevent them from imitating the tactics of other state governments when the compulsions of governance warrant.[89]

Congress state governments can also demonstrate techniques for the successful political management of reform that find takers among non-Congress governments in other states. Seeking to mollify farming interests that had suffered losses on account of other liberalisation measures, Maharashtra's former chief minister Sharad Pawar announced plans to amend existing land reform legislation that placed ceilings on the amount that individual farming families could hold. (A larger story of which this is a part is discussed later in this chapter.) This was eventually passed as the

[88] 'Survey: India', *Financial Times*, 17 November 1995, p. 10. Indeed, the Gujarat government, among others, has viewed the Orissa 'experiment' as a model. See also 'Looking Beyond Enron', *India Today*, 31 January 1996, p. 3.

[89] Several aspects of Rajasthan's sales-tax reform, for instance, directly influenced efforts by the Maharashtra government (when it was controlled by Congress) to effect changes of its own. Interview with a high-ranking official in Maharashtra's finance department, 1 September 1996, Bombay. Moreover, the efforts of Tamil Nadu and Maharashtra to evolve a form of value-added tax have involved a process of mutual learning. See S. Gurumurthi, 'Sales Taxation: Evolution and Reform – Lessons from Tamil Nadu' (Part I of II), *Economic and Political Weekly*, 18 January 1997, pp. 111–26.

Maharashtra Agricultural Lands (Ceiling on Holdings) (Amendment) Ordinance, 1993. Though it required the assent of the central government in order to have the force of law, as a signal of Pawar's benign intentions towards prosperous farmers the amendment took some of the edge off of his unpopularity among this important group. It also proved to be a trend-setter.

According to a senior aide to former Karnataka chief minister Veerappa Moily, Pawar is something of a 'guru' among chief ministers: 'They don't necessarily like or trust him', he said, 'but they respect his political intelligence. Especially when it comes to liberalisation . . . because he was the first', referring to the fact that Pawar started liberalising Maharashtra's economy well before the central government began overhauling the policy regime in mid-1991.[90] The political logic of Pawar's revisions to the existing land-ceiling legislation made sense to chief ministers in other states – though, crucially, each had to adjust it to local circumstances. Similar amendments were later put forward by governments in Gujarat, Madhya Pradesh, West Bengal, and Karnataka, while the AIADMK-ruled Tamil Nadu government was seriously considering the matter before losing power in 1996.[91] Like Maharashtra's amendment, these require the approval of the President of India, acting on the advice of the central government.

Karnataka's 1995 amendment was promoted by then-chief minister and future prime minister H. D. Deve Gowda who, though not a Congressman, recognised the political value of such a move, and the opportunity provided by the climate of liberalisation. Indeed, his decision to pursue such a risky reform – lip service to land reform had long been a 'litmus test' issue – demonstrated more than just the 'federal learning effect'. First, his decision stemmed at least in part from a belief that such reforms were politically viable if they could be blamed on the conditions created by the centre, in the same way that the examples outlined earlier in this chapter were. Second, the amendment included a large degree of discretionary control over how it was to be implemented. In addition to raising the land ceiling for specific categories of land usage, such as educational institutions and places of worship, it also allowed the state government to exempt any other category of land from land-ceiling limits 'in public interest and for reasons to be recorded in writing'.[92] By adopting the specific idea of amending land-reform legislation, blaming its

---

[90] Interview, 23 March 1994, Bangalore.

[91] *Hindustan Times*, 14 April 1994. The West Bengal amendment was subsequently withdrawn.

[92] Janaki Nair, 'Predatory Capitalism and Legalised Landgrab: Karnataka Land Reforms', *Economic and Political Weekly*, 3 February 1996, p. 251.

necessity on the central government, and ensuring that the reforms could be implemented selectively (and in a manner suited to the configuration of political forces in Karnataka),[93] Deve Gowda tore a whole sheaf of pages from the playbooks of colleagues in other states.

Other formal institutions

The containment of political resistance to economic reform occurs through a variety of formal institutions. The focus thus far has been on one such institution, the federal political structure, because: (1) it has been of immense value to the strategists of economic reform at the apex of the system; and (2) it represents an accommodation which in the years since independence has permitted alien political institutions to adapt to, and therefore strike deep roots in, Indian society. To place the contribution of the federal system in perspective, to stress that it is not the only formal political institution that contributes to the process of reordering politics in a way amenable to sustaining policy change, and to highlight the connection between this conception of institutions and arguments advanced elsewhere in this book, let us briefly examine one other formal institution which helps to absorb the political strain resulting from economic reform.

National tripartite committees were created in November 1991 to examine the impact of the new economic policies on the small minority of the Indian labour force that is unionised and to consider the problem of 'industrial sickness'. These included representatives of industry, organised labour, and government. The committees were coordinated by an inter-ministerial working group, marking them out as formal, if necessarily *ad hoc*, institutions of government. While their impact on problem-solving has been marginal, according to an ILO report they have provided an important channel through which labour's positions on specific companies and specific reform mechanisms could be aired – in the process reducing the possibility that more strident versions of trade union resistance would spread to and overwhelm other institutions, such as legislatures and political parties.[94] The operation of the tripartite process has also provided governing elites an opportunity to probe poten-

---

[93] Detailing the design and impact of Deve Gowda's amendments to existing land-reform amendments, Narendar Pani argues that '[the] spirit of liberalisation was also used to meet the changing requirements of those who had benefited from [previous] land reforms'. See his 'Political Economy of Karnataka – 1950–1995: An Overview', *Journal of Social and Economic Development*, vol. 1, no. 1 (Jan.–June 1998), p. 81.

[94] Ajeet N. Mathur, 'The Experience of Consultation During Structural Adjustment in India (1990–92)', *Occasional Paper No. 9* (Geneva: International Labor Organization, April 1993).

tial points of contradiction in the trade union agenda that could be exploited through other means at a later date. This is precisely the type of systemic transparency cited earlier as a crucial ingredient in the effective political management of economic reform. It is not the type to which accounts of democracy which ignore existing power relations are capable of giving proper emphasis.

Countering this image of transparency, however, has been the way in which the tripartite committees have functioned in parallel with other formal institutions designed specifically to reduce the burden on national ministries and political decision-makers.[95] At roughly the same time that the apex and sector-specific tripartite committees were established, the government also announced an extension of the Sick Industrial Companies Act to include public-sector firms. This expanded the jurisdiction of the Bureau for Industrial and Financial Reconstruction (BIFR), the body charged with determining whether chronically loss-making firms should be closed or resuscitated with a package of public and private financing.[96] Consequently, trade unions representing workers in PSEs were engaged in a 'two-track process', which, according to the president of the National Confederation of Public Sector Officers' Associations, was made even more confusing and ambiguous by the finance minister's long-standing offer, voiced in *informal* consultations organised through party-affiliated unions, to transfer sick PSEs to workers' cooperatives with 'viable' turnaround plans.[97]

In this case, then, the proliferation of formal institutions served to distribute the political burden of implementing adjustment by creating what one representative of the Communist Party of India-affiliated trade union called 'a constantly moving target . . . a process which raises hopes by appearing orderly, but then reverts to the usual routine of passing the buck'.[98] Increasingly, state governments have used the BIFR as a way of

---

[95] The United States Congress has also on occasion found it politically expedient to devolve decision-making authority on difficult issues to 'non-partisan' bodies. The relatively autonomous Federal Reserve Bank, created by an act of Congress, is an obvious example. Less well known is that in the 1980s the question of which domestic military bases would be closed to meet deficit-reduction targets was referred to an 'independent base-closing commission'. The objective was to avoid the usual horse-trading that would allow individual members of Congress to protect installations in their home districts, and to provide representatives from districts where bases *were* to be closed with a ready excuse to their constituents – that the matter was out of their hands and not a reflection of their lack of political influence relative to other members of Congress.

[96] The lack of transparency that this example is meant to highlight does not imply that the BIFR itself is corrupt. According to well-known trade unionist D. Thankappan, '[t]he BIFR is one of the least corrupt institutions in this country'. *Business World,* 8–21 April 1992, p. 23   [97] *Business India,* 28 February–13 March 1994, p. 167.

[98] Interview with a leading member of a national trade union, 23 March 1994, Bangalore.

'taking the pressure' off elected officials.[99] That this is part of a discernible pattern of government ambiguity and obfuscation will become apparent in Chapter 6, where the introduction of 'backdoor' labour reform is discussed.

Informal political institutions: parties, networks, and conflict mediation

This section of the chapter focuses on the role of party-affiliated political networks in: (1) calculating the political trade-offs of risky policy decisions; and (2) negotiating the political bargains which underwrite the sustainability of economic reform. Our chief concern is not with Indian parties themselves, but with the network of relationships they help to sustain. This requires a brief explanation, which will help to frame our discussion of the empirical material.

The dynamics of informal political institutions are difficult to capture with precision, but no less important than the formal institutions of state. An appreciation of their complex role is vital if the arguments in this book are to make sense. In explaining the capacity of India's democratic political system to produce sustainable economic reform we stress two key factors: (1) the willingness and capacity of governing elites to take calculated policy risks; and (2) the willingness of socio-economic elites to engage in negotiations with both other interests and governing elites, and ultimately to strike acceptable bargains. Neither orientation is uniquely associated with democracy, and yet both are observable behaviour patterns in India. This is where a focus on institutions becomes necessary.

One of the reasons why institutions have become such a popular focus of study in recent years is their crucial role in shaping behaviour patterns among actors in the political process.[100] Only a complex interaction among many different institutions – formal and informal – is capable of explaining the two types of behaviour listed above. But one informal institution whose contribution is particularly worth assessing is the political party. The main attribute of Indian political parties that we emphasise

[99] For instance, the particularly difficult issue of loss-making firms in industrially backward portions of Maharashtra – such as the Textile Corporation of Marathwada – was 'something that no minister wanted on his desk'. Referring it to the BIFR was seen as the easiest 'escape route . . . because neither the workers nor the management nor the opposition would be quite sure what it meant'. Interview with a senior official in the Department of Textiles, Government of Maharashtra, 17 February 1994, Bombay. See also *Times of India*, 17 March 1993. Even the communist government of West Bengal referred nine public-sector units to the BIFR. *Business Standard*, 17 February 1994.

[100] For an excellent review of the literature which emphasises the diversity of conceptions of institutions, see Peter A. Hall and Rosemary C. R. Taylor, 'Political Science and the Three New Institutionalisms', *Political Studies*, vol. 44, no. 5 (1996), pp. 936–57.

in assessing their behaviour-shaping impact as an institution is their relative porousness. The argument is that the fuzziness of boundaries separating party and non-party political networks, combined with the ease of exit for faction leaders, inclines politicians to take policy risks because of the expectation that they will be able to quell resultant political resistance by: (1) arranging suitable conflict-avoiding (or conflict-deferring) compromises among contending interests; (2) exploiting the faith of privileged interests in the sanctity of their privileges by assuaging these opponents of liberalisation with promises that may never be fulfilled; and/or (3) harnessing the political potency of nascent groups which might emerge as key supporters in the future if offered tacit support. All three behaviour-shaping expectations are structured by the nature of parties as an informal institution operating within a context of formal democracy. And yet all three involve the use of underhanded tactics that seem to subvert the ideal of transparency. (This aspect will be addressed in Chapter 6.)

But most importantly, all three extend the time-horizons of India's governing elites. This is the second half of the explanation for how structural adjustment, which imposes immediate costs to well-organised interests and only the possibility of deferred gains for latent or disorganised groups, can be successfully introduced by politicians notorious for privileging the short term over the long haul. The first half of the explanation has to do with the nature of reform itself: when reforms are implemented gradually, the initial reforms often produce economic impacts that reconfigure interests. They can sow discord among powerful groups, and sometimes awaken a sleeping giant that might provide backing to later reforms. This is the 'policy feedback' effect, discussed in the latter portion of Chapter 4.

The second half of the explanation, stemming from the behaviour patterns to which Indian political institutions give rise, reinforces the efficacy of the policy feedback effect in promoting sustainable economic reform. The economic impacts of first-generation policy reforms on an interest group are less likely to generate political correlates (either in the form of attitudinal adjustments or an alteration to its coherence as a lobbying unit) when politicians are disinclined to exploit high-payoff risks and interests have little faith that negotiating with governing elites will allow them to land on their feet. In other words, for policy feedback effects to work their political magic, they require a supportive institutional climate, of the type which India's fluid party-centred political networks provide. This usage of the term institution finds its closest parallel in the work of historian Romila Thapar, whose essay on cultural patronage in ancient India defines an institution as 'an integrated, organized behaviour-pattern through which social control is exercised'.[101]

Abstract discussions of this kind often cause us to lose sight of the important role played by democracy in the operation of informal institutions such as parties and party-based networks of influence. There are two aspects that need highlighting. First, the existence of electoral contestation *under Indian conditions* has shaped the particular institutional trait with which we are concerned – the porousness of parties. This is not to argue that democracy as such *must* give rise to such institutional features; otherwise all democracies would have porous parties. But in the context of an extremely heterogeneous society in which individuals have a multitude of identities on which to draw, it is perhaps no surprise that political mobilisation is so rapid and political alignments so unpredictable. It is beyond the scope of this study to provide a cultural genealogy of Indian democracy; but it will suffice for the present to note that democracy has combined with indigenous political forms in ways that provide fertile ground for porous parties composed of enterprising individuals whose networks of influence span party and non-party activities and are often easily detachable from any individual party. Porousness, in short, may be a systemic adaptation to conditions of uncertainty.

The second aspect of democracy's relationship to institutional evolution that needs to be noted here is its influence upon the way in which individual politicians who operate within this system of political modularity go about pursuing their interests. That is, certain features of Indian democracy help to ensure that the institutional form we have identified – porous parties composed of enterprising individuals, controlling networks of influence that shade imperceptibly into other organisational arenas – actually produces the two key behaviours that we have identified as critical to the political sustainability of policy reform. This is a key role for democracy. After all, parties in many political systems are at least as porous (if not more so) than those found in India. Yet, they do not necessarily give rise to similar behaviours and change-promoting capacities. Why, in non-democratic systems, might risk aversion be so much more prevalent among politicians, and the willingness of socio-economic interests to engage in bargaining and strike deals so much less in evidence? There are innumerable plausible explanations for this discrepancy because there are an infinite number of differences between India and other political systems.

But for the present there are three worth highlighting. The first is that democracy makes forecasting and adapting to change a necessity. The job-insecurity of elected politicians might, by one reckoning, make them

---

[101] Romila Thapar, *Cultural Transaction and Early India: Tradition and Patronage* (Delhi: Oxford University Press, 1994), p. 38.

particularly risk-averse. But another way of looking at it is that elected leaders who expect stasis are inevitably bypassed by change – to the composition of their electoral bases, to social attitudes, to new opportunities for building a political career, and to economic transformations. As for interest groups, their representatives are all too aware that their competitors in civil society are busy courting both holders of political power and those in opposition. Open competitive politics makes both continuous reassessment and continuous coalition-building a necessity.

The second way in which Indian democracy affects the behaviours of key political and socio-economic elites concerns its longevity. Both Indian politicians and representatives of social and economic interests have operated in the type of climate discussed above for long enough to understand the need for flexibility, whether regarding ideological or practical matters.[102] A large enough proportion of elites have sufficient experience of constant change that they tend not to fear it. The flip side to their deep cynicism, paradoxically, is a chronic optimism about their ability to strike a deal with virtually any other group, no matter how many principles might separate them. The success of democratically accountable politicians at negotiating such bargains makes them confident enough occasionally to throw the dice of policy reform. Operating within a democratic system has also given them the political skills to assemble new coalitions from new interest-group fragments.

This ability to assemble coalitions is aided by a third aspect of democracy: what we will call here its signalling mechanism. Many crucial and creative compromises are brokered through prolonged closed-door negotiations between governing, party, and interest-group elites. The efficacy of the resulting agreements relies, in large measure, on the extent to which leaders are able to deliver the support of the constituencies they purport to represent. In this sense, the openness of the Indian political process – 'transparency' of a sort – must be regarded as a critical factor in facilitating politically sustainable adjustment. This is because it allows the negotiating parties to evaluate each other's strength and cohesiveness. Governing elites which have some moderately reliable basis for calculating the political costs of competing risks are more likely to take at least one of them. Their networks of influence, often independent of the party's official chain of command, also help to produce this behavioural pattern by serving as instruments for political intelligence-gathering.

Before turning to the case-study evidence, it may help to recapitulate, in condensed form, the logic which it is meant to support: the systemic

---

[102] Indeed, R. S. Khare considers ideological, social, and political 'fluidity' a distinct cultural characteristic of Indian democracy. See his *Culture and Democracy: Anthropological Reflections on Modern India* (London: University Press of America, 1985).

uncertainty produced by Indian democracy, combined with both its longevity and signalling function, has provided the climate in which parties, and the networks of influence to which their structure gives rise, can perform their catalytic institutional role as shapers of individual behaviours, including calculated risk-taking and negotiation, without which sustainable economic reform would be highly unlikely.

Tax reform in Rajasthan

An example of liberalisation which illustrates many of these points is tax reform in Rajasthan. Two types of tax reform were effected: to the sales-tax regime and to the system of taxation on goods transport. Both of these upset long and deeply entrenched sets of interests. Both were masterminded at the highest levels of government – by the chief minister in association with his political lieutenants and administrative aides, which are often indistinguishable from one another. Both were, in effect, propelled by events at the national level. And both relied upon the manipulation of political relationships that had become regularised through the creation of individual leaders' networks of influence, embedded within a fluid party structure. Transactions were arranged that, but for the far-ranging links and mediating authority of key leaders within the ruling party, would not otherwise have taken place. For reasons of space, let us examine only the more substantial of the two sets of reforms – the one relating to sales tax.

As we have seen, state governments have used tax policies to vie with one another for private investment. This has often worked to the short-term detriment of state exchequers. Sales tax is one of the few revenue areas over which states have complete control, as stipulated in no. 54 of List II (State List) in the Constitution's Seventh Schedule. Given the reduced resource flows from the central government, there were both incentives to make the sales-tax system more efficient (the state government needed the funds), as well as disincentives (concern that streamlining might lead to a reduction in revenues). To the extent that the fiscal constraint was largely created by self-interested actors in New Delhi, this situation already possessed political overtones.

But, as one civil servant closely connected with Rajasthan's tax reforms has pointed out, there were more overt political factors involved: 'There were also very well entrenched vested interests who did not want change'.[103] These interests consisted mainly of groups who were able

---

[103] This quotation is taken from an unpublished report on the Rajasthan tax reforms prepared by a senior government administrator: 'State Level Reforms in the Financial Sector: A Case Study on Rajasthan', March 1996, p. 11 (mimeo).

effectively to evade taxation, a corrupt tax administration, the lawyers who amassed large fees from tax litigation, and politicians who derived benefits by patronising each of the three former groups. The complex provisions of the more than 200 amendments to the Sales Tax Act 1954 made the system both flexible and confusing, and therefore open to corruption as well as harassment of honest taxpayers.

Chief Minister Bhairon Singh Shekhawat of Rajasthan, who also held the finance portfolio, began the tax-reform process in 1992. As with many of his most sensitive projects, his strategy for effecting a reform that had few backers (and even fewer willing to predict that radical change would ultimately result) was to engage the affected constituencies on two levels. On the official level, he and the finance secretary, the chief civil servant in the finance ministry, engaged in an extremely comprehensive process of consultation with business associations. Representatives of trade and industry were invited to air their views on the draft legislation before an advisory committee. Subsequently, when the bill was submitted to the state legislature in March 1994, the chief minister immediately referred it to a fifteen-member all-party select committee, which also invited business associations to provide testimony. The select committee took six months to effect modest changes to the bill. The final bill passed after just five minutes of debate on the floor of the legislature.

The real work had taken place elsewhere – in the formal consultation process and the informal negotiations between the chief minister's team and representatives with a stake in one of three areas: (1) an aspect of tax reform itself; (2) a different issue on Shekhawat's agenda; or (3) another issue of interest to the groups affected by tax reform.[104] Each of the important changes that constituted the new sales-tax act required trade-offs. These bargains required a degree of trust – in the willingness and ability of both the chief minister and various economic interests to make good on pledges made during the negotiations. It was only Shekhawat's ability to maintain a political network integrating party and non-party arenas that enabled him to convince diverse groups that he could deliver on his promises. The key point is that he was able to expand the sphere within which trade-offs could take place. As one former IAS officer described this dynamic: 'A promise by the CM is negotiable currency anywhere in Rajasthan'.[105] While this exaggerates, the main point is valid: a political broker's ability to defuse conflict is enhanced in proportion to the diversity of deals he can arrange. This, in turn, is dependent upon the

---

[104] The political details of this process were revealed in interviews with government and private-sector actors involved in this process during 1–5 September 1996, Jaipur.

[105] This was a man who worked closely with Shekhawat during his first stint as chief minister in the late 1970s. Interview, 10 December 1993, Jaipur.

breadth of agents he can deliver to a system of exchange. Just as importantly, it was the information-gathering capacity of Shekhawat's personal
political organisation – which is by no means synonymous with the party
organisation[106] – that enabled him to exert the pressure necessary to strike
bargains that entailed minimal political costs for him.

On the official level, the chief minister's careful stewardship of the Sales
Tax Advisory Committee had neutralised some of the opposition to the
bill. In part this was a by-product of his intimate knowledge of the
business community. Sectors of trade and industry that had natural
business conflicts with one another were invited to the same committee
meetings together, and means were found for compensating each. Shekhawat transformed the prevailing political dynamic from one in which the
primary conflict was between government and sectoral interests, to one in
which the conflicts between sectoral interests themselves were the main
point of negotiation. The chief minister's complex and longstanding
relationships with representatives from each group helped to 'guarantee'
the inter-sectoral understandings that were arranged. It is important to
recognise that it was not simply the fact that he occupied the office of chief
minister that made these arrangements possible.

In unofficial meetings the chief minister pursued a slightly different
strategy. He would often invite to a single meeting representatives from
two sectors that stood to lose substantially from the proposed legislation.
One of these would be 'friendly' to the chief minister, and was briefed by
his men in advance. The friendly group's representative was prompted to
make what appeared to be one or two large concessions. This was
designed to create an atmosphere in which the other group's representative would feel obliged to offer something as well, lest he be seen as
comparatively intransigent. In a number of instances, the friendly group's
concessions were not incorporated into the final bill. They had served
their purpose by getting the other group's representatives to offer support
to one of the bill's more unpopular provisions. This backing, in turn, was

---

[106] The existence of this network has been a major source of unease among Shekhawat's
rivals in the state party, particularly those affiliated with the RSS, and has served as the
basis for repeated efforts to have him ousted. Their stated concern is that his links outside
the party, and the way in which he utilises them, undermines 'party discipline' and 'the
integrity of the party organisation'. However, these anti-Shekhawat campaigns failed to
remove him from office largely because the BJP's national executive was aware that
Shekhawat's far-reaching networks were the main reason why the party was able to retain
power in the state. I am grateful to both Sunny Sebastian, special correspondent of *The
Hindu*, and Sanjiv Srivastava, formerly of the *Indian Express*, for describing this dynamic
to me at great length. Interviews, 2 September 1996, Jaipur; and 7 September 1996, New
Delhi, respectively. For the role of these networks in the context of electoral politics, see
Rob Jenkins, 'Where the BJP Survived: Rajasthan Assembly Elections, 1993', *Economic
and Political Weekly*, vol. 29, no. 11 (12 March 1994), pp. 635–41.

used as a lever to gain similar support from other groups, thus perpetuating the cycle of concessions.

It is difficult not to notice how closely this process resembles a confidence trick. This was a consultative process, to be sure, but one involving underhanded tactics on the government's part. These would not have worked had the chief minister not been able to command the loyalty of friendly shills, willing to trust that their 'concessions' would not become reality. In some instances their complicity was bought with favours arranged from groups not in the least concerned about tax reform, but nevertheless engaged in an ongoing relationship with Shekhawat or one of his faction followers. One case involved the chief minister promising to have a mafia-infiltrated union in eastern Rajasthan 'restrained', which would make life easier for Shekhawat's friendly accomplices.[107]

Undermining interest-group resistance to tax reform, in other words, did not always require Shekhawat to devote government resources. His ability to call on the services of other clients within his network could substitute for material patronage, especially when an interest-group's representative was willing to sacrifice his constituents' interest for a personal favour. More often than not the complicity of the 'friendly' shill group rested upon the certainty that a failure to cooperate would mean the end of their 'friendly' relations with the chief minister. Like the leader of any organisation that functions on the basis of 'diffuse reciprocity',[108] Shekhawat had made them an offer they could not refuse.

But such subtle balancing acts are not always possible. Political management can often require a ruthless approach to gauging the value of relationships. In fine-tuning the details of the new tax regime – determining the levels of taxation for commodities, production inputs, luxury goods, as well as policy regarding new industries – some former clients had to be abandoned. The ability of the Shekhawat government to do so has implications for the conventional wisdom surrounding the operation of democratic politics. Interest groups are often portrayed as 'entrenched' merely on the basis of the favoured treatment previously extended to them. While a history of privilege necessarily implies contacts in government, it is by no means a clear indicator of staying power.

One group that had become very well connected politically over the years were the manufacturers of hydrogenated oil, or vanaspati, which is considered 'the poor man's ghee' (clarified butter). Because of the large subsidies provided by the Rajasthan government's Directorate of Vanas-

---

[107] Interview with an actor involved in this transaction, 4 September 1996, Jaipur.
[108] For an elaboration of this notion, see the case studies collected in Ernest Gellner and John Waterbury (eds.), *Patrons and Clients in Mediterranean Societies* (London: Duckworth, 1977).

pati, the installed capacity in this sector had become far greater than the market could bear, creating a vicious subsidy-inflating cycle.[109] The men who controlled these ventures were considered so well entrenched politically – contributing healthy sums to the coffers of all political parties – that they would be spared any adverse consequences from policy reform. Indeed, their confidence in the continuation of their privileged positions helped to lure them into what they expected to be rather tame negotiations.

The vanaspati sector's main competition is from edible oil, which appeals to increasingly health-conscious Indians and, because of its export potential, was commanding higher prices. Shekhawat's government had promoted this sector over the years, as had his Congress predecessors, and corruption in the state-run edible oil cooperatives was well known.[110] Still, the response from Rajasthan's oil-seed farmers to the incentives had been impressive. The market for edible oils was growing, and Rajasthan was now increasingly processing its own oil seeds rather than watching them be sold to processing centres in other states. One of the tax-reform programme's objectives was to reduce or eliminate sales tax on raw materials that were used as production inputs. While the government could not afford to give up the entire Rs. 1 billion it was receiving in the form of input tax on raw materials,[111] it focused its tax-remission efforts on sectors which might ultimately provide more revenue for the state through sales tax on the final product. One of these was edible oil, and oil seeds were duly exempted from sales tax.

Upset by the additional advantage extended to their competitors, vanaspati producers called on their political connections. Using party members with access to the chief minister, they arranged a deal whereby edible oil itself, because it was an input in vanaspati production, was exempted from sales tax. Once the tax system was functioning, however, the government revoked this exemption. Despite their well-honed lobbying machine – and much-vaunted clout – the 'vanaspati barons' were humbled. It is significant that the government's willingness to do this only materialised once an alternative constituency – the edible oil lobby – had emerged to neutralise the political cost. Moreover, the edible oil industry did not require anywhere near the level of government subsidy consumed by the vanaspati sector, which was plagued by high levels of industrial

---

[109] There were fifteen plants in Rajasthan in 1998. *The Hindu*, 8 April 1998.

[110] According to two key officials in the state's cooperative bureaucracy, who claimed to be keen to 'clean up the mess', the oilseed cooperatives were 'corrupt from top to bottom'. Interviews, 8 November 1993, Jaipur.

[111] This figure is taken from an unpublished report on the Rajasthan tax reforms prepared by a senior government administrator: 'State Level Reforms in the Financial Sector: A Case Study on Rajasthan', March 1996, p. 17 (mimeo).

'sickness'. In fact, edible oil provided the government with tax revenues which it could use for other important patronage projects. It was a lower-cost political client. Yet, many developing country governments are loath to abandon long-time allies. This makes the promotion of change in such circumstances more difficult. Contrary to the conventional wisdom, the range of options that Indian democracy offers to its practitioners tends to militate against such stasis.

State governments throughout India have had to make such difficult choices. As we saw in Chapter 4, the axe often falls on business groups operating in the small-scale sector. For instance, in a bid to shore up its financial position, the West Bengal government in April 1994 decided to disallow intra-state stock transfer of olefin products to consignment agents. This was not good news for big producers. But the impact on small-scale industry in this sector was disastrous.[112] In this case, and in many others like it,[113] the small-scale producers were sacrificed in the process of apportioning the costs associated with state-level fiscal adjustment. In accordance with the logic outlined earlier in this chapter, because sacrifices of this type happen in isolated incidents in different states, it allows certain small-scale producers to be picked off one at a time – rather than removing in one stroke the blanket protection provided to the small-scale sector as a whole. Assessing which industries are particularly vulnerable to an assault on their small-scale component is best done at the state level, where the informal networks of governing elites provide them with a means of evaluating the political consequences of dispensing with a particular group.

Liberalisation, sugar politics, and business interests in Maharashtra

Our second example of the functional role played by informal institutions comes from Maharashtra, where, during the first two decades following independence, a network of powerful farmer-controlled sugar cooperatives for organising production, processing, and marketing emerged as a major political force. Politicians play an active part in the fierce battles waged for the leadership of cooperative boards, and during local, state, and national elections cooperative leaders throw the full weight of the cooperative's resources – vehicles, manpower, institutional influence, and often finance – behind their chosen candidates. They are

[112] *Economic Times*, 15 April 1994.
[113] One example is the Rajasthan state government's reversal of its policy of favoured treatment for operators of 'mini-cement plants'. In late 1993, their representative was amazed that the state government was turning its back on them (interview with the chairman of the Rajasthan Association of Mini-Cement Plants, 20 November 1993, Jaipur). By 1994, the state government had done a deal with them.

the linchpin of many a Maharashtrian politician's network of influence.

But this context of inter-penetration has resulted in the cooperatives being viewed, justifiably, as 'a privileged sector'. Leaders of cooperatives, which include a number of senior figures in the Congress Party, are naturally suspicious about the implications of economic reform for the future of the institutions around which they have built their political careers. The fact that between 1991 and 1996 Maharashtra had the largest Congress parliamentary delegation of any state invested their perceptions with added significance. Former chief minister Sharad Pawar's response to this potentially serious source of opposition, like Shekhawat's, was to play a two-level game.

On the one hand, he exploited nascent divisions within the sugar lobby. The stagnation in public investment in agricultural infrastructure during the 1980s had substantially exacerbated infighting between the state's 'sugar barons'. A decline in the rate at which new land came under irrigation led to declining yields of sugarcane. Under pressure to continue processing activities on an economic scale, cooperatives began increasingly to defy the legally mandated zonal system, under which farmers in a geographic region are required to sell their output only to their zone's designated cooperative processing factory. By illegally offering higher prices to farmers whose lands were not assigned to their zones, the more efficient factories were able to poach on the cane supply of other cooperatives. By turning a blind eye to this practice, and by hinting at the eventual abolition of the zonal system, the Pawar government succeeded in pitting the efficient cooperatives against their victims in the battle for scarce cane supplies.

On the other hand, Pawar understood that his political base was the sugar belt of western Maharashtra. He therefore took steps to assuage the fears of *selected* cooperative leaders concerning the potentially negative impacts of liberalisation. His objective was to blur distinctions, particularly to counter the impression that the advance of the private sector (with which he had strong ties) must necessarily be at the expense of the cooperative sector. For instance, in private meetings with individual cooperative leaders, he gave assurances that their factories would benefit from opportunities in other agro-processing activities.[114] This went beyond the vague public rhetoric about the vast potential of the agro-processing sector in a liberalised India. A number of promoters of newly established or expanded private-sector agro-processing units were connected with prominent cooperatives. Regardless of whether the new enterprises flourished, or whether the cooperative itself benefited, the

---

[114] Interview with a senior official in the state's sugar bureaucracy, 22 February 1994, Pune.

promoters almost always turned a profit. This was reportedly because of assistance from the state government in helping to arrange the details of share-rights issues, and in obtaining the state-level clearances required for foreign technology tie-ups.[115] Those that have been helped in these and other ways have been conspicuous by their failure to join factional intrigues that have attempted to use the new economic policy as a lightning rod for anti-Pawar dissidence.

The same is true for cooperative leaders who saw the potential future benefits of a provision in the revised Maharashtra Industrial Policy of 1993 which permitted certain types of industrial units to own land in excess of existing land-ceiling laws.[116] By proposing a liberalisation-induced loophole in land-reform legislation that is open only on a discretionary basis, the state government created yet another mechanism to reward collaborators. Far from publicly highlighting this provision of the industrial policy statement, the Maharashtra government went to great lengths to downplay its significance, and certainly did not publicise its discretionary nature.

These and other forms of favouritism have served to undermine the unity of the sugar lobby, and overcome resistance to a number of adjustment-related measures. This series of events is another illustration of the role played by Indian politicians' networks of influence in: (1) accentuating the divisive impact of first-generation liberalisation measures on the structure of interest groups; and (2) subsequently exploiting the lack of interest-group unity to pursue further reforms. This again relies on a well-honed appreciation for the inclination of interest groups to adapt to new incentives, whether they involve the desire of efficient cooperatives to gain at the expense of the inefficient, or the willingness of some cooperative leaders to strike individual deals on diversification. Non-transparent tactics – which, paradoxically, are reliant upon the openness of the political system – are crucial to this process. So is the ability to mobilise networks built around personal loyalty to party leaders. The integration of quasi-party organisations, in the form of Maharashtra's sugar cooperatives, is an extreme example of this phenomenon, but one suited to the state's high level of economic diversification. It is, however, just one facet of a considerably more complex mechanism for articulating and reconciling interests. For instance, Sharad Pawar's far-flung network of influence, including reported links to organised crime, allowed him to broker solutions to a wide range of conflicts, such as disputes within a

---

[115] Interviews with the general manager of a sugar cooperative which had been shut out of this process, 24 February 1994, Ahmednagar District; and a senior IAS officer in an agriculture-related department, 28 January 1994, Bombay.

[116] Government of Maharashtra, 'New Industrial Policy for Maharashtra, 1993' (Bombay: Government Central Press, 1993).

family-run business house[117] and protests arising from new industrial projects.[118]

The success of Pawar's two-level game of reassuring the sugar lobby while undermining its capacity to act unitedly permitted him to manage the distributional conflicts that arose as a result of another central government policy decision. In April 1993 the Government of India removed controls on the price at which molasses, a major by-product of the sugar factories, could be sold. The gain for Maharashtra's sugar cooperatives during the last eight months of 1993 was estimated at Rs. 1.5 billion.[119] Manufacturers of alcohol-based chemicals, one of the main consumers of molasses, were hit with massive price increases – from roughly Rs. 240 per tonne before decontrol, to between Rs. 1,500 and Rs. 2,000 per tonne thereafter. Pressure mounted on the chief minister to take action when two major alcohol-based industrial chemical units, one of which is controlled by one of Pawar's associates, closed due to 'economic unviability'.

Pawar's solution was to introduce 'partial recontrol' of molasses pricing. A proportion of molasses could be sold on the open market, while a quota system would ensure that the price rises facing the chemical industry would not be as dramatic as under total decontrol. According to actors close to the negotiations, this compromise would not have been possible without the active participation of representatives from the chemical industry and the sugar cooperatives.[120] Both had over the years become integrated into Pawar's political network, which extends far beyond the Congress Party. (A key member of one of the groups had in fact built a relationship with Pawar during the early 1980s when he was outside the Congress Party.) This allowed them to trade concessions on this issue in exchange for help on outstanding matters over which Pawar had influence by virtue of his connections with yet other groups. Particularly important in facilitating this process was the divided state of the sugar lobby, which had been one of Pawar's other short-term objectives.

This sequence – national-level reform, followed by mediation and a compromise formula – paralleled the pattern set in other states. Uttar Pradesh followed a policy in which 65 per cent of production was subjected to a controlled price (Rs. 400 in late 1995) and 35 per cent is available at open-market prices of roughly three times the controlled price. Karnataka removed price controls, but introduced controls over the movement of molasses. Punjab's solution was similar to Maharashtra's. But

---

[117] *Business World*, 8–21 September 1993.

[118] See Charudatta Deshpande, 'The Man Behind Maharashtra Inc.', *Economic Times*, 4 March 1994.

[119] 'Sugar Industry: An Investor Survey', *Business India*, 3–16 January 1994.

[120] Interviews with a representative of the All-India Alcohol-Based Chemicals Manufacturers' Association, 16 February 1994, Bombay; a senior IAS officer, 28 January 1994, Bombay; and a leading figure in a major sugar cooperative, 6 April 1994, Bombay.

Maharashtra itself eventually changed its policy, by removing price controls and earmarking a certain percentage of production for specific sectors.[121] As with the abandonment of the vanaspati interests in Rajasthan, this was effected only once circumstances had appreciably reduced the political cost to Pawar. One important factor was the reduced level of prices reigning in the decontrolled portion of the market.

It is important to appreciate that such compromises, when brokered by state-level political elites, can have a range of downstream political consequences. First, they can further accentuate inter-state rivalries of the type outlined earlier in this chapter – in this case pitting molasses-producing states against those that are net consumers. Second, they can reduce the future prospects for subsequently enacting national policy. In December 1995, the governments of states which produce molasses fiercely opposed the central government's move to impose a uniform policy, which had been prompted by rapid increases in molasses prices.[122] Though it was politically expedient for reformers in the central government to saddle states with the task of mediating the conflicts that arose from its initial decontrol order, it also made subsequent reform more difficult.

The tactic of mediating conflicts that arise between winners and losers from specific reforms has been applied to other cases by both the central and state governments. For instance, the increased export opportunities that the liberalised trade regime offered to manufacturers of cotton yarn (the primary production input in the cloth-weaving industry) had increased its domestic price. While the large-scale mill sector could absorb the price increase, the small-scale handloom weavers, an important interest group with a presence in a vast number of rural constituencies, were hard hit. In 1992, through a combination of threats and incentives, the textiles minister, Ashok Gehlot of Rajasthan, persuaded the yarn producers to siphon some of their windfall profits to a parastatal agency that would help to subsidise purchases for the beleaguered handloom sector. (This tactic was repeated in 1995–96.)[123] It was the minister's contacts with key individuals within both lobbies – in one case a caste fellow who could expect future unspecified favours – that made this arrangement possible.[124] That many mills subsequently violated this agreement did not detract from its short-term political utility.[125]

[121] *Business Standard*, 5 December 1995.
[122] Ibid.   [123] *Observer of Business and Politics*, 3 September 1996.
[124] Interview with a former president of the Rajasthan Textile Mills Association, 1 December 1993, Jaipur. Similar far-reaching political networks have helped to defuse many an impasse, including conflicts between the Rajasthan government and the central government over environmental aspects of the Dholpur Power Project. *Economic Times*, 16 January 1994.
[125] For details, see K. Srinivasulu, 'Handloom Weavers' Struggle for Survival', *Economic and Political Weekly*, 3 September 1994, pp. 2331–3.

A comparable example relating to deeper, institutional reforms – that is, changes which alter the underlying structure of economic actors, rather than just the level of competition they face – can be found in the case of proposed changes to the Companies Bill, 1997. The bill aimed to increase transparency and accountability within the corporate sector by reducing the opportunities for corporations to clandestinely divert funds from one subsidiary to another, and by making non-executive directors legally liable actors. These had been issues of major concern to one (increasingly internationally oriented) segment of the investment industry, which found investor confidence waning, and its own profits shrinking. The proposals were to abolish the pyramidal structure of Indian companies by stipulating that only one set of subsidiaries be permitted, and to insist that non-executive directors be liable for boardroom decisions. Ultimately, a compromise formula was negotiated by two United Front politicians – one with close links to a major financial-sector firm, and the other with a longstanding personal relationship with the CEO of one of India's most well known conglomerates.[126] Two levels of subsidiaries would be allowed; and non-executive directors, rather than being considered company officers by default (as the proposed legislation originally envisaged), or receiving the blanket protection of non-liability (the status quo), would be legally liable only to the extent their involvement in misdeeds was provable in a particular case.[127] The intervention of politicians not only overcame an impasse; it helped to reinforce in the minds of their private-sector clients that, despite liberalisation, political access would remain critical to protecting their interests from the unpredictable winds of change – which, as noted in Chapter 4, was a major reason why much of the business community had remained publicly supportive of reform.

The key to the effective exercise of this brokerage function – whether the issue is corporate governance, molasses pricing, or textile production – is the political system's ability credibly to foster hope among a broad cross-section of elites that they will be provided for in the process of economic transition, and that there will in any case be future opportunities brought on by new circumstances. Like an airline that has to overbook its flights in order to stay in business, or a bank that holds only a percentage of depositors' assets in liquid form, Indian politicians must often make many more promises than they can keep. The trick is to prevent all of the depositors in the 'favour bank' from turning up at once to make withdrawals. Indian reformers have done this through shrewd sequencing tactics, and by blurring the edges of their adjustment programmes with the use of ambiguity – a subject which will receive more attention in the next chapter. The key point is that socio-economic elites

---

[126] Interview with a sectoral specialist in a major business association, New Delhi, 17 December 1997.   [127] *The Pioneer*, 26 January 1998.

believe in the democratic political system's essential adaptability, and the capacity of their patrons to arrange suitable compromises. Any fear that party discipline will undermine this capacity is severely reduced by the nature of Indian parties, in which faction leaders have great latitude. Our focus on the seamier side of this process may throw a new and perhaps more sober light on Adam Przeworski's observation that '[p]olitical forces comply with present defeats because they believe that the institutional framework that organized democratic competition [provides] will permit them to advance their interests in the future'.[128]

Democracy, of course, also provides forms of discipline to check any excesses that may arise in the use of such tactics. The Congress Party under Sharad Pawar's leadership received an electoral drubbing in the state assembly elections of 1995 and the parliamentary elections of 1996. Much of the blame must go to the way in which he attempted to balance interests within the state. The divisions within the sugar lobby which he played upon in order to tame its influence, and thus facilitate the introduction of policies more conducive to industrial growth, clearly helped to undermine both Pawar and the party, and not only in the western portions of the state. As Shankarrao Bajirao Patil, a disaffected sugar cooperative chairman who ran unsuccessfully against Pawar for parliament in 1996, put it: 'The sugar barons are turning against the Congress. This is mainly because of the behaviour of Pawar. He never speaks the truth. Never keeps his word. Self-interest is his guiding principle'.[129]

Though Patil lost that election, his sentiments were shared by enough other members of the sugar-cooperative lobby that the Congress vote, in both 1995 and 1996, was heavily depleted in many constituencies by Congress dissidents contesting as independent 'rebel' candidates. The main complaint was that Pawar had sold out to industrialists, upon whom he relied increasingly for political funds.[130] This does not make his political strategy, or its consequences for the line of argument this book seeks to advance, any less significant. It not only achieved its short-term aims, but also entrenched the logic of liberalisation to such a degree that the Hindu nationalist Shiv Sena–BJP coalition which succeeded the Congress in Maharashtra continues to pursue recognisably liberal economic policies to this day.

In fact, some businesses reportedly find it easier to work with the new

[128] Adam Przeworski, *Democracy and the Market: Political and Economic Reforms in Eastern Europe and Latin America* (New York: Cambridge University Press, 1991). Quoted in Khare, 'Ten Headlines in Search of a Regime', p. 31.

[129] *Outlook*, 8 May 1996, p. 26. Interviews with two senior IAS officers responsible for industrial development, 7 and 8 February 1994, Bombay; and with a political rival of Pawar who was a minister in his government, 5 April 1994, Bombay.

[130] Interview with an MLA from the sugar belt, 10 September 1996, Bombay.

government. Two reasons are cited in this connection. First, because the Shiv Sena controls so many labour unions in the state, employers can strike a deal under the auspices of the state government confident in the knowledge that the Shiv Sena will be able to deliver on its promises. One trade union activist and writer argued that the Shiv Sena was better able to deliver on its promises than other parties with affiliated trade unions, such as Jyoti Basu's CPI-M in West Bengal, which is constantly engaged in confrontation with the CPI-M's affiliated union, the Centre for Indian Trade Unions (CITU).[131] This was because being part of a governing coalition committed to economic reform held different implications for lower-level leaders in these respective unions. Such grassroots organisers in the Shiv Sena-affiliated unions would have many other spin-off activities available to them were trade unionism to decline, such as mobilisation of religious, linguistic, and caste identities to build a political following. Many such leaders are also engaged in protection rackets and dubious 'social work' projects. For CITU's middle-ranking officials, on the other hand, trade unionism 'is their life . . . where else are they going to go?' Indian democracy thus provides paths for political diversification, which do not arise in political systems in which 'winner-take-all' institutions tend to undercut moderation.

Second, the Shiv Sena–BJP coalition is less reliant upon one powerful section of rural society. Indeed, the government has taken several steps since assuming office in 1995 to effect even further divisions within the cooperative sector. Some of these have been far more ruthless than what any Congress government would have dared to attempt. While there has been a parallel effort to recruit prominent cooperative leaders who could swing votes to Shiv Sena and BJP candidates, this has relied mostly upon threats by state cooperatives minister Jayprakash Mundada to take legal action against corrupt sugar barons. The Shiv Sena–BJP government is continuing what its Congress predecessor had begun – the taming of a major interest group capable of forming the core of an anti-liberalisation political movement. As one analyst put it, '[s]ince most of the cooperatives are steeped in corruption and mismanagement, the [Shiv Sena–BJP] alliance is in a better position to bring them to heel'.[132] Its less cosy relationship with the cooperative sector means that it need not tread so warily when dealing with domestic business interests.[133] For example, the Shiv Sena–BJP government set up a combined trade and industry

---

[131] Interview, 10 April 1995, Bombay.
[132] See 'Targeting Sugar Cooperatives: Shiv Sena Comes of Age', *Indian Express*, 7 June 1996.
[133] Because of its economic nationalist rhetoric, however, the Shiv Sena–BJP government is on more difficult ground in dealing with foreign capital, though it has shown itself capable of finessing this issue on important occasions.

ministry to secure financing for ambitious infrastructure projects, under the leadership of businessman-turned-politician, Suresh Jain, of the Jain Irrigation Group, a highly reputable and extremely successful firm.[134] Even Sharad Pawar would have shied away from such a blatant exhibition of pro-business sentiment.[135]

Finally, it is important to recognise that a democratic framework provides other, less visible, means of support for politicians facing the arduous task of mediating conflicts among contending groups during the process of reform. Perhaps most importantly, associations in civil society themselves take up some of the slack, arranging compromises between narrowly defined interest groups within their ranks. The Confederation of Indian Industry (CII), for instance, evolved a complex policy position which combined support for higher duties for capital-goods imports (favoured by members producing engineering equipment) with a set of proposals to increase productivity in the steel sector (which, as a major importer of engineering equipment, wanted lower tariffs). The CII was able to present a broadly agreed compromise formula to government, and as a result policy-makers were able to enjoy a slightly reduced level of interest-group cacophony on a sensitive issue. Such intra-association agreements are usually accompanied by griping from aggrieved members who feel cheated by a biased leadership.[136] Their threats to join other, competing business 'chambers' foster the sorts of rivalries within civil society that, in was argued in Chapter 4, further increase politicians' room for manoeuvre.

Other informal institutions

Just as the federal system is only one among many formal institutions, India's porous parties and the 'regularised interactions' that arise from them in the form of relationships between governing and socio-economic interests are just one cluster among the diverse array of informal institutions that shape political life. For the same reasons that brief mention of an additional formal institution was made in closing the discussion of the federal system, we must now also consider at least one other informal institution which absorbs some of the political burden which economic reform carries in its wake.

An informal institution of particular importance is the round of annual

---

[134] *Economic Times*, 12 and 13 June 1996.
[135] Interview, Sanjoy Narayan, deputy editor, *Business World*, 11 September 1996.
[136] One editorial writer argued that the CII had a pro-engineering bias on this issue, which stemmed from its roots in the Confederation of Engineering Industries, the institutional predecessor of the CII. See 'Still Living in the Past', *Business Standard*, 9 September 1996.

consultations, held before and after the finance minister's budget speech to parliament, between senior government officials (including the finance minister himself) and various sectoral interests. These meetings are more than window dressing, and to the extent that they are regularised, indeed perennial, forms of interaction which influence the expectations and strategic calculations of the actors involved, they qualify as an institution. Because they take place behind closed doors it is difficult to know the substance of the deliberations. They are part of the 'interior world' of democratic politics, to use Gordon White's evocative phrase. Yet, they provide an important forum for bringing specific concerns to the finance minister's team. The *post*-budget exercises are particularly significant, since they often result in refinements to the original budget proposals. Most such changes tend to represent concessions to one or another group. But the important point is that successive governments have shown themselves capable of making concessions without caving in entirely to the demands of individual groups. In 1996, for instance, finance minister P. Chidambaram stood reasonably firm in the face of demands, made in post-budget consultations with representatives of India's largest business houses, that he withdraw his proposal for the Minimum Alternative Tax (MAT), which was designed to ensure that corporations did not escape tax through accounting practices that allowed them to show losses year after year.[137]

Usually, however, what emerges is a compromise: the type that splits not only the difference, but also the unity of lobbying groups. In the case of the MAT in 1996, the finance minister's decision, following the post-budget consultation exercise, to exempt companies established in designated 'backward' areas helped to appease a significant section of the aggrieved business community, thus dissipating the force of the protests. The finance minister managed to buy some goodwill among small-scale producers within the irate export sector by offering them exemptions from certain import duties theretofore available only to large firms.[138] Similar lobby-dividing concessions were made in 1994 following post-budget consultations and political deliberations within the cabinet. The original budget proposals called for expanding the number of industries subject to excise tax. Finance minister Manmohan Singh later announced a series of specific exemptions, as well as concessions for small-scale producers in selected industries.[139]

The complex configuration of trade-offs, concessions, and future

---

[137] *Economic Times*, 10 September 1996.

[138] The percentage of exporters likely to benefit from this extension of the Special Import Licence scheme was estimated at 30 per cent by the Director General of Foreign Trade. *Economic Times*, 29 August 1996.   [139] *Business Standard*, 26 April 1994.

guarantees makes straightforward interest-group lobbying extremely difficult. In some cases, for instance, what the national finance minister gives with one hand, the state government can take away with the other, as happened when a national excise-duty reduction for the jute industry was announced at the same time as the West Bengal government introduced a marketing tax on parts of the jute trade.[140] The divisive impact of the informal institution of the budget consultation process was thus compounded by the effects of the formal institution of federalism.

Two aspects of the budget consultation process are relevant to how it is viewed as an institution. First, contrary to conventional wisdom, concessions to sectoral interests that result from this mechanism do not necessarily encourage unrealistic demands in the future. Instances in which the government shows flexibility on an issue affecting a particular interest can convince other groups that there are benefits in maintaining cordial relations with the government, rather than launching a pitched battle.[141] The knowledge that there will be future rounds of negotiation moderates adversarial behaviour by lengthening time horizons, which it will be recalled is one of the functional contributions of political institutions.

Second, because these consultations are a regular feature of the budget exercise, they are closely watched and reported on by the media, thus drawing in a wider cross-section of civil society and opening up the potential for unexpected consequences. Because of media scrutiny, representatives of sectoral interests find it easy to get their views on even rather mundane and technical matters reported in the national press. They thus marshal statistics to make their case to the wider audience of public opinion. This can backfire, as it did in the case of the MAT. Leading export houses protested that the tax would adversely affect the country's foreign-exchange earnings. In an effort to make their case publicly, they ended up unwittingly supplying information which revealed a large number of prominent firms to have paid little or no corporation tax in recent years.[142] This was plastered across the front pages of national dailies.[143] It is impossible to judge the extent to which a cabinet minister might be persuaded that it is worth implementing a budget provision because bad publicity has weakened an interest group's bargaining position. But such factors can have a contributory and cumulative impact.

---

[140] *Business Standard*, 27 April 1994.
[141] The symbolic nature and value of some such concessions was commented upon in an editorial entitled, 'Small Mercies as Usual', *Business Standard*, 27 April 1994.
[142] After the exporters' loud protests, Prime Minister H. D. Deve Gowda reportedly asked for details of the companies that would be affected by the new tax. *Financial Express*, 31 August 1996.   [143] For instance *Financial Express*, 8 September 1996.

This chapter has examined the role of institutions in reducing the political potency of resistance to economic reform. Some of the change-promoting capacities of India's political institutions stem from the formal division of state power in a federal system. It is important to stress, however, that it is not just the federal provisions in the constitution that provided the political breathing space for reformers in New Delhi. The active engagement in matters of policy formulation and implementation by state governments was crucial to both the creation of reforms supportive of those announced by the central government, and the development of a political process whereby representatives of key socio-economic elites were drawn into local political arenas, where they were comparatively less powerful. It was not the mere existence of the provincial tier of government but its capacity to manage conflict that was critical.

This, in turn, relied crucially upon informal political institutions. This chapter identified one such institution as especially important – the political party. The specific feature of Indian parties that was highlighted was their porousness, which under Indian conditions gives rise to a system in which enterprising leaders are able to construct networks of influence which span a vast array of interests, both within and outside parties. (These relationships were themselves considered institutions, in the sense that they created expectations among actors about future behaviour.) This wide-ranging influence, when combined with the impacts of reform itself (the policy feedback effect), allowed these leaders to arrange political bargains that would likely have been impossible for a leader operating in a political context in which his personal networks were more firmly entrenched within a specific party, and his effective autonomy curtailed.

The democratic context itself has not been without its impacts upon this process. It is no coincidence that uncertainty is a prominent feature of both democracy and theoretical explanations for why institutions are born. As Heiner put it in his seminal article, 'The Origins of Predictable Behavior', institutions are 'regularities in the interactions between agents that arise because of uncertainty in deciphering the complex interdependencies created by these interactions'.[144] The conditions in which Indian democracy functions have furnished governing elites with a good deal of short-term autonomy in the exercise of state power. But, as we will see in the next chapter, it also requires of them a distinct set of skills. While these are found, to varying degrees, in all political systems, they are honed to their most acute level in democratic environments.

---

[144] Ronald A. Heiner, 'The Origins of Predictable Behavior', *American Economic Review*, vol. 73, no. 4, (1983), pp. 560–95.

6   Political skills: introducing reform by stealth

Political skills are vital to effecting a sustainable reorientation of development policy. But like the journalistic cliché 'political will', invoking the
notion of political skill comes dangerously close to constructing a residual
category, a last resort when substantive variables are insufficient to explain events. To argue for political skill as a contributing factor in achieving any outcome is to risk entering into the realm of circular reasoning:
actions which are deemed to reveal skill on the part of their practitioner
can be verified as skilful only with reference to the outcome which the skill
itself was meant to explain. Thus, A occurred because B is skilful; and we
know that B is skilful because of the very fact that A occurred.

To put this more concretely, the same political gambit which succeeds
for one leader can fail miserably for another. The former's skill, according
to conventional standards, is his ability to judge when 'appropriate'
circumstances were in evidence. But in virtually every such instance the
specific circumstances identified as decisive in influencing the timing of
the gambit turn out to be highly ambiguous. They could as easily have
been interpreted to support a different course of action.[1] In short, the
gambit was skilful because it was successful, not the other way around.
Politicians considered skilful are those who produce such outcomes with
surprising frequency, though even this is rarely subjected to verification.
But is someone who calls a coin-toss correctly 75 out of 100 times skilful
or lucky? This question acquires particular salience when, as in politics,
an early lucky streak (say, three out of four) effectively generates better
odds for future tosses by creating a power base which can act as a cushion
for errors that would be fatal for politicians at earlier stages in their
careers.

This is a rather insurmountable methodological shortcoming. And,
yet, if we are to believe in anything other than a determinism of random-

---

[1] An oft-cited case of 'successful' decision-making, based upon inherently ambiguous cues,
and yet subsequently attributed to political skill, is the Cuban missile crisis. See Graham
Allison, *Essence of Decision: Explaining the Cuban Missile Crisis* (Boston: Little, Brown,
1971).

ness, it is difficult not to believe that political skills exist. Indeed, there is a good deal of support for a focus upon political skills in the literature on economic reform and democracy. Guillermo O'Donnell has argued that if there is any hope of solving the prisoner's dilemmas that confound efforts to manage economic and political change simultaneously, 'it probably lies in finding areas . . . in which skilled action (particularly by the government) can lengthen the time horizons (and, consequently, the scope of solidarities) of crucial actors'.[2] Peter Gourevitch grudgingly concedes that 'even leadership' may be important in determining variations in the relationship between markets and democracy given a set of 'structural constraints'.[3] In the Indian context, even the usually sober Economist Intelligence Unit remarked that the 1995–96 budget was 'skilfully presented to make politically popular gestures seem more generous than they are'.[4]

In fact, if the discussion of incentives and institutions in this book is itself to avoid deterministic conclusions, we need to understand how human agency can exploit the opportunities to which incentives and institutions give rise. As previous chapters have stressed repeatedly, neither the political incentives thrown up by economic reform nor the political institutions prevailing in India necessarily dictated the outcome of politically sustainable economic reform. They provided breathing space and conducive conditions for governing elites seeking to outmanoeuvre entrenched interests. But would-be reformers required distinct skills in order to exploit these openings. We have seen many of these on display in the two previous chapters – especially the ability to perform the complex utility calculations which are instrumental in the creation and maintenance of political networks and, ultimately, in the capacity to broker the agreements which underwrite policy change. But if we revisit the logic which underpinned the arguments about incentives and institutions, it is possible to see the need for a somewhat different, though complementary, type of skill.

One of the arguments was that, in responding to the uncertainties that arise when policy change is initiated, governing elites are able to rely upon the tendency of socio-economic elites to operate according to established patterns of interaction. Politicians were thus able to broker arrangements on this basis – while, crucially, retaining the capacity to deviate from the

[2] Guillermo O'Donnell, 'On the State, Democratization and Some Conceptual Problems: A Latin American View with Glances at Some Postcommunist Countries', *World Development*, vol. 21, no. 8 (1993), p. 1376.
[3] Peter A. Gourevitch, 'Democracy and Economic Policy: Elective Affinities and Circumstantial Conjunctures', *World Development*, vol. 21, no. 8 (1993), p. 1271.
[4] Economist Intelligence Unit, *Country Report – India*, 2nd Quarter, 1995 (London, 1995), p. 32.

accepted norms when new incentives and constraints presented themselves. Accomplishing what in game-theoretical terms amounts to a disguised 'defection' requires mastery of a range of political skills, particularly those which democracy tends to breed in its practitioners. In particular,
it depends upon a talent for obfuscation, the use of intentional ambiguity,
and the exploitation of other politically expedient means in the pursuit of
constantly shifting policy objectives.

These tactics disrupt and complicate the utility-calculating capacity of
interest groups, which tends to disarm them, while the prospect of future
rounds of negotiation means that the result is rarely open revolt. It also
needs to be pointed out that interest groups themselves are not averse to
misdirection and the use of clandestine lobbying. One study of reform to
the intellectual property-rights regime argued that the business association representing the largest transnational pharmaceutical companies
operating in India 'has run a stealthy, behind-the-scenes campaign to
convert the opinions of Indian policy elites regarding patent reform'.[5]
This, it seems, was only fitting, given the government's approach to
bringing Indian patent law into conformity with its treaty obligations,
which one editorial referred to as reform 'by stealth'.[6]

The extent to which actually existing democracy appears to make the
skilful use of such tactics essential calls into question the validity of rather
more naïve conceptions of democracy. Lest this be mistaken for a teleological form of reasoning, it is important to stress that democracy not only
makes such skills *necessary*; it also makes their prevalence *possible*.[7] It does
this, chiefly, by permitting governing elites to use the openness of the
political system to assess continuously the relative worth of political
backing from competing socio-economic groups. This, in turn, enables a

[5] Michael W. Bollom, 'Capturing Ideas: Institutions, Interests and Intellectual Property
Rights Reform in India', paper presented at the Annual Meeting of the American Political
Science Association, Washington, DC, 28–31 August 1997.

[6] 'In a premeditated ploy to bypass parliament, [the government] waited for parliament's
winter session to end and then, just days later, took brazen recourse to ordinance raj to
amend the patents and customs laws . . . [which were then] presented to the president for
his signature at the very last moment'. See 'By Stealth', *Economic and Political Weekly*, 7
January 1995, p. 3.

[7] Teleological reasoning, which is based upon the fallacy that the inevitability of a given
end-state 'requires' the emergence of a corresponding process in order to facilitate its
achievement, is not uncommon in political analysis. A good overview of this pitfall can be
found in Jose Serra's critique of Guillermo O'Donnell's attempt to 'explain' the rise of
authoritarianism in Brazil with reference to the structural requirements of capitalist
development. See Jose Serra, 'Three Mistaken Theses Regarding the Connection between
Industrialization and Authoritarian Regimes', in David Collier (ed.), *The New Authoritarianism in Latin America* (Princeton: Princeton University Press, 1979), pp. 99–164. For
another good example, see Theda Skocpol, 'Wallerstein's World Capitalist System: A
Theoretical and Historical Critique', *American Journal of Sociology*, vol. 82, no. 5 (March
1977).

better appreciation of which to accommodate, which to abandon, and which to leave in limbo. A studied ambiguity on policy, allowing relatively low-cost subsequent revisions, is vital to this process.

Political skills, however, are important to any political system, democratic or authoritarian. They are an adaptation to the prevailing political context. In India, a premium has been placed on the ability to blur conflicts of interest between social groups. Often this has been accomplished by allocating 'hidden' subsidies, and holding out the promise of future rewards, particularly in the form of government posts. During this period of economic reform, however, the flexibility of India's political actors (including politicians and non-elected elites) has proven extremely helpful in taking advantage of the institutions which the specific nature of Indian democracy puts at their disposal. Indeed, it is a skill that has been honed through a prolonged exposure to an environment of fluid competitive politics, in which cultivating new groups without necessarily abandoning long-time supporters is a common practice. Indian politicians and other political figures routinely alter policy positions and transfer party or factional loyalties, with seemingly little cost to their credibility within the system. Democracy breeds politicians that are good at exploiting what they consider the advantages of a democratic system (the ability to gauge reactions to ambiguous policy decisions) in order to overcome what they see as its disadvantages (the pressure of the ballot box). This is not circular reasoning of the 'political will' variety. It is an adaptation to an institutional constraint. Satish Saberwal argues that the 'satisfactory operation' of India's formal and informal 'democratic political structures' requires

support from substantial, extensively learned matching skills, ideas, motivations, and practices. That is to say, the formal structures and processes can follow from relatively simple legislative and bureaucratic acts, while their functioning on the ground asks for a great deal more from the participants.[8]

Attempting to divorce an analysis of institutions from an examination of the skills necessary to operate within them effectively – to say nothing of the skill involved in their creation and rejuvenation – is in some ways as artificial as distinctions between economic and political factors in the process of policy reform. But this problem is inherent in the study of any system. Separating the parts from the whole, or from each other, leads ultimately to distortions of meaning. The hope is that the analytical value of identifying the functional role played by each part outweighs the

[8] Satish Saberwal, 'Democratic Political Structures', in T. V. Sathyamurthy (ed.), *Social Change and Political Discourse in India: Structures of Power, Movements of Resistance – Volume I: State and Nation in the Context of Social Change* (Delhi: Oxford University Press, 1994), p. 177.

danger of misrepresenting the whole.

The remainder of this chapter examines the use of these tactics. The first section concerns the skill of governing elites at maintaining the appearance of essential continuity with the past, while simultaneously undermining the basis upon which previous institutions have operated. The second section focuses on the inverse of the first: disguising continuity as change.

Cloaking change in the guise of continuity

One of the skills which reforming governments must possess is the capacity to cloak change, which tends to cause anxiety among those privileged by the status quo, in the appearance of continuity. The need to find innovative ways of accomplishing this considerable feat was emphasised by Robert Packenham in his study of why reform became politically sustainable in Argentina under Menem. His argument was that Menem 'combined continuity and change in such a way that the symbols of continuity facilitated the changes rather than hindered them'.[9]

There would seem to be ample precedent for achieving such a transformation in India. According to Ashis Nandy,

the tradition in India is to alter the dominant culture from within, by showing dissent to be a part of orthodoxy or by reinterpreting orthodoxy in terms of the needs of dissent. This is especially true of ideological deviations or innovations, the type of challenge the society has repeatedly faced and become experienced at handling.[10]

Without arguing that there exist cultural preconditions for political change, it is possible to stress the conducive cultural context within which the skills of Indian politicians have been used to justify a break not only with a set of economic policies, but with a way of thinking about the relationship between public authority, social mobility, and economic justice. Certain cultural proclivities clearly provided fertile ground for political strategies reliant upon intentional obscurity and ambiguity. As Nandy has elsewhere argued,

[9] Robert A. Packenham, 'The Politics of Economic Liberalization: Argentina and Brazil in Comparative Perspective', *Working Paper No. 206*, Kellogg Institute for International Studies, University of Notre Dame (April 1994), p. 9.

[10] Ashis Nandy, *At the Edge of Psychology: Essays in Politics and Culture* (Delhi: Oxford University Press, 1990), p. 51. This may not be a peculiarly Indian trait. It may even have been reinforced by the encounter with the British. Eric Hobsbawm has argued that most of the major changes to British economic, social, and political life since 1750 involved a marked preference for maintaining the form of old institutions, but with a profoundly changed content. *Industry and Empire* (Harmondsworth: Penguin, 1968), p. 18.

Indian culture emphasized continuities so much that even major breaks with the past passed as minor reforms, till the full implications of the break became evident after decades or centuries, when the metaphors of continuity and permanence could no longer hide the fundamental changes that had already taken place in the culture.[11]

By then, presumably, change would have been deeply entrenched, and far more difficult to reverse. This is what India's reformers have tried to achieve since at least 1991, if not longer. To the extent that economic reform was considered a non-issue in the general election campaigns of both 1996 and 1998 (despite the BJP's swadeshi rhetoric in the latter contest), they have for the time being succeeded.

While we are arguing that change can take place within a context which appears to favour continuity, we are not arguing for the rhetorical or visionary powers of India's politicians. As we saw in Chapter 3, even sober World Bank economists can be seduced by the notion of politicians creating a 'vision' which enables them effectively to promote change. Other World Bank-funded research contains similar views. To the extent that such studies recognise the importance of creative leadership, and the capacity to transcend transitory interest-group configurations, they correspond to much of what this thesis is arguing. For instance, Leila Frischtak, a World Bank consultant in the Private Sector Development Department, argues that in some developing countries,

[t]he continual need to anticipate society, to generate new realities that are not yet under the control or on the agenda of powerful interests, becomes the primary means for not succumbing to the control of these interests, and for simultaneously resolving disputes among them.[12]

So far so good. Frischtak, however, extends this logic to claim that a government possesses governance capacity 'only to the extent that it can achieve sufficient autonomy from society by articulating a vision of the future that is distinct from, and goes beyond, the diverse interests of this society'.[13] We need not reject the notion that providing a 'meta goal or meta idea'[14] *can* be an important aspect of governance in order to state that, in India, politicians have relied far less on this positive form of vision-creation than they have on the ritual intonation of developmental shibboleths to conceal reform's radical implications and thereby reassure those groups who may be threatened by them. This approach has the advantage – for Indian politicians as well as for the plausibility of our

---

[11] Ashis Nandy, *The Intimate Enemy: Loss and Recovery of Self under Colonialism* (Delhi: Oxford University Press, 1983), p. 61.
[12] Leila L. Frischtak, 'Governance Capacity and Economic Reform in Developing Countries', *World Bank Technical Paper No. 254* (Washington, DC: The World Bank, 1994), p. 23.   [13] Ibid., p. 24.   [14] Ibid., p. 25.

argument here – of demanding far less impressive rhetorical skills. In fact, the few attempts of India's reformers to project encompassing visions of what liberalisation means have involved tired clichés that emphasise continuity with the past. Narasimha Rao's orations, for instance, often returned to Gandhian themes of village self-reliance and their purported relevance to a market economy.[15] At other times they stressed the compatibility of nationalism and entrepreneurship, as he did on the occasion of the birth centenary of pioneering Indian industrialist G. D. Birla.[16] Most often, Narasimha Rao reaffirmed his commitment to social welfare. As he stated in a speech at the London Guildhall:

No multinational will build a primary school in India, no foreign investor will set up a health centre. These are jobs for the government. Let the multinationals handle the top sector, we will manage the grassroots. This is the way forward as I see it.[17]

Attempts to reinterpret past doctrines, such as Manmohan Singh's repeated claim that liberalisation was simply an alternate means to the cherished goal of self-reliance, or that freeing the market was the culmination, rather than the abandonment, of Nehru's development vision, went largely ignored.[18] They did not capture anyone's imagination. At most, they may have served a limited goal of reinforcing a default impression of 'politics-almost-as-usual'.[19] Projecting such an image is more useful than standard accounts of visionary leadership allow. By lulling enemies of change into a false sense of security, obfuscatory tactics play a large role in supporting this sort of rhetoric, which on its own would serve little purpose.

Even the altered dynamics between the central and state governments outlined in Chapter 5 illustrate the importance of both imperceptible change and the exploitation of power differentials rather than the consensus-generating capacities for which democracy is usually praised. In so far as reformers in New Delhi were able to rely upon state governments to

[15] For instance, his speech to a seminar on 'Panchsheel and Global Diplomacy' in New Delhi in June 1994 (*Asian Age*, 28 June 1994).   [16] *Hindustan Times*, 20 April 1994.

[17] *Sunday*, 27 March–2 April 1994, p. 14. As one commentary pointed out, the emphasis on continuity, which Rao called 'the middle path', was much closer in style to Indira Gandhi's approach to reform in the early 1980s than to Rajiv Gandhi's brash attempts at liberalisation in the second half of the decade. *Business India*, 11–25 April 1994, p. 51.

[18] This was most forcefully articulated in his budget speech to parliament for fiscal year 1992–93. See *Times of India*, 1 and 2 March 1992. Singh also claimed in other speeches that liberalisation would correct urban-biased development policies, and thus rectify the Nehruvian over-emphasis on industrial development by bringing India closer to a Gandhian vision. See the report on his speech at the National Institute of Advanced Studies, *Asian Age*, 5 July 1994.

[19] This phrase was suggested by Sanjaya Baru, editorial page editor of the *Times of India*. Interview, 29 April 1995, New Delhi.

perform many of the unpleasant tasks arising from adjustment, without openly acknowledging the coercive means by which their services were enlisted, this represents a relatively untransparent method of effecting sustainable policy reform. That triggering state-government involvement in reform involved pitting states against one another, starving states of resources, and providing new opportunities for patronage and profiteering at the state level was, of course, never admitted. It was in many ways an opaque and gradual process which only revealed its radical consequences much later.

Indeed, the political benefits accruing from the conflictual relationship underlying this burden-transferring process even escaped the notice of S. Guhan, the commentator quoted in Chapter 5 to illustrate the importance of state-level political arenas. Voicing the standard diagnosis of federalism's ills, Guhan pleaded for the tidy public-administration solutions of which good-government theorists are enamoured:

> the reforms cannot be approached in a dichotomous, segmented manner with the Centre playing its own narrowly conceived part, leaving the States to play theirs at the pace and manner determined by each of them. Quite clearly, the reform process will have to be conceived and pursued in a framework of *cooperative* federalism that takes into account the distribution not only of economic burdens and benefits between the two levels, but also of the political constraints.[20]

Yes, it *would* be nice if various levels of government worked in a coordinated fashion. But in reality politicians at different levels have different concerns and different interests, and they often represent different parties. Unloading thankless responsibilities on to others is part of the time-honoured tactic of shifting blame, which as we saw in Chapter 3 was a winning strategy for both Reagan and Thatcher in the pursuit of their policy objectives. An idealised notion of democracy should not blind us to its pervasiveness in the process of promoting policy change in democratic India. The *conflictual* nature of federalism provided some of the tools with which accomplished buck-passers in the central government were able to generate competition as a way of furthering their preferred agenda.

An examination of government policy in three areas will illuminate the existence and political function of this pattern of obfuscation. The first concerns aspects of anti-poverty policy; the second deals with subsidised credit; and the third involves policies relating to privatisation and labour.

---

[20] S. Guhan, 'Centre and States in the Reform Process', in Robert Cassen and Vijay Joshi (eds.), *India: The Future of Economic Reform* (Delhi: Oxford University Press, 1995), p. 101 (emphasis added).

Economic reform, shell-game politics, and the poor

Two examples from policy in the 'social sectors' are worth exploring. The first relates to food subsidies. The government of India's approach to the food subsidy bill, according to one observer, is 'as close to shell game politics as you will find'.[21] The government has loudly trumpeted its steadfast refusal to comply with World Bank recommendations that it drastically curtail the Public Distribution System (PDS), through which rice, wheat, sugar, kerosene, and other essential commodities are sold at subsidised prices to 'ration card' holders. National leaders are able to portray this as a determined stand against attempts to undermine India's sovereignty.[22] It is held up as proof of their continued commitment to India's poor and downtrodden. Government officials make frequent mention of the fact that the budgetary allocation for the food subsidy has risen or remained constant in the years since liberalisation began.

What this masks, however, is that this level of budgetary support for the food subsidy has not been sufficient to offset the steep rise in government support prices offered to cultivators of wheat and rice.[23] As a result, poor consumers have been forced to pay far higher prices. The fact is that it would have required *even higher* increases in the level of budgetary support in order to stabilise the price at which grains are sold to 'ration card' holders in the PDS's 'fair-price shops'. While 'increasing the level of budgetary support' for the PDS, the government has nevertheless made essential commodities more expensive for the poorest of the poor.[24] But that was not all. Through a deft display of political legerdemain, it transferred a substantial portion of the subsidy from consumers to farmers. This was deemed necessary to compensate for the government's failure to take other measures demanded by farmers. For instance, it did not increase fertiliser subsidies in line with the previous trend or extend the loan-waiver scheme initiated by the V. P. Singh government. The

---

[21] Interview with Narendar Pani, acting resident editor, *Economic Times* (Bangalore edition), 18 April 1995, Bangalore.

[22] In order to quell speculation that India was considering the abolition of food subsidies in response to international pressure, Civil Supplies and Public Distribution Minister A. K. Antony told a press conference: 'Whatever may be the constraints, there is no question of reducing or abandoning the food subsidy because food security is as important as national security, if not more'. *Asian Age*, 9 July 1994.

[23] It also masks the fact that much of this subsidy – indeed a rising proportion – goes to pay for storage costs, which have been increasing as rising prices have reduced offtake by consumers. According to Partha Pratim Mitra, Controller of Accounts in the central government's power ministry, while the 'total food subsidy between 1984–85 and 1994–95 grew at an annual average rate of 19.5 per cent . . . the consumer subsidy went up by about 9 per cent during this period'. See his 'Economics of Food Security: The Indian Context', *Social Action*, vol. 46 (July–Sept. 1996), p. 281.

[24] See 'Illusion of Plenty', *Economic and Political Weekly*, 15 October 1994, p. 2073.

result was to change the way subsidies were delivered. It is significant that the government did not increase its commitments through *overt* subsidies. Instead, it handed out enormous increases in the form of 'price incentives' for farmers, while recouping as much of this outlay as possible from those who rely on subsidised foodgrains, the poor. While maintaining the appearance of continuity (maintaining the food subsidy), the government effected a dramatic change (massive increases in the prices at which consumers bought them through the PDS).

It would be a mistake to consider this an isolated episode.[25] Moreover, the downstream implications are important if we are to comprehend the ways in which incentives, institutions, and skills can work together in support of change. This is because the opaque manner of bringing about a qualitative shift in the food subsidy – increasing need, while reducing outlays as a percentage of GDP – will influence the government's capacity to effect further reform in this area. As we saw in Chapter 5, the policy feedback effect (originally introduced in Chapter 4) requires a supportive institutional climate in order to produce results. It also relies upon the application of tactical skill. The rise in the prices at which foodgrains are sold through the PDS – the 'issue price' – shortened the distance between the 'subsidised' and market prices, leading to a very large decline in consumption through the PDS, from 20.8 million tonnes in 1990 to 14 million tonnes in 1994. This is because PDS issue prices during that period rose even faster than the consumer price indices for the groups most in need of subsidised foodgrains.[26]

Ashok Gulati and Shashanka Bhide, two economists specialising in subsidy issues, argued that this policy of retaining an administrative network of subsidised fair price shops, while slowly removing incentives for people actually to use them by bringing their prices closer to market levels, was a strategic way of deferring open conflict on the issue. It was also, they argued, an extremely shrewd way of softening the introduction of a system better targeted towards the poor. Preventing leakages to the middle classes had always been the avowed goal, but the introduction of the 'revamped' PDS (RPDS) in 1992 – which targeted subsidies towards the poorest districts in India – had remained a limited experiment.

---

[25] For instance, another example of adjustment's burdens being shifted on to the poor involves the activities of the National Cooperative Development Corporation (NCDC). 'In the context of adjustment', argues Raghav Gaiha, 'the level and pattern of assistance by NCDC . . . [indicates that] the share of cooperatives for the weaker sections in total assistance declined from about 10.5 per cent in 1991–92 to 7.5 per cent in 1992–93'. See his 'Structural Adjustment, Rural Institutions and the Poor in India: A Comparative Analysis of Andhra Pradesh, Maharashtra and Karnataka', paper prepared for the UN Food and Agricultural Organization, 27 September 1994, p. 78.

[26] *Frontline*, 26 January 1996, p. 79.

However, they argued,

> if one can read between the lines, raising [the price for PDS consumers] to keep the food subsidy within reasonable limits makes the *general* PDS (not the RPDS) almost defunct, which can be used as an argument to withdraw it at a later stage. If this is being done as a calculated move, perhaps one can term it as an attempt towards targeting on area basis as the only functioning component would be RPDS, which caters to backward and poor blocks where the issue price is lower than in the non-RPDS blocks.[27]

We cannot know whether this was, in fact, a 'calculated move', and any effort to ascribe such strategic genius to Indian reformers should rightly be greeted with suspicion. But the ability to respond skilfully to opportunities that arise from previous decisions is arguably something that democratic politics engenders in its practitioners. To use Saberwal's phrase, it is a product of 'extensive learning'. Gulati and Bhide's further point was that if rises in PDS issue prices were a prelude to a focus on greater targeting, it would be 'better for the government to come out openly with its policy and have the courage to announce the withdrawal of the untargeted PDS'.[28] This, of course, it did not do. After roughly a five-year delay, during which many pro-poor activist groups had been thrown on the defensive, the United Front coalition which succeeded Narasimha Rao's government did continue the process of PDS reform in the way predicted by Gulati and Bhide's account: the concept of targeting became further entrenched with the introduction of the Targeted PDS (TPDS).

Imploring reformers to avoid taking paths of lesser political resistance is a favourite pastime of neo-liberal economists,[29] though if anyone should know that such pleas will fall on deaf ears it should be neo-liberal economists themselves. They would do better to probe the additional political implications of the central government's *de facto* retreat from food subsidies to the poor. One reason why it was able to get away with such sins of omission is that it is state governments, the first line of political defence, that must face the irate public. Electorates vent their frustrations at the most accessible level of government, not necessarily the one most responsible for their problems. This may be unfair, but so is the abuse hurled at ticket clerks when trains are late or cancelled. The laying of blame is a political process, one that by no means follows strict rationality. Tactics matter, as the Republican-controlled Congress learned when it

[27] Ashok Gulati and Shashanka Bhide, 'What Do the Reformers Have for Agriculture?' *Economic and Political Weekly*, 6–13 May 1995, p. 1091.   [28] Ibid.

[29] Anne Krueger told an Indian journalist that, in the area of economic reform, 'the main thing . . . is for the government to make its intentions very clear' (*India Today*, p. 49). While this might hold true if the only objective were to reassure 'entrepreneurs waiting to see if the reforms are there to stay' (ibid.), it ignores the political logic which must simultaneously inform policy implementation.

lost the battle of public opinion against President Clinton over which arm of the U.S. government was responsible for shutting down essential services during prolonged budget negotiations in 1995–96.

Faced with protests, and the futility of blaming New Delhi, many state governments in India were, in effect, forced to substitute their own food subsidies to offset what the central government had withdrawn. The most notable example was the highly expensive Rs. 2 per kilogram rice scheme in Andhra Pradesh, which emerged as a result of a campaign promise during the 1994 assembly elections. In that case, not only was the newly installed non-Congress state government forced to clean up the mess created by the central government's PDS price increases, it was also blamed for its lack of fiscal prudence when it had done so. With a good deal of the responsibility firmly rested upon its shoulders, honouring this commitment at the lowest possible cost by cutting corners became a major preoccupation of the state government. Obfuscation at the centre begat more obfuscation in the states.

Andhra Pradesh had the most expensive subsidy scheme, but others took similar actions, and for similar reasons. In Karnataka, the Congress government of Veerappa Moily in 1994 reduced the prices at which PDS outlets in the state sold rice and wheat. This cost the state's exchequer Rs. 420 million. As a newspaper editorial noted:

> The decision to reduce the end prices of grains also represents the additional financial burden that the States are forced to carry on account of the Centre's fiscal stabilisation programme. While the Centre raised issue prices to contain food subsidies, Mr Moily reduced it to ensure demand among the weaker sections.[30]

As the central government continued its withdrawal from the PDS, Moily's successor as chief minister, H. D. Deve Gowda, felt compelled to extend the state-level subsidised rice scheme, at a cost of Rs. 2.2 billion per year, more than five times the amount Moily was willing to commit. In 1995, Deve Gowda announced that the scheme would be extended to urban consumers.[31]

If we recognise that only *some* states found it necessary to cushion the blow of the central government's PDS price rises, it is possible to gain an even greater perspective on the extent to which the politically unpalatable consequences of underhanded tactics are masked by the veneer of continuity. Slowly emerging in India is a system in which the states with the most assertive populations – not necessarily the most deserving – take remedial action. In practice, the distribution of public resources thus takes a *politically* more efficient form: it apportions the price rises in

[30] *Deccan Herald*, 24 March 1994.   [31] *The Pioneer*, 18 October 1995.

accordance with regional, rather than national, thresholds at which such hardships translate into widespread political discontent. After all, poorer groups are not as politically assertive in Rajasthan and Orissa as they are in Karnataka and Andhra Pradesh. In this sense, it is valid to ask, as Mick Moore's study of the politics of adjustment in Sri Lanka did, whether one unintended consequence of how liberalisation has been implemented in India has been to 'remedy an historic "weakness" of the . . . political system: the relatively indiscriminate and inefficient distribution of relatively large volumes of material patronage such that they purchase little lasting support for the party in power'.[32] To whatever extent this has taken place, it has not been advertised.

The approach of central and state governments to other anti-poverty measures has clearly conformed to a similar pattern, in which political expediency is masked by a continued official commitment to social welfare.[33] In the hope of maintaining office, elected politicians at the state level direct the government's poverty-alleviation efforts towards constituencies they consider most likely to provide the support necessary to retain power. This is why state-level and intra-state data are so important. Even among states that have reduced poverty, it is clear that biases exist, biases which cannot be explained away as unrelated to political calculations of state-level governing elites. West Bengal, for instance, registered reductions in poverty in rural areas by less than the national average reduction between 1987–88 and 1993–94, while over the same period it reduced urban poverty faster than did the nation as a whole.[34]

The second example of shell-game politics is the proliferation of employment-generation schemes, which have been among the major 'safety net' programmes during the period of economic reform. The massive expansion of such schemes was an attempt to enhance the government's

[32] Mick Moore, 'Economic Liberalisation versus Political Pluralism in Sri Lanka', *Modern Asian Studies*, vol. 24, no. 2 (1990), p. 352, fn 20.

[33] It also conforms to the political logic underlying changes to welfare policy in such economically advanced federal countries as the United States. In 1996, the US began the process of allowing individual states rather than the federal government to define welfare eligibility requirements. This was coupled with 'block grant' funding from the federal government. See the *Financial Times*, February 1996. Extending this premise, Theodore J. Lowi argues that federalism in the United States allows state governments to exercise the political control which the national government has forfeited in its movement towards privatisation and deregulation: 'Our new globalization proceeds within this context of [federally] divided government'; and thus, he argues, 'the costs [of globalization] will simply be devolved and, along with the poor, less visible'. See his 'Think Globally, Lose Locally', *Boston Review*, April/May 1998.

[34] These figures are derived from a study conducted by the Delhi-based Indian Statistical Institute, which attempted to estimate poverty from the expenditure surveys carried out by the National Sample Survey (NSS). Reported in Amaresh Dubery and Shubhashis Gangopadhyay, 'Poverty and Economic Reforms', *Economic Times*, 23 February 1998.

pro-poor credentials (or at least curtail their erosion), while still finding ways to benefit groups whose clout might pose a serious threat to reform. This was possible because employment-generation programmes in India have been prone to leakages, benefiting individuals outside the official target groups. Joan Nelson's cross-national research, discussed in Chapter 3, pointed to such leakages as a significant contributor to the sustainability of anti-poverty programmes during the period of adjustment.

The national schemes which have been so much more in evidence during the reform period are modelled on Maharashtra's Employment Generation Scheme (EGS), which continues as a separate programme. Both the EGS and the national Jawahar Rozgar Yojana (JRY) – in theory, and for the most part in practice as well – guarantee daily wage employment to citizens willing to contribute their labour. Because the work is physically demanding, and the pay minimal, the EGS (and to a lesser extent the JRY) is widely considered extremely well targeted at the poorest of the poor. But the nature of the programme has encouraged the formation of a considerably more broad-based constituency to support its continuation, and indeed expansion.[35] The rationale of both the EGS and JRY is not only to put people to work, but also to enhance the value of rural public assets, such as roads and irrigation canals. But, in reality, the work that is performed by poor labourers, paid from public funds, is often used to upgrade facilities used primarily by prosperous and middle-class landowners who otherwise despair of having canals desilted or roads maintained. In some cases, much of the work carried out under the EGS actually 'turns out to be land improvements . . . on land belonging to richer rural households'.[36] The JRY, as it evolved as a national programme administered by state and local governments, followed a similar pattern.[37] Both the JRY and EGS also provide opportunities for local politicians and bureaucrats to intervene in the selection of works projects and the recruitment of labourers.[38]

If politically sustainable adjustment requires continued commitment to poverty alleviation programmes – and if such commitment is likely only to arise when a solid constituency remains to support it – then the emerg-

[35] See Robert S. Jenkins, 'The Politics of Protecting the Poor During Economic Adjustment in India: The Case of Maharashtra', in Usha Thakkar and Mangesh Kulkarni (eds.), *Politics in Maharashtra* (Bombay: Himalaya Publishing, 1995), pp. 195–212.
[36] Harry W. Blair, 'Success and Failure in Rural Development: A Comparison of Maharashtra, Bihar and Bangladesh', paper presented at the annual meeting of the Association of South Asian Studies, San Francisco, 25–27 March 1988, p. 7.
[37] Interviews with a senior IAS officer in the accounts and audits bureaucracy, 9 October 1993, New Delhi; and a middle-ranking IAS officer knowledgeable about the JRY in Maharashtra, 1 March 1994, Pune. See also *The Hindu*, 18 October 1995.
[38] For example, see the study conducted by the Institute of Regional Analysis, reported in *India Today*, 15 February 1995, p. 98.

ence of the 'targeted-yet-leaky'[39] JRY as a major plank of the Indian social safety net must be viewed as an important contributor to the political sustainability of economic reform. It may not represent the most economically efficient allocation of resources, or the most equitable means for helping the poor.[40] But given Indian realities it is remarkably well adapted to the need for satisfying groups other than the poor, as well as the need for a concealing mechanism to mask this fact.

Shifting priorities but not official policy

The government's approach to the issue of 'priority-sector' lending also relied upon tactical skill. Banking regulations stipulate that 40 per cent of financial institutions' total outstanding credit must be allocated to priority sectors, mainly agriculture and small-scale trade and industry. Rather than taking a stand that 'directed credit programmes' lead to allocative inefficiencies, and then 'selling' this reform by persuading farmers and small-scale industrialists that they will be more than compensated by other fiscal and regulatory reforms,[41] the government decided to proceed quietly. Officials of the finance, agriculture, and industry ministries loudly proclaimed at every opportunity their undying commitment to priority-sector quotas and their determination not to cave in to World Bank and IMF pressure on this issue.

Unofficially, banks were consistently permitted to fall short of the stipulated targets – a phenomenon that the erring bank officers themselves admit is largely caused by liberalisation. A general manager at the Bank of Baroda in charge of priority-sector lending said: 'After the

---

[39] This was the phrase used by a middle-ranking IAS officer knowledgeable about the JRY in Maharashtra. Interview, 1 March 1994, Pune. This paradox was further confirmed in the report of the Comptroller and Auditor General of India for the financial year ending 31 March 1994. Though it criticised the Rajasthan state government for accounting irregularities and diversion of funds between programmes, the report also found that the level of employment generated exceeded programme targets. Even accounting for falsification – such as the inclusion of bogus names on employment registers – this was a considerable achievement, made possible in part by payment (in at least two districts) of wages lower than the prescribed minimum. That workers would nevertheless turn out in large numbers suggests that targeting works despite pervasive graft. See *Observer of Business and Politics*, 2 May 1995.

[40] Two evaluations of the JRY conducted by central government ministries found that roughly one-third of village panchayats implementing JRY schemes did not possess a copy of the JRY guidelines. It is therefore not surprising that, even according to official records, 18 per cent of JRY workers in 1992–93 were from ineligible economic categories – i.e., households with incomes exceeding the poverty line. *Economic Times*, 20 January 1998.

[41] This was the recommendation of the Narasimham Committee report on financial-sector reform, which argued that fiscal policy was the least distorting means for achieving redistributive ends. Credit policy, on the other hand, was considered an unnecessarily blunt instrument.

government kicked off its liberalisation drive, a lot of credit is being pumped into export finance. So banks have been finding it rather difficult to maintain the level of agricultural disbursements'.[42] This was also partly because the banking sector had been exposed to competitive pressures. As another bank executive admitted, 'at a time when we have to worry about staying afloat, we are just not prepared to take such risky assets in our books'.[43] In fact, twenty-two of the twenty-eight nationalised banks failed to meet their targets in 1993.[44] As of March 1993, only 33 per cent of gross bank credit was directed to priority sectors, considerably less than the target of 40 per cent.[45] No action was taken against the banks.

The Reserve Bank of India, the agency responsible for setting targets and monitoring compliance, was aware that slippage on priority-sector lending would take place. According to one official, this was tacitly permitted because the banks had already been subjected to considerable shocks that year as a result of new accounting procedures instituted to prepare Indian banking for a more open market economy.[46] In order not to upset the banks too greatly, it was decided to allow them, temporarily, to reduce their commitment to 'directed credit'. The calculation was that changes then being made to the definition of 'small-scale industry' – allowing larger firms to qualify – would in future years make it possible for banks to increase lending to this 'priority sector'. In other words, a behind-the-scenes compromise permitted one interest group (banks) to withstand the costs of policy reform at the cost of another (the small-scale sector), until such time as the latter could be redefined in ways that would privilege yet another group (slightly larger firms). Through such means was the charade of continuity maintained.

In fact, several changes to the priority-sector guidelines were quietly introduced. New banks were exempted from priority-sector quotas for their first three years in business. For the first time, a firm's export-orientation made it eligible for priority status, thereby increasing the size of the 'target' group for directed credit and making it easier for banks to meet their quotas. The rules regarding which housing loans would qualify as priority-sector lending were also relaxed. Previously, only housing loans of Rs. 5,000 or less made to members of scheduled castes or scheduled tribes counted under the priority-sector heading. The limit was raised to Rs. 200,000 per loan, and the restriction to scheduled castes and tribes withdrawn.[47] 'Indirect lending' was also permitted to count to-

---

[42] *Business World*, 28 July–10 August 1993, p. 89.
[43] *Business India*, 25 October–7 November 1993, p. 99.   [44] Ibid.
[45] 'Banking: Lost Priority', *Economic and Political Weekly*, 18 December 1993, p. 2756.
[46] Interview with a senior RBI official, 11 April 1995, Bombay.
[47] *Business Standard*, 25 March 1994.

wards meeting the banks' quotas, meaning that loans to state electricity boards for rural electrification projects,[48] for instance, could be treated as agricultural loans, as could lending for high-tech agricultural activities such as tissueculture and greenhouse-based floriculture.[49] Retail trading, usually considered less deserving than other sectors, increased its share of priority-sector lending substantially between 1990 and 1994.[50] This was unsurprising, given that the ceiling for qualification was hiked from Rs. 25,000 to Rs. 200,000.[51] The government permitted some commercial banks to close loss-making branches,[52] and private domestic and foreign banks were allowed to meet priority-sector obligations by parking funds with the National Bank for Agriculture and Rural Development (NABARD). Even with these crucial (unpublicised) concessions, priority-sector lending as a percentage of net bank credit fell from 42.4 per cent in 1990 to 35.3 per cent in 1994.[53] The priorities changed – especially as banks began to focus their efforts on loans above Rs. 200,000 – but the official commitment to directed credit remained untouched.[54]

This division was mirrored institutionally in the RBI's bureaucracy: the department of rural planning and credit would publicly prod the banks to increase lending to agriculture and the small-scale sector, while the department of banking operations and development was itself encouraging the scaling back of such lending practices.[55] The latter's goal of improving the profitability of public-sector banks paid off when it was announced that twenty of twenty-seven posted operating profits for 1994, which compared favourably with the fourteen which had done so in 1993.[56] Finally, in early 1998 it was leaked that the RBI's bank-inspection reports would not make mention of banks' exposure to the priority sectors. Quietly, almost imperceptibly (but for the thoroughness of the Indian press) the RBI was, according to one official, 'distancing itself from such issues'.[57]

Through the back door: indirect approaches to state-owned firms and labour

The approach to reforming state-owned firms and the industrial relations regime has relied upon similarly indirect methods. Even some foreign

[48] *Business World*, 5–18 April 1995, p. 131.
[49] 'A Matter of Priority', *Business India*, 3–16 June 1996, p. 106.
[50] *Business Today*, 22 April–6 May 1995, p. 36.   [51] *Business Standard*, 25 March 1994.
[52] 'Monkeying with Rural Credit', *Economic and Political Weekly*, 18 September 1993, pp. 1959–60.   [53] *Business World*, 5–18 April 1995, p. 131.
[54] 'A Matter of Priority', *Business India*, 3–16 June 1996, p. 106
[55] *Economic Times* (editorial), 24 November 1993.   [56] *Asian Age*, 14 September 1995.
[57] *Economic Times*, 12 March 1998.

observers have begun to recognise that the government has not only faced political constraints, but has also attempted to overcome them through relatively unconfrontational tactics. As one put it:

It would be nice if privatisation were speeded up, but the government is allowing companies to compete against state-owned companies, and that's a back-door way of doing it. China has followed a similar policy of ignoring some very tricky issues, and concentrated on getting private investment to increase.[58]

In fact, compared to some of the other means the government has employed, subjecting public-sector firms to competition is a relatively above-board approach. Automobile manufacturer Maruti, for instance, has remained nominally a government enterprise, though the Japanese firm Suzuki has slowly been permitted to increase its joint-venture equity participation from 26 per cent, to 40 per cent, and then to a controlling 50.2 per cent. Former finance minister Madhu Dandavate termed this 'back door' privatisation, and considered it consistent with the government's general policy of 'double-faced liberalisation'. That he is right is less significant than the fact that protests such as his failed to generate the political backlash that he and others clearly expected.[59]

Another example of the skill with which Indian politicians have practised reform by stealth is the coal sector. The long history of trade-union militancy in this sector has made governments particularly wary of taking decisive action. Disruption in the supply of this vital input has the capacity to cause serious economic disorder. The existence of powerful political patrons behind the monopoly supplier, state-owned Coal India Limited (CIL), added an extra measure of caution to the statements of reformers and political managers in Narasimha Rao's circle.[60] Diverting coal supplies to clients willing to pay a premium above the state price was over the years a lucrative source of illegal income for politicians with connections at various levels of CIL's operational hierarchy.[61] During the first four years of reform, the result was a spate of government denials that the coal sector would be thrown open to the private sector.[62] Even limited

---

[58] This was the view of Malcom S. Forbes, Jr., president and editor-in-chief of *Forbes*, the US-based business magazine. *India Today*, 15 March 1995, p. 133.

[59] See Madhu Dandavate, 'Patronage to Maruti: Government's Policy of Double-Faced Liberalisation', *Indian Express*, 1 December 1993.

[60] One newspaper editorial argued that over-regulation had 'led to the emergence of unofficial premia on different grades of coal, which was usually realised by the coal mafia. Indeed, many people believe it is because of the mafia that it is difficult to dismantle the present system'. *Economic Times*, 15 January 1994.

[61] In January 1997 the Central Bureau of Investigation arrested CIL's former director of finance, Suresh Jha, for misappropriation of public funds. *Asian Age*, 8 January 1997.

[62] For instance, *Financial Express*, 18 March 1993.

disinvestment of CIL's shares to raise resources was deemed too sensitive to risk.

Nevertheless, a quiet start was made towards deregulation. It began with a bidding process that resulted in twenty private firms being shortlisted to set up coal washeries. The most significant move, however, was the decision in 1994 to allow firms investing in power-generation, steel, and cement projects to establish 'captive' coal mines – a step which was the result of intense lobbying by a group of firms that ultimately included those bidding for the coal washery projects.[63] Permission was to be granted only to those firms which could justify the need for a captive supply on the basis of projected productivity gains from vertical integration. According to Pranab Bardhan, the process of 'indirect' liberalisation in the coal sector subsequently took other forms consistent with this logic. CIL had its monopoly further undermined when the Government of India permitted certain businesses to import coal if the supply from CIL was 'erratic', which it almost always was. This is another means of building a constituency for future policy reform.[64]

This type of policy modification has three important implications. First, the criteria in such *ad hoc* policies are notoriously imprecise, leading to decisions being made on a discretionary basis. This allows a new source of corrupt income to emerge. Second, because this happens at the same time as the old system of CIL favouritism is still relatively intact, a period of overlapping patronage defuses opposition from within the political and bureaucratic elite.[65] Third, and most importantly, the overlap period helps to nurture an actual, concrete 'proto-constituency' – the firms with captive mines – capable of contributing to the battle for more direct forms of reform at a later stage. It is a process which relies on systematic obfuscation about future intentions, if not outright deceit.

This state of affairs is also very significant for our understanding of why traditional approaches to modelling the political economy of economic reform do not produce the expected results. Most models envision the substitution of a constituency of 'winners' from reform for those groups who 'lose' in the redistributive process. Yet this often – perhaps even in a majority of cases – does not take place. To reiterate, the reason is that the winners are always *potential* winners, most likely dispersed and poorly organised because of the extreme uncertainty that they will actually reap the promised benefits. The costs to the usually well-organised losers, on

[63] *Observer of Business and Politics*, 18 April 1994.

[64] Seminar on 'The Politics of Liberalisation', Birkbeck College, University of London, 17 June 1998.

[65] The nurturing of a transitionary constituency was also facilitated by the government's decision to allow downstream users of coal to resell it, which was part of a more market-oriented approach to distribution. *Economic Times*, 15 January 1994.

the other hand, appear very real indeed. When, as in the case of the coal sector in India, the winners have been able to taste some of the rewards, they are a more potent source of support to reformers, who likewise are that much more inclined to believe that they can effect a relatively costless substitution of their support base. The potential losers, for their part, are more likely to have been lulled into a false sense of complacency as a result of their apparent ability to prevent the government from taking the most serious steps towards reform.

The result of this strategy of 'back door reform', then, is to strengthen the government's political position when the economic logic reaches its ultimate conclusion and a decision on more substantial deregulation and privatisation becomes unavoidable. As the Economist Intelligence Unit put it: 'The question must inevitably be raised soon as to why the nationalised company is needed at all and why prices should be set administratively'.[66] Allaying the apprehensions of powerful figures about what the future might hold for the sectors in which they have interests is not easy. An economist who has served on the boards of several public-sector firms argued that it requires 'an approach reeking of business as usual'.[67]

It bears reminding that this capacity can rely substantially on tactics of obfuscation. Even the sale of shares in public-sector firms 'is a kind of privatisation by stealth'.[68] With most of the attention focused at the national level, state governments have seized limited opportunities to take action. By early 1995, for instance, Orissa, Meghalaya and other states were 'quietly selling off state electricity distributors and generators'.[69] The communist-controlled government of West Bengal also preferred 'to privatise quietly, often through under-the table deals'.[70] The West Bengal State Electricity Board's Kasba gas turbine, for instance, was effectively sold to the R. P. Goenka industrial group in the guise of a leasing arrangement. In this and other instances, chief minister Jyoti Basu has used his personal popularity with the electorate as a lever with which to pressure the leaders of his party's affiliated trade union to take a more 'pragmatic' approach to foreign investment, privatisation, and tax reform.[71]

Perhaps the best example of reform by stealth is in the area of indus-

[66] Economist Intelligence Unit, *Country Report – India*, 4th Quarter, 1994 (London, 1994), p. 32.   [67] Interview, 26 November 1993, New Delhi.
[68] Economist Intelligence Unit, *Country Report – India*, 2nd Quarter, 1995 (London, 1995), p. 22.   [69] Ibid., p. 23.
[70] 'If Government is Frank, PSUs [Public-Sector Undertakings] Only Mean Cash', *Asian Age*, 8 November 1994.
[71] Interview with Jayanta Sarkar, correspondent for the *Far Eastern Economic Review*, 26 April 1995, Calcutta.

trial-relations policy. As we saw in Chapter 5, state governments have been waging a guerrilla war on this front, taking action in isolated incidents and sapping the power of unions to resist encroachments upon their rights. This has taken place without alterations to official policy. The central government can claim to have left India's labour-relations regime in tact. Indeed, India still has some of the most pro-worker labour laws in the world. Implementation is another matter.

Several means have been employed for bringing about the sort of flexible labour environment that a market economy is deemed to require. Voluntary Retirement Schemes (VRSs) have been among the most popular. The government originally devised the VRS framework as an integrated programme for redeploying surplus labour, and one or two retraining centres were opened with great fanfare. Companies opting for the VRS route are officially required to abide by specified procedures, including extensive consultation with unions. These are routinely ignored. By September 1996, 85,000 workers in state-owned firms had been retrenched through one or another VRS – there were many more in the private sector – but only 2,000 had been given retraining. The number actually redeployed through the VRS machinery is anyone's guess.[72]

The strong sense of complicity between government and employers has contributed to an atmosphere in which trade unions perceive few options other than to make massive concessions. Even business leaders recognise the change of attitude. P. K. Dutt, vice-president of the West Bengal Chamber of Commerce and Industry, stated in 1994 that 'without a shade of doubt, the attitude of the unions and politicians has turned around'.[73] While the increasing willingness of workers to opt for VRSs is cited by industrialists as evidence that labour has woken up to business realities, trade-union leaders argue that it is the 'uncertainty' created by government betrayals that causes workers to lose hope and take what they can get.[74] The point is that even a 'non-policy' can generate results by creating an impression that unofficial continuity might be worse than

[72] *Times of India*, 6 September 1996.
[73] *International Herald Tribune*, 8 September 1994. See also, 'Rethinking Reform', which analyses the AITUC's questioning of its traditional hostility to economic reform. *Business India*, 10–23 April 1995, p. 141; and 'Labour Turns its Back on Militancy'. *Business World*, 1–14 July 1992, pp. 28–33. The secretary of the union at Maharashtra government-owned Mafco actually voiced his support for privatisation of the company. *Business India*, 11–24 March 1996, p. 100. Perhaps the best example of this trend is the position taken by the union leaders of the public-sector engineering company Jessop, who argued that instead of immediately paying workers the three months' back wages owed them (even though the firm had just been given Rs. 58.40 million from the central government), the company should use the funds to improve future business prospects – by buying raw material to keep production going, and taking employment preservation into account when choosing among future business strategies. *Economic Times*, 4 February 1998.
[74] *Economic Times*, 17 March 1994.

official change.[75] This is especially true in a climate in which unions have been subjected to divide-and-rule tactics by both national and state governments.[76] Moreover, the tendency for union leaders to be secretly in league with governments has led to divisions between rank-and-file members and their representatives.[77] Government decisions which discriminate arbitrarily among different classes of employee have even served to sow discord among workers within firms which have initiated a VRS.[78]

Another way in which governments made progress on 'back door' labour reform without having actually to reform labour legislation was by allowing firms to substitute their regular employees with contract employees. As one account put it, '[w]hen it became clear that there may be no legal Exit Policy, contract employment ballooned'.[79] While the law states that employers are permitted to hire workers on a contract basis only in certain types of seasonal jobs, governments have turned a blind eye to the abuse of this provision.[80] The contract labour approach is complemented by the corporate restructuring techniques used by many firms to skirt labour laws.[81] A study conducted by the All-India Management Association found that the absence of labour-market reform had

[75] A study by the Maniben Kara Institute reported that of workers who accepted VRS packages, 63 per cent did not do so voluntarily, but due to physical intimidation by hired thugs and employers' threats of illegal lockouts. Reported in Ernesto Noronha, 'Wages of Globalisation', *Humanscape*, March 1998, p. 12.

[76] In 1994, for instance, the Maharashtra state government allegedly worked with the management of Otis Elevators to stoke inter-union rivalries at its Kandivli plant in Bombay. *Business India*, 14–27 March 1994, p. 131. At the national level, one faction of the National Federation of Indian Railwaymen deplored the 'blatant partisan attitude of the railway ministry in favour of the small minority group'. *Business Standard*, 25 January 1994.

[77] *Business World*, 12–25 January 1994, p. 115.

[78] This happened in the case of the public-sector Coffee Board. *Economic Times*, 17 April 1994.

[79] Gurbir Singh, 'Who Needs an Exit Policy Anyway?', *Economic and Political Weekly*, 10 June 1995, p. 1360.

[80] In fact, the Tamil Nadu state government itself, through its state electricity board, was eventually found by the Supreme Court to have been one of the worst violators of contract-labour regulations. *Business India*, 5–18 June 1995, p. 149. CITU general secretary M. K. Pandhe accused Coal India Ltd. (CIL) of pursuing a concerted strategy of increasing coal production through contract labour. He also criticised the central government for failing to take action against these malpractices, though he admitted that some trade union leaders had themselves become contract labour middle-men, under false names, supplying casual labour to CIL subsidiaries. *Economic Times*, 28 December 1994.

[81] For instance, the B. K. Birla group, which planned to transfer a business unit that had experienced chronic labour unrest to a dormant subsidiary. *India Today*, 15 August 1992, p. 57. And in an effort to retrench workers in its electronics division, Ceat's personnel manager claimed that there were in fact two separate business units, each with fewer than 100 workers, the minimum required for India's pro-labour laws to take effect. *Times of India*, 11 September 1996.

not prevented firms from using restructuring as a way of closing unviable production units.[82]

Companies, with the assistance provided by cooperative state governments and trade unions affiliated to state-level ruling parties, have become skilled at combining this array of indirect tactics. It is worth citing one such case to provide a taste of the possibilities that have been opened up by governments which nevertheless refuse to take concrete action on labour-market reform. Industrial giant Hindustan Lever Ltd. (HLL) decided to close down Indian Perfumes Ltd. after acquiring the firm as part of a large corporate merger. Since industrial-relations laws presented an obstacle, it was decided that taking action on the grounds of health, safety, and environmental problems at the plant would suffice. The state government regulators, on orders from their political bosses, were willing to oblige. Still, labour regulations required that scheduled output not be stopped, so production was shifted to a new site where sub-contracting was used to lower costs. But since there were still more than 100 salaried workers in the unit – the minimum required for the no-closure provisions to apply – HLL offered workers VRS packages, 85 of whom accepted, fearing that waiting might get them nothing, given the state government's clearly pro-management stance. This pushed the workforce well below 100, freeing the firm from the shackles of India's officially tough, but unofficially malleable, labour-relations regime.[83]

Given such *de facto* labour reform, it is perhaps no surprise that the World Bank's Country Economic Memorandum for 1996 and its Country Study for 1997 made less noise than usual about the need to reform labour legislation. In September 1996, a western diplomat remarked that foreign investors visiting India no longer considered labour-market reform a top-priority issue.[84] The government's sins of omission had, for the time being, begun to produce the intended results by other means.

The mirror image: continuity masquerading as change

The types of skills that support the tactics outlined above have been practised by ruling parties in India from across the ideological spectrum. But the task of managing the politics of economic reform was (and is) considerably more difficult for those non-Congress governments, at the centre and in the states, which campaigned on an anti-liberalisation

[82] *Economic Times*, 7 December 1993. Bush India, to take one example, ceased operations and re-registered as a way of moving its workers on to contract status. *Economic Times*, 7 February 1994.
[83] See Mahesh Gavaskar, 'Labouring Over a Capital Task', *Humanscape*, May 1997, pp. 17–19.
[84] Interview, 7 September 1996, New Delhi. This was also the view of a senior executive of a major British multinational firm. Interview, 29 August 1996, New Delhi.

platform. They must effect new reforms while simultaneously undertaking efforts to undo some of the reforms introduced under Congress rule, or at least *appear* to be doing so. In this sense, they must cloak continuity (with earlier liberalising policies) in the garb of change (reverting to illiberal policies).

Policy decoys and political camouflage

One way that such governments reduce their vulnerability to charges of betrayal by their supporters is by pursuing 'decoy' policy measures which can be portrayed as evidence of their commitment to resisting reform. These help to make the overall thrust of policy reform more ambiguous. The cancellation of the Enron power project by Maharashtra's incoming Shiv Sena–BJP government in 1995 is a good example of a high-profile symbolic issue which arguably helped to distract attention from the many liberalising steps taken by its ministers.[85]

While such decoys are useful, some policies require additional political camouflage. In Maharashtra, one of the most controversial concerned land reform. The preceding Congress government under Sharad Pawar had pushed through an amendment to existing legislation to raise the ceiling on individual holdings, and relax norms on the transfer of agricultural land to corporations. While it is in no party's political interest to press too hard for the repeal of legislation prohibiting the sale of agricultural lands to corporations, the Shiv Sena–BJP government in Maharashtra nevertheless wanted to pursue this option. Again demonstrating the federal learning effect (outlined in Chapter 5), it stole a page from the playbook of its Congress counterpart in Madhya Pradesh, which had found creative ways of facilitating corporate farming without subjecting itself to the bruising political battle that would have accompanied an attempt to amend existing legislation. In June 1995, the Madhya Pradesh government, on an *ad hoc* basis, began awarding exemptions from the land-ceiling laws for contract farming and agro-development projects.[86] In the process it found a new role for a troubled public-sector firm, using the Madhya Pradesh State Agro-Industrial Corporation, which owns vast tracts of land, as a joint-venture partner for private-sector investors.

While continuing its public denunciations of the Pawar land-reform amendments, which had yet to become law because they were still awaiting the assent of the president of India, the Maharashtra government proceeded in the same way that Pawar had by acting quietly to circumvent the existing legislation. It even went a step further than Madhya

---

[85] When the project was subsequently reinstated, the Shiv Sena chief minister claimed to have negotiated a better deal for the state's consumers than had his Congress predecessor.

[86] *India Today*, 15 March 1996.

Pradesh's government by allowing individual company directors to buy plots within the land-ceiling limits. The plots were then sold to individual investors, such that no individual held more than the law allowed. Maxworth Orchards (India) Ltd. used this method for developing 15,000 acres of land. The land is owned by individuals, but managed by the company. Both states were thus able to skirt the spirit of the law, and avoid opening themselves up to damaging public debates over the propriety of corporate farming. 'Selling' the benefits of this type of reform to the rural electorate is not considered smart politics.[87]

Part of the skill in performing this delicate balancing act comes from choosing issues that can be portrayed as evidence of a commitment to economic nationalism, but that will not unduly constrain future policy choice. During the last year of the Narasimha Rao government the commerce and finance ministries studied the feasibility of introducing more stringent 'local content' regulations for manufactured products – rules which would require specific product sectors to contain a stipulated percentage of locally produced parts. One reason why this particular policy appealed to astute political managers was that it would have had little impact.[88] It was designed as window-dressing. In the automotive industry, the targeted sector, a marked move in the direction of increased local content was already being propelled by economic exigencies. The decline of the rupee's value against the dollar (down by more than 16 per cent between mid-1995 and early 1996) had inclined many joint ventures to increase the indigenous content of their assembled products as a way of reducing production costs. DCM Daewoo Motors Ltd., for instance, was pressing towards total in-house production. It hoped to have 90 per cent of its components (in value terms) produced locally by 1997–98.[89]

Such politically low-cost 'indigenisation' strategies were followed by both United Front and BJP economic strategists, allowing both governments to make good on their economic nationalist rhetoric without taking difficult decisions. This is in the tradition of the Narasimha Rao government, which preferred to introduce reform measures by stealth, rather than trumpet them loudly. In fact, it is the mirror image: the tactic is to accentuate fairly insignificant areas of governmental resistance to the neo-liberal agenda, even as market forces are heading inexorably in the same direction. It is wrapping the logical culmination of existing economic trends in the garb of deliberate policy change.

The objective of such manoeuvres is to find policy solutions with an optimal political cost–benefit ratio, which given the complexity of the

---

[87] Interview with a bureaucrat who previously held senior posts in state agricultural agencies, 12 September 1996, Bombay.

[88] This strategy was revealed in an interview with a former policy adviser to the Government of India, 5 September 1996, New Delhi.   [89] *Times of India*, 25 February 1996.

constraints facing India's reformers is not an easy task. Proponents of the local-content strategy, for instance, had to calculate whether the rupee's slow decline against other major currencies was likely to continue. They were swayed by the fact that gradual slippage suits increasingly powerful economic lobbies: a cheap rupee means that exporters will find their products easier to sell in foreign markets, while firms producing for the local market will find greater protection from competing imports, provided they are not too reliant on imported production inputs. Moreover, all of this can be done without antagonising the multilateral lending institutions, since it implies neither an explicit subsidy to exporters (a major drain on the budget in the pre-reform days), nor higher direct tariff barriers against foreign imports. These kinds of creative (and undeniably sly) solutions to the political difficulties associated with implementing economic liberalisation are a speciality of India's politicians.

The impure motivations of opposition politics

A decided lack of transparency was also integral to the means by which the Shiv Sena–BJP government in Maharashtra went about systematically undermining the sugar cooperative sector – a process discussed in Chapter 5 to illustrate the capacity of informal institutions to tame economic interests. In this case, the 'invisible methods' used to threaten them into supporting the government were said to have 'sent shivers down the spines of sugar barons'.[90] This refers primarily to a reversal of one of the means–ends relationships stressed in the first part of this chapter. Instead of using decidedly untransparent tactics of intimidation to threaten groups into supporting liberalisation, the Shiv Sena–BJP government has used the language of liberalisation to justify regulatory changes that it hopes will threaten a substantial segment of this Congress party bastion into joining its ranks. The key element in this still-unfolding plan is the government's standing threat to formalise a phenomenon that Sharad Pawar had merely, on occasion, turned a blind eye to – allowing sugarcane farmers to sell their cane to cooperatives other than those of which they are members. The government claims that such a move would be consistent with the notion of fostering a free market that would benefit farmers. It also, of course, knows that it would mean the death of many cooperatives.

The threat to implement this proposal is combined with clandestine offers of financial support,[91] as well as protection from various environ-

---

[90] *Indian Express*, 24 February 1996.
[91] Some of these inducements have borne fruit. The chairman and entire board of one sugar cooperative quit the Congress and joined the Shiv Sena in exchange for promises of financial support. *The Hindu*, 21 January 1996.

mental regulations and corruption investigations, for groups that lend backing to the ruling-party alliance. A prominent Congress MP from the sugar belt calls this strategy 'a classic carrot and stick approach. The [Shiv Sena–BJP] combine is trying to woo the belt with tickets [i.e. party nominations for local, state, and national elections], licences, seed capital and, of course, punitive action'.[92] The Shiv Sena–BJP government's hand is strengthened in pursuing this strategy by the lack of sympathy for the sugar sector among the Maharashtra electorate at large. Moreover, Congress indignation at the government's tactics rings hollow, especially when most people regard the Shiv Sena–BJP offers of favouritism as little more than an extension of what Congress state governments have done for decades. As for the intimidation, we have seen that Sharad Pawar played that game, as did one of his predecessors. As chief minister in the mid-1980s, S. B. Chavan, who did not emerge into politics through the sugar-cooperative route, attempted to counter his rivals in the party by clamping down on corruption and irregularities in cooperative elections. Because he operated from within the Congress Party, Chavan's efforts were fairly easily thwarted.[93]

The logic of democratic competition has unleashed a more capable enemy in the form of the Shiv Sena–BJP government. It has, moreover, been able to cloak its political intentions in the guise of promoting economic efficiency. While some of its other tactics would not find a place in a World Bank manual on good government, the Manohar Joshi administration's attack on one of the main strongholds of its political enemies is, as a secondary effect, helping to introduce a greater degree of market orientation. This is certainly true in the case of the cooperative banking sector in Maharashtra.[94] Jayaprakash Mundada, minister for cooperatives, cited market-friendly motivations, rather than political self-interest, for the government's decision to split the state's Congress-dominated cooperative banking system by creating a state-level urban cooperative bank free from the predations of the rural banks:

We have only tried to bring about some competition which is both necessary and healthy. It will help streamline the functioning of the MSCB [Maharashtra State Cooperative Bank]. After the urban co-operatives' apex bank began to function, the MSCB hiked its interest rates on deposits from 12 to 15 per cent.[95]

[92] *Indian Express*, 24 February 1996.
[93] B. S. Baviskar, 'Leadership, Democracy, and Development: Cooperatives in Kohlapur District', in B. S. Baviskar and Donald W. Attwood (eds.), *Finding the Middle Path: The Political Economy of Cooperation in Rural India* (Boulder, Colo.: Westview Press, 1995), pp. 157–75.
[94] Interview with Mayank Bhatt, special correspondent for *Business India*, 9 September 1996, Bombay.
[95] *Business India*, 23 September–6 October 1996, p. 132. See also *The Hindu*, 6 January and 24 February 1996.

Similar motivations underlie the Shiv Sena–BJP government's efforts to replace the Bombay Industrial Relations Act of 1948. The Maharashtra Harmonious Labour and Industrial Relations Bill is designed primarily to undermine the hegemony of the Congress-affiliated Rashtriya Mill Mazdoor Sangh in the textile industry, and to replace it with BJP and Shiv Sena unions.[96] Such spiteful attacks are a mainstay of the democratic process in advanced capitalist democracies, as the Conservative government's undermining of local-government autonomy in the United Kingdom during its eighteen years in power amply demonstrated. Indian democracy, by providing the means for parties ostensibly opposed to economic reform to take power and dismantle systems of state control which have benefited their political rivals, is further entrenching the principles of a market economy. The result in many instances are patronage networks, controlled by new patrons with different political affiliations. But the argument of this book is that democracies can uproot interest-group coalitions to promote change, *not* that market relations will characterise all aspects of economic life, or that new interests will not become entrenched in power.

Economic reform, identity politics, and political discontent

A political system's capacity to cope with issues which are not, strictly speaking, related to the politics of economic reform can nevertheless have a decisive impact on the political sustainability of adjustment programmes. A potent combination of economic dislocation and the assertion of identity politics, for instance, has the potential to disrupt political and economic life in any socially or ethnically heterogeneous state. As one commentator remarked, while 'China's super-charged economic growth and the spread of modern commercial communication and transportation links are widely supposed to be further integrating the country . . . this dynamism has the potential to fuel ethnic and linguistic divisions'.[97]

---

[96] *Indian Express*, 21 June 1996. The Shiv Sena–BJP government, like its Congress predecessor, has resolutely refused to announce a clear-cut policy on the selling of the valuable central-Bombay land owned by textile companies. As a result, a number of firms were permitted, without the announcement of any specific policy, to go into the property-development business themselves. As of April 1995, three major firms had taken this circuitous route, precisely because of 'the absence of a clear-cut policy' by the state government. *India Today*, 30 April 1995, p. 101. Many more had taken unauthorised, but unofficially tolerated, action by early 1996. An activist working on behalf of displaced textile workers stressed the clandestine nature of what is taking place: 'The mill area is being destroyed quietly and systematically . . . Crores [tens of millions] of rupees are passing hands in the land deals of Girangaon, most of it in the black'. *Frontline*, 26 January 1996, p. 94.
[97] D. C. Gladney, 'Unity vs. Diversity in China', *Asian Age*, 6 March 1995 (originally published in the *International Herald Tribune*).

As uneven capitalist development intensifies, the Chinese government's capacity to promote a 'unified multinational state' through official programmes aimed at fostering the economic development of its fifty-five 'minority nationalities' – those not from the majority Han group – has come under severe strain.[98] Moreover, the burgeoning of cultural identity among different subsections within the Han grouping, which accounts for 91 per cent of the population, has at least part of its roots in the growth of voluntary associations that have arisen alongside private-sector initiative.[99]

Arguably, the threat of an ethnic reawakening grafted on to regional disparities is as much a challenge to the sustainability of economic reform in China as is the government's inability to manage the details of sectoral reform in ways that solidify cohesion among party elites. By the same logic, the stalled reform programmes of Kenya and Nigeria might have much to do with the distractions of ethnic politics, and those undemocratic states' inability to manage the political predicaments associated with economic reform on top of it all. To consider the politics of economic reform in analytical isolation from the rest of political life – particularly the realm of identity politics – is to distort the nature of the dilemmas facing most adjusting countries.

A useful way to conceptualise the interaction between reform-related and identity-based politics is to assume that every government has its breaking point – as variable, uncertain, and self-defined as it may be. If this is true, then we cannot assume a clear division between reform-related strains and those stemming from other political pressures. This is not to say that the pressure emanating from different issues – such as economic reform and identity politics – can be plugged into a simple formula in which the reform-related stresses are added to identity-issue strains to arrive at a political-pressure quotient. In some cases, the salience of one type of issue diverts attention from the other. The destruction of a sixteenth-century mosque in December 1992 by Hindu nationalist extremists in the north Indian town of Ayodhya certainly stole some of the limelight from less dramatic reform-related events of that period, like changes to import-export regulations. But the 'distract-and-reform' process does not always unfold so neatly, and it is certainly not always a conscious strategy. Even the Ayodhya incident subsequently entered into the government's calculations of what new reform measures were poss-

[98] For an analysis of the shifting nature of regional inequality during different phases of the reform period, see Tianlun Jian, Jeffrey D. Sachs, and Andrew M. Warner, 'Trends in Regional Inequality in China', *Working Paper 5412* (Cambridge, Mass.: National Bureau of Economic Research, January 1996).

[99] Gordon White, 'Market Reforms and the Emergence of Civil Society in Post-Mao China', *IDS Working Paper*, no. 6 (Brighton: Institute of Development Studies, 1994).

ible. Referring to a failure to reduce the government's food-subsidy bill in
1993–94, the finance minister alluded to this issue:

There were extraordinary circumstances. Last year our country's energies had to
be devoted to the more important issues, which came in the wake of Ayodhya, to
see that this country's cohesion is not destroyed by the divisive forces which
suddenly appeared much stronger than they later turned out to be. If we had let a
cat loose among the pigeons in that atmosphere, it could have been misused by
our opponents to strengthen themselves. I think there were valid political reasons,
therefore, for raising procurement prices while a decision on issue prices was
deferred.[100]

What is necessary is to avoid overload of the type that would undermine a
government's willingness to gamble on its ability to contain the political
disruption that might accompany further reform. This, in turn, requires
an ability to assess when identity issues are additive (requiring a resort to
stealthy means), divertive (furnishing an opportunity for major new reforms), or potentially overlapping (making them susceptible to an attempt at integration).

Indeed, the substantive divide between identity politics and economic
reform is not always so great. The identification of many caste groups
with traditional occupations provides a potent focal point for projecting
resistance to reform. This is true among small traders, who often use caste
associations to organise lobbying efforts and general strikes to protest
against increases in sales tax. The large percentage of landless labourers
who come from the 'scheduled', or ex-untouchable, castes is another
example of the power of social identity to infect the political struggles that
emanate from changes in economic policy. As one analyst of the political
fallout of the 1994–95 budget observed, '[p]olitical workers realise that it
will be easier to convince a Harijan [scheduled caste] or a tribal about his
own economic disabilities as a [low-caste] *chamar* rather than as an
agricultural worker'.[101] Since Indian politicians generally conceive of
electorates as mosaics of caste and community 'vote banks', this linkage
between social and economic identity is a source of much worry.

An example of how these factors affect the political management of
economic reform is the issue of 'reservations' in government employment
for members of 'backward castes'. There is great concern among political
representatives from these communities that the shrinkage of the state
associated with liberalisation will marginalise reservation policy as a tool
of political mobilisation. Some even suspect that one of the motivations
behind the privatisation of the economy is the desire among more privi-

[100] *Business World*, 9–22 March 1994, p. 39.
[101] P. Raman, 'Political Fallout of the Budget', *Business Standard*, 7 March 1994.

leged castes to remove decision-making from the public 'political' realm at precisely the moment when backward castes have begun to assume unprecedented state power.[102] In the two years prior to the initiation of the current programme of economic reform in 1991, India's two most populous states, Uttar Pradesh and Bihar, elected governments headed by backward caste chief ministers heading explicitly backward-caste-oriented parties.[103] In 1990 and 1991, the country had witnessed a serious backlash from upper-caste activists against the V. P. Singh government's attempts to broaden the scope of reservations for lower castes, the first substantial attempt to make this an issue of national scope.

Because of this deep suspicion among backward-caste political leaders, Indian reformers have been forced to guard against the possibility that 'reservation agitations' will be transformed into emotionally charged political movements against economic reform. Finance minister Manmohan Singh told the annual session of the Confederation of Indian Industry that the process of reforms could be affected by the apprehension of the scheduled castes and tribes that their opportunities will shrink as the role of the public sector diminishes, stating that '[i]f this thought acquires momentum, it will hurt the process of reforms'.[104]

This possibility must be treated with particular care in the state of Karnataka, where reservations in government employment were introduced early this century and have proven an explosive issue on many occasions in subsequent years. Former Karnataka chief minister H. D. Deve Gowda demonstrated his sensitivity to this challenge shortly after taking power in the state assembly elections of late 1994. His method for doing so represented a carefully calibrated strategy to defuse the potential for destructive protest without in the process causing greater harm.

Deve Gowda's government announced a policy whereby half of new positions in the *private* sector were required to be filled by persons residing in the state for at least the preceding fifteen years.[105] After initial consternation that this requirement would deter new investors from coming to Karnataka and impinge on the productivity of firms already operating in the state, it became clear that the policy contained enough

---

[102] A variation on this theme is the statement by Bihar chief minister Laloo Prasad Yadav, a major political leader of the backward castes: 'Brahminism in this country has been conspiring with US imperialism in implementing the Dunkel [GATT] proposals and reducing the backward classes to slaves'. *Sunday*, 13–19 March 1994, p. 7.

[103] Mulayam Singh Yadav became the chief minister of Uttar Pradesh in 1989, and Laloo Prasad Yadav took power in Bihar in 1990. After a period of BJP rule from 1991–92, and a subsequent year of centrally imposed president's rule, Mulayam regained power in December 1993, only to lose it again in 1995. In Bihar, Laloo Prasad Yadav's government served its full five-year term, and was re-elected in 1995.

[104] *Economic Times*, 20 April 1994.

[105] In lower-level jobs the percentage would be even higher. *The Hindu*, 21 April 1995.

loopholes to impose only minimal constraints on the operation of business activity. Deve Gowda was able to soothe the concerns of outside investors with projects in the pipeline, while doing nothing to disabuse in-state business leaders of the notion that their intimate knowledge of the state bureaucracy would give them an advantage in exploiting the policy's loopholes, and that the new requirements might impose barriers to entry for potential competitors considering investing in the state.

Deve Gowda displayed impressive skills of political management, notable for their reliance on ambiguity and obfuscation. He succeeded in taking pre-emptive action on an identity-based issue of great significance in the local political culture which threatened to take on a reform-related dimension. He did so by transforming its basis of identity from caste to region, in the process playing on an emotive substratum of political consciousness surrounding the state's perceived exploitation by the wielders of national power in New Delhi. This appeal to regional pride – in the form of 'sons of the soil' rhetoric – is very important, as a great deal of the anti-liberalisation sentiment has been cast in terms of its 'imposition' on the states from New Delhi. Before taking power in New Delhi in 1996, Deve Gowda's party was one of the loudest voices among those arousing this sentiment. Having embraced large portions of the liberalisation programme after taking power in Karnataka in 1994, he was at pains to immunise himself against charges of complicity with an agenda formulated in New Delhi. To the extent that his private-sector reservation policy also contained loopholes to render it ineffective, its politically effective promulgation represents a skill which is the reverse of the one outlined in the first part of this chapter – the capacity to cloak change within the appearance of continuity. Deve Gowda's reservation policy is continuity masquerading as defiant change.

Appealing to a shared sense of regional identity in order to justify politically difficult policy reversals has proved to be an effective tactic in other states as well. Rajasthan chief minister Bhairon Singh Shekhawat couches his government's embrace of market-oriented policies in terms of defending the state's people from nefarious forces outside the borders of Rajasthan. The New Mineral Policy of 1994, for instance, was required because 'the centre had left the states to fend for themselves'.[106] In addition, the Government of India's failure during the years of central planning to help set up industries in Rajasthan had made it an unattractive prospect for private investors as well. As a result, Rajasthan's 'indigenous entrepreneurs', the Marwari community, members of which head some of India's best known industrial houses, were forced to leave

[106] *The Hindu*, 17 August 1994.

their 'homeland'. This has undermined the 'integrity and self-reliance of Rajasthan's culture', according to Shekhawat. Helping them to 'come home to Rajasthan' was how Shekhawat described his efforts at liberalisation. This, he argued, was just one part of his larger effort to rebuild the people's pride in Rajasthan.[107] To understand the associations of regional pride in Rajasthan's current political climate one must take account of the Rajasthan BJP's strategy of mobilising religious identity around a regionalised form of Hindu nationalism, one which holds a special place for Rajasthan in the national Hindu reawakening and tends to emphasise the political dominance of the Rajput caste.[108] Regionalism, Rajput revivalism, and Hindu nationalism have become very closely intertwined. In such a climate, efforts to justify support for liberal economic reform with claims of restoring Rajasthani pride and the integrity of its indigenous culture – an appeal to regional identity – tap into a stream of associations that includes issues of religion- and caste-based mobilisation. It deflects political criticism by, in Nandy's terms, 'showing dissent to be a part of orthodoxy'.

Even when promoting liberal economic policies that are little different from those promoted by his Congress opponents, Chief Minister Laloo Prasad Yadav of Bihar claimed to be ushering in a revolution in the relationship between Biharis and the outside world. Laloo used the occasion of the inauguration ceremony for a new private-sector cement plant to demand that the central government abolish the Mines and Minerals Regulation Act, the foundation of state control in the mining sector. The act vests most powers with the central government. Stating that the operation of the act deprived Bihar's exchequer of Rs. 3 billion in royalty and cess revenues annually, Laloo justified his demand for deregulation with a rousing defence of the Bihari peoples' honour: 'When I hear that Bihar is rich, but the Biharis are poor, I feel insulted. It is because of racketeering by a few powerful people at the centre that Bihar is being deprived of its own resources'.[109] His strong leadership was going to reverse centuries of humiliation and return Bihar to its former glory, Laloo thundered at public meetings across the state.[110]

---

[107] Interview with Bhairon Singh Shekhawat, 20 April 1994, Jaipur.
[108] This idea has been developed in greater depth in Rob Jenkins, 'Rajput Hindutva: Caste Politics, Regional Identity, and Hindu Nationalism in Contemporary Rajasthan', in Christophe Jaffrelot and Thomas Blom Hansen (eds.), *The BJP and the Compulsions of Politics in India* (Delhi: Oxford University Press, 1998).
[109] *Times of India*, 31 March 1994.
[110] See *The Telegraph* (Calcutta), 25 March 1994. Laloo peddled a more business-friendly version of the strong-leadership line when he told a 1,000-strong gathering organised by the CII in April 1995: 'You tell me when and where in Bihar you want to invest. The decision will be taken in a day. Bihar has a single-window system as I have kept all the portfolios with myself'. *Times of India*, 27 April 1995.

Laloo has used different forms of identity politics to soften the edges of other economic issues. One mechanism which has proved fruitful with respect to labour issues is to subsume them within the identity-based political dynamics at the state level, thereby diluting the potency of organised labour as an interest group. This sometimes involves appealing to social identities that have come to occupy important positions in the mobilisation strategies of state-level political parties. In early 1994, for instance, junior doctors of the medical services in the state of Bihar went on strike demanding higher pay and guaranteed employment for all medical graduates. The Bihar chief minister responded by invoking the weapon of caste-based quotas, a major feature of political life in most Indian states, but particularly rampant in Bihar. He announced that of the 644 vacancies in the medical services, 333 would be filled by members of the 'backward castes'. This served to sow discord between high- and low-caste members of the Bihar Junior Doctors Association, effectively ending the strike.[111]

This was not an isolated incident. The rise of caste-based unions was lamented by none other than the president of the Communist Party of India-affiliated All-India Trade Union Congress (AITUC), who called this one of the most important trends preventing an effective trade-union response to liberalisation. Moreover, this trend is most evident at the state level, where caste identity is strongest and most clearly articulated. The AITUC president cited as an example the Brahman Employees' Welfare Associations, which have sprung up in a majority of public sector enterprises in Karnataka.[112] Divisions based on religious identity, particularly between Hindus and Muslims, are also rampant within trade unions, providing yet another opportunity for reforming governments to undermine trade-union unity.[113] Similar afflictions have long thwarted coor-

[111] Similar tactics were reportedly used in Haryana by chief minister Bhajan Lal to end a strike among government employees. *The Hindu*, 19 December 1993. Rajasthan's Shekhawat is also well known for 'playing the Rajput card' in his dealings with potentially hostile public employees' unions. Interview with two office-bearers of a public employees' union, 10 November 1993, Jaipur.

[112] See the editorial by M. S. Krishnan, AITUC president, in the official CPI journal, *New Age*, March 1994.

[113] The communalisation of trade unions was commented on by a leader of a national trade union federation in Karnataka. Interview, 23 March 1994, Bangalore. It has also been demonstrated by survey data on Bombay factories in a study entitled *Communalism and Industrial Workers* (Bombay: Centre for the Study of Society and Secularism, 1994). See also Kiran Saxena, 'The Hindu Trade Union Movement in India: The Bharatiya Mazdoor Sangh', *Asian Survey*, vol. 33, no. 7 (July 1993), pp. 685–96. Even Bombay-based communist trade-union organisers such as Vivek Monteiro consider 'the communal virus' a major obstacle to coordinated labour opposition. Monteiro claims that all parties are engaged in manipulating religious identities in order to divide labour organisations. Interview, 31 March 1994, Bombay. See also 'Religious Divide', *Business World*, 10–23 February 1993, p. 103. Some commentators argue that 'the consumerist

dinated action among rural interests. Ashutosh Varshney has argued that the failure of democracy to prevent urban-biased development policies in predominantly rural India stems from the social divisions in society based on caste, religion, and language.[114] It is worth pointing out, however, that it is at the state level that such tactics are most likely to work.[115]

Pushing through reform measures involves a broad range of underhanded tactics, only a small sampling of which have been outlined in this chapter. It is important to emphasise that many of these would not be out of place in a western democracy. For instance, in April 1995, in an effort to rally votes to defeat an opposition-sponsored budget-related motion, which would have amounted to a vote of no confidence, Congress Party managers reminded first-time MPs who might be flirting with dissidence that they would lose their pensions if the government failed to complete four years in office.[116] The variations on this theme are almost endless. In the same month, it was revealed that, 'in a notable instance of lack of transparency', the Foreign Investment Promotion Board (FIPB) allowed Indian firms to circumvent a law which prevents royalty payments to multinational firms by permitting them to pay American and British wholly-owned subsidiaries what it termed an 'R&D access fee'.[117] The FIPB also signed agreements with two American firms for the extraction of methane gas from coal beds, though the government had not previously published guidelines or announced its intention to attract foreign investment in this sector.[118] In April 1994, representatives of service industries were outraged by the finance minister's authorisation of an unpublicised circular by the Central Board of Direct Taxes which brought them into the tax net for the first time. When contacted by reporters for comments on this 'quiet' move, many service industry companies had not even heard of the circular. Those that had were amazed at the flouting of 'recognized norms of consultation', particularly as they had been involved in the pre- and post-budget discussions with the finance minister (one of the informal institutions mentioned

---

ethos that accompanied [liberalisation] . . . created, in fact, new spaces into which communal discourse inserted itself'. Arvind Rajagopal, 'Ram Janmabhoomi, Consumer Identity and Image-Based Politics', *Economic and Political Weekly*, 2 July 1994, p. 1659.

[114] Ashutosh Varshney, 'Self-Limited Empowerment: Democracy, Economic Development and Rural India', *Journal of Development Studies*, vol. 29, no. 4 (July 1993), pp. 177–215.

[115] This is because, as Rathin Roy has argued, even during the pre-reform era states served as 'the political conflict-resolution mechanism that attempted to resolve the demands of federal public policy with far more *primordial* regional and local demands'. Rathin Roy, 'State Intervention, Interest Groups and the Politics of Fiscal Policy', *Discussion Paper No. 36*, Institute for Development Policy and Management, University of Manchester (1994), p. 33 (emphasis added).   [116] *The Telegraph* (Calcutta), 25 April 1995.

[117] *Financial Express*, 27 April 1995.   [118] *Indian Express*, 27 April 1995.

in Chapter 5). As one executive put it:

It is, therefore, hard to believe that the government would bring service contracts within the tax net through the backdoor. In the first place, if at all it was to be introduced, the finance minister should have done it through the Finance Bill and not through a circular.[119]

Hard to believe, that is, unless one has had a chance to step back and discern the pattern of obfuscation and manipulation which has characterised the implementation of reform over nearly eight years in India.

Most studies of democratic governance capacity, especially those preoccupied with the contrasts between new democracies and their authoritarian predecessors, fail to recognise the vital importance of these types of tactics in allowing adjustment to become politically 'consolidated'. The architects of the good-government agenda have instead advanced a vague, sanitised, and ultimately unconvincing version of how transparency (implicitly equated with formal democracy) will assist reformers by facilitating the 'selling' of reform to a vibrant, well-organised civil society. The sort of manipulative and obfuscatory tactics employed regularly in the implementation of reform, however, are a much truer representation of the political reality in India. Above all, they are an integral part of the democratic political process wherever liberal democracy is practised successfully, whether in the developed or developing world.

[119] *Economic Times*, 15 April 1994.

7   Implications

Rather than recapitulate the entire book in miniature, this chapter probes some of the unexplored implications of its main arguments. The aim is to identify additional questions arising from the explanation offered for why India has been able to sustain policy reform in the face of the political obstacles imposed by its democratic framework. This, it is hoped, may highlight some of the ways in which the findings of this study might inform future research. The first section considers the implications of this book's interpretation of the Indian case for the logic which underpins the good-government agenda. Particular emphasis is laid upon the shortcomings of what is currently the linchpin of this agenda – namely, the attempt of aid agencies to foster the emergence of 'civil society' in developing countries. The second section asks whether the means by which economic reform has been made politically sustainable in India may present problems for the implementation of future reforms, and for the health of democracy itself. The focus is on the extent to which the use of underhanded tactics during this first phase of reform may have seriously depleted India's institutional capital.

Before turning to these concerns, however, we must stress what this book is *not* arguing. The previous three chapters have attempted to demonstrate the crucial contribution of three features of India's democratic political system to making economic reform politically sustainable. Each has played a role in enabling change to take place, either by testing the boundaries of the possible or by altering perceptions among individuals and groups. Despite the neat categorisation furnished to contain and structure the evidence, emphasis has been laid upon the unpredictability of change in India. The political actors are engaged more in an ongoing improvisation than a scripted piece of theatre. Audience participation – in the form of elections, agitations, perceived currents of public opinion – provides cues for the next act. A few lines of stage direction can be culled from India's rich political tradition. But nothing inherent in the structure of India's polity, society, or economy determined the outcome, nor will any such 'law of history' do so in the future. Democracy has provided the space and tools for actors to seize fleeting opportunities. That it has done this at all is significant. That it has done so in ways that challenge quaint conceptions of how democracy works should provide a source of reflection for those who believe that the operation of such a complex organism can be managed, much less created, by means of official development assistance. Democracy's impact on governance capacity is ambiguous. After all, it also proved amenable to the creation of the highly regulated, import-substituting, state-dominated economy that economic reform was intended to supplant.

We must also resist the temptation to generalise from the specific. Two caveats are paramount in this connection. First, no single-country study can support generalisations about the relative change-promoting capacities of democratic or authoritarian forms of government. What this study has argued is that democracy *per se* need not be viewed as an impediment to large-scale shifts in policy direction simply because it must contend with avaricious politicians, demanding electorates, and rent-seeking interest groups. The opportunism of politicians allows them to find new resources for sustaining their political careers, and the skills on which democracies place a premium provide them the means with which to manipulate a complex set of interlocking institutions. Electorates act as a check on this process, providing early-warning signals against the more extreme forms of liberalisation that can make it unsustainable for any government, not just a democratic one. Rent-seeking interests are an intrinsic part of a free, pluralistic society, but when given the space to craft alternatives, they favour limited battles rather than total war in pursuing their objectives, which are in any case continually open to reinterpretation. All of these actors operate within institutions that lengthen time horizons, which helps to avoid the intransigence that characterises winner-take-all systems.

Second, just as we cannot make firm statements about the relative capacity of democracies *vis-à-vis* authoritarian political systems, neither can we infer sweeping generalisations about democracy itself. India's is just one form of democracy, embedded in a specific cultural context.[1] The strongest statement we can make is that a well-institutionalised democracy[2] is a flexible instrument, which works best when wedded to

---

[1] See Judith M. Brown, *Modern India: The Origins of an Asian Democracy* (Delhi: Oxford University Press, 1985); Bikhu Parekh, 'The Cultural Particularity of Liberal Democracy', *Political Studies*, vol. 40, Special Issue (1992), pp. 160–75 (especially pp. 171–2); Sudipta Kaviraj, 'Dilemmas of Democratic Development in India', in Adrian Leftwich (ed.), *Democracy and Development: Theory and Practice* (Cambridge: Polity Press, 1996), pp. 114–38; and David Held (ed.), *Prospects for Democracy: North, South, East, West* (Cambridge: Polity Press, 1993).

[2] Precedent for citing both formal and informal entities as indicators of India's institutional

indigenous forms of social organisation, and that on this basis the arguments advanced concerning the Indian case could be expanded to suit other democracies as well, subject to local variations. But even this highly qualified assertion must contend with untidy historical contingencies. The emergence of liberal democracy in India was a slow, painstaking process, linked to a unique struggle for national identity and sovereignty. The gradual process by which Indians took control of state power – as a result of reforms enacted during the Raj – provided an incubation period found in few other nations. It allowed a political organisation of the complexity that characterised the Indian National Congress at its zenith to mature under conditions which inculcated a taste for compromise, negotiation, deliberation, and continuous mobilisation in support of political action. Congress during the pre-independence phase proved itself capable of both aggregating diverse interests and defining intricate national goals beyond simply self-rule. Perhaps the closest parallel is the African National Congress, which under the leadership of Nelson Mandela, a figure of Nehru's stature, has been able to negotiate a moderate path towards democratic rule in which accommodation is the dominant theme. The African National Congress also faced a protracted period of struggle, in the process forging an inclusive political organisation capable of containing great social diversity and ideological friction.

Economic reform, civil society, and good government

The profound influence of historical contingency – a variant of which can be found in the concern of some forms of institutional analysis with 'path-dependence'[3] – must also temper the enthusiasm which democratic India's thus-far successful reorientation of development strategy may raise among aid agencies.[4] Any attempt to derive lessons from the Indian experience in order to replicate its success must recognise that the three key assets of India's political system which have aided the sustainability of adjustment – political incentives, institutions, and skills – are the product

health can be found in Samuel Huntington's assessment of Indian democracy twenty years after independence. Huntington's focus was on the Indian bureaucracy and the Congress Party: 'So long as these two organizations maintained their institutional strength, it was ridiculous to think of India as politically underdeveloped no matter how low its per capita income or how high its illiteracy rate'. Samuel P. Huntington, *Political Order in Changing Societies* (New Haven, Conn.: Yale University Press, 1968), pp. 84–5.

[3] See, for instance, David Collier and Ruth Collier, *Shaping the Political Arena* (Princeton: Princeton University Press, 1991); and Margaret Weir and Theda Skocpol, 'State Structures and the Possibilities for "Keynesian" Responses to the Great Depression in Sweden, Britain and the United States', in Peter B. Evans *et al.* (eds.), *Bringing the State Back In* (Cambridge: Cambridge University Press, 1985), pp. 107–63.

[4] In private discussions with the author, some officials of the UK's Overseas Development Administration voiced great enthusiasm for what they consider replicable 'lessons' from the Indian experience.

of half a century of constitutional democracy. Unfortunately, there is no way to ensure that newly democratising countries will be capable of constructing and nurturing the complex state–society linkages that underlay these assets. Guillermo O'Donnell, among others, stresses the difficulty of building institutions capable of overcoming the tendency for political conflict in democracies to devolve into prisoner's dilemmas:

> The best-known invention for such achievement is the strengthening of social and political institutions. But under the conditions I have depicted [in Latin America] this is indeed a most difficult task. In the contemporary world, the joyful celebration of the advent of democracy must be complemented with the sober recognition of the immense (and, indeed, historically unusual) difficulties its institutionalization and its rooting in society must face.[5]

Indeed, there are contingencies within contingencies. Arguably, the consolidation of Indian democracy itself rested upon the creation of a pool of state spoils for which established and emergent groups could contend, using the means the new political system placed at their disposal.[6] In other words, we are faced with a historical paradox that limits the ability to replicate the virtues of the Indian political system: a highly *dirigiste* policy regime may have been required to nurture the democratic institutions capable, ultimately, of dismantling it without fatally undermining either the reform effort or democracy itself. If this is substantially true, then the role of historically contingent processes is ignored by proponents of good government at their own peril.[7] The Indian experience should serve to temper the optimism among donors about the prospects for an ill-defined 'civil society' to serve as the foundation for newly constituted democracies in Africa and Latin America. The reasons for the durability of Indian democracy are more complex, as are the reasons why its evolving form of democratic politics has been able to foster and adapt to policy change. As Richard Jeffries has argued,

> the tendency of some Africanist scholars to wax optimistic about a new era of hand-in-hand economic and political liberalisation, both supported by a reflowering of civil society . . . is wishful thinking on a par with 1960s modernisation and 'political development' theory.[8]

His conclusion is that '[t]here seems little reason to doubt that economic

[5] Guillermo O'Donnell, 'On the State, Democratization and Some Conceptual Problems: A Latin American View with Glances at Some Postcommunist Countries', *World Development*, vol. 21, no. 8 (1993), p. 1376.

[6] See James Manor, 'How and Why Liberal and Representative Politics Emerged in India', *Political Studies*, vol. 38, no. 1 (March 1990).

[7] This point is made in greater detail in Section 4 of Robert Jenkins, 'Liberal Democracy and the Political Management of Structural Adjustment: Conceptual Tensions in the Good Government Agenda', *IDS Bulletin*, vol. 26, no. 2 (April 1995), pp. 37–48.

[8] Richard Jeffries, 'The State, Structural Adjustment and Good Government in Africa', *Journal of Commonwealth and Comparative Politics*, vol. 31, no. 1 (March 1993), p. 20.

and political development in African states . . . will have to go through something like the same historical stages' seen in the case of the East Asian NICs.[9] The Indian case demonstrates that, in Asia at least, an alternative path exists. Nevertheless, it does not negate Jeffries' underlying criticisms of the good-government agenda: that outcomes are historically contingent; that the processes involved cannot readily be speeded up; and that attempts to apply the lessons of political and economic systems across space and time are usually misguided.

The difficulty of replicating historical sequences is one reason why aid agencies have in recent years begun to dig deeper in their search for the underlying mechanisms which underpin democracy, and which might link democracy with positive developmental performance. In the process they have retreated further from political reality. Foreign aid programmes have identified civil society as the key ingredient in promoting 'democratic development'. The United States Agency for International Development (USAID) has developed perhaps the most fully elaborated statement of the logic underlying this hope. It runs roughly as follows. Development requires sound policies and impartial implementation. These can only be delivered by governments that are held accountable for their actions. Accountability, in turn, depends upon the existence of 'autonomous centers of social and economic power'[10] that can act as watchdogs over the activities of politicians and government officials. Civil society consists of both the associations that make up these 'centers' and the 'enabling environment' that permits them to operate freely. It is an arena of public space as well as a set of private actors. By funding organised groups within developing countries, aid agencies seek to create a virtuous cycle in which rights to free association beget sound government policies, human development, and (ultimately) a more conducive environment for the protection of individual liberties.

From the standpoint of the role into which civil society has been cast in promoting this equilibrium, there are several problems with this model.[11] The most serious shortcoming is that aid agencies expect too much of civil society. In order to justify its reliance on civil society for so many different missions, USAID, to take the most prominent example, has assigned a *range* of meanings to the term. Each use is, in effect, context-

[9] Ibid., p. 30.

[10] USAID, Center for Development Information and Evaluation, 'Constituencies for Reform: Strategic Approaches for Donor-Supported Civic Advocacy Programs', *Program and Operations Assessment Report No. 12*, February 1996, p. viii.

[11] These problems are addressed in greater detail in Rob Jenkins, 'Mistaking Governance for Politics: Foreign Aid, Democracy and the Construction of Civil Society', in Sudipta Kaviraj and Sunil Khilnani (eds.), *Civil Society: History and Possibilities* (Cambridge: Cambridge University Press, forthcoming).

dependent – that is, the definition of civil society changes, depending on which goal is under discussion. There is nothing inherently wrong in this, since civil society is in fact an ever-changing phenomenon. The problem arises when efforts are undertaken to operationalise these varying conceptions by building (or 'fostering', or 'supporting', or 'nurturing') civil society through the application of foreign aid. The main difficulty is that the definitions used are incapable of producing the three-part sequence towards which civil-society funding is aimed: (1) transitions to competitive politics; (2) the 'consolidation' of fledgling democracies; and (3) the establishment of market-oriented economic policies, and subsequently positive developmental performance.

To put it slightly differently, in order to make the case for civil society's pivotal role in achieving any one of the three objectives, the concept is defined in ways that preclude it from contributing to the other two. This disjunction is remedied by specifying, when referring to the other two objectives, alternative definitions of civil society that render its ability to achieve them more plausible. Since the three objectives are meant to reinforce one another in a virtuous cycle, the aid-agency conception of civil society is fatally flawed. Their instrumental usage of the term cannot contain these multiple meanings. To understand why this is the case, we must pay particular attention to the ways in which dynamics within one process can have 'spillover effects' for the other two. Despite its pronouncements on the need for careful sequencing, USAID's policy, *in effect*, pretends that the three objectives operate in isolation – and therefore that civil society can be represented differently in each case.

Consider, for instance, just one aspect of the transition from a 'movement for democratisation' to 'democratic consolidation' – that is, from 'phase one' to 'phase two'. For the purpose of dislodging an authoritarian regime, USAID is willing to stretch its definition of civil society to include virtually any mass organisation that can bring pressure to bear on the offending government. This even encompasses 'first-tier associations' – that is, those of 'a more ascriptive nature (kin, clan, ethnic, or religious)'.[12] When discussing the later task of consolidating democracy, however, these groups are nowhere to be found in USAID's vision of civil society. They have been surreptitiously erased from the 'strategic logic' which informs their funding of 'Civic Advocacy Organizations'.[13]

But political reality works rather differently. Such mass movements have a tendency to live on beyond the transition phase. As mobilisers of identities which cut across sectoral interests, their actions continue to affect the organisations contained within the more restrictive (phase two)

---

[12] USAID, 'Constituencies for Reform', p. 2.   [13] Ibid., pp. 5–11.

definition of civil society. These organisations need to be integrated into the matrix of competitive politics – as they have been in India[14] – rather than cast as obstacles on the road to modernity and good governance. While this book has not offered a full explanation for how this can take place within the context of a transition to a market-oriented development strategy, it has highlighted the importance of such concerns, as well as the failure of both aid agencies and rational-choice political economists to accord them the importance they deserve. It also provides some insights that may be of use to future research which addresses this issue directly, especially concerning the purposes which a blurring of the boundaries between formal and informal institutions can serve.

While the issues which arise in the transition from democratisation to democratic consolidation are important, it is the interaction between democratic consolidation and market orientation (phase two and phase three), and how these are treated by aid-agency conceptions of civil society, that are more directly relevant to the arguments advanced in this book. At the root of the tortured attempts of development practitioners to equate civil society with all that is wholesome in political life – citizen involvement, public-interest advocacy, self-help – is a preoccupation with promoting good governance. This is understandable, even admirable. In practice, however, it turns out to be something of a mirage. The problem is with how the conception of good governance is formulated – in particular, the explicit bias towards neo-liberal economic orthodoxy. Market-centred policies, it is everywhere implied, are 'sound', while those that deviate from this logic undermine both efficiency and welfare.[15]

The concept of good governance, in short, has transcended democracy. It no longer refers simply to authority which is accountable. It denotes the taking of actions consonant with sound policy, which, in turn, is con-

---

[14] The classic account of how caste identities have adapted to democratic politics in India is Lloyd I. Rudolph and Susanne Hoeber Rudolph, *The Modernity of Tradition* (Chicago: University of Chicago Press, 1967).

[15] The most zealous expositions of this view are to be found in World Bank publications. See *Sub-Saharan Africa: From Crisis to Sustainable Growth* (Washington, DC: The World Bank, 1989); *Governance and Development* (Washington, DC: The World Bank, 1992); and *Governance: The World Bank's Experience* (Washington, DC: The World Bank, 1994). For more detailed statements, see the publications of the World Bank's Senior Policy Adviser in the Africa Region's Technical Department (written in his 'personal capacity' and therefore expressing views that 'should not be taken as reflecting those of the World Bank'): Pierre Landell-Mills, 'Governance, Civil Society and Empowerment in Sub-Saharan Africa', paper prepared for the Annual Conference of the Society for the Advancement of Socio-Economics, 1992; P. Landell-Mills and I. Serageldin, 'Governance and the External Factor', *Proceedings of the World Bank Conference on Development Economics* (Washington, DC: The World Bank, 1991); and P. Landell-Mills and I. Serageldin, 'Governance and the Development Process', *Finance and Development*, vol. 29 (1991), pp. 14–17.

strued as market-oriented economics. This raises a fundamental dilemma for the efforts of USAID and other donors to promote civil society as the basis for ensuring good governance: many of the associations which inspired the original faith in the power of civil society to act as a check on state power arose in *opposition* to the imposition of market-oriented policies by authoritarian regimes. They were formed to bury neo-liberal economics, not to praise it. Were subsequently installed democratic governments to be swayed by such voices they would, by definition, be providing *accountable* governance but not *good* governance. This is an anomaly that further undermines the credibility of the aid agencies' conception of civil society. The assumption that nascent grassroots associations will support market-oriented economic policy is rooted in the type of democracy that aid agencies envisage – that is, 'democratic capitalism'.[16] If a government fails to embrace liberal economics, then it is not seen to be operating within the context of liberal politics. The adoption of neo-liberal policies thus becomes the *sine qua non* of civil society's existence.

On a more basic level, what USAID and other donor agencies fail to recognise (or at least openly to acknowledge in their policy statements) is that free-market economics removes many decisions from the purview of not only the state, but also the political community, democratically constituted or otherwise. In their zeal to see dominant social groups stripped of their power to subvert public institutions for private gain, they simultaneously disempower subordinate social groups: the associations that come closest to the ideal of citizen involvement will find the political basis for pursuing even mildly radical redistributive projects undermined. The most important reason why this fallacy has remained relatively unchallenged is the ability of aid agencies to point to the adoption of market-oriented economic reform in democratic countries. Thus the case of India, which is not only democratic but also possessed of a vibrant civil society, has thus become a powerful weapon in the rhetorical arsenal of donor agencies. It would be a shame for a misreading of this book to contribute to such a project.

As discussed in Chapter 2, the expectation among many commentators at the outset of India's reform programme was that powerful economic interests (threatened by the potential withdrawal of their perquisites) would join forces with advocates of the poor (who feared that reform

[16] One internal assessment, referring to USAID's support of business associations, argues that '[i]n civil society terms, such assistance could be called a "democratic capitalism" strategy'. USAID, Center for Development Information and Evaluation, 'Civil Society and Democratic Development in Bangladesh: A CDIE Assessment', *USAID Working Paper No. 212*, August 1994, p. 29.

would not come with a 'human face') to thwart efforts to restructure the Indian economy. Because this has not happened – not yet, at least – the Indian case would seem to support the aid-agency view that governments of countries in which civil society is clearly free enough to hold them to account are nevertheless willing and able to provide good governance (in the form of neo-liberal economic prescriptions). The Indian experience, in this reading, helps to maintain the equation between good governance, accountability, market economics, and civil society.

The details of the Indian case, as we have seen, reveal a more complicated picture – one which by no means justifies such facile assumptions concerning how civil society is best conceptualised. One of the main reasons why the Indian reform programme has been able to overcome the political forces arrayed against it is the existence of functional subnational political arenas. The logic of economic reform brought many more decisions about economic life to the state level. Politicians heading state-level governments – representing parties of the left, right, and centre – pursued liberal policy reforms of varying intensities. These leaders were free to indulge in such activities because the main electoral preoccupation of politicians operating at the state level is with courting the support of organisations engaged in the mobilisation of politicised social identities, based on affiliations of caste, sub-caste, religion, language, sect, and tribe. 'Modern', functionally defined sectoral interest groups, which under other circumstances might have had more success with their efforts to undermine reform, found themselves subsumed within the matrix of local, primordial politics – an arena and idiom in which they were relatively less powerful. Thus, in this instance, it was the existence of a particular form of civil society – one in which primordial politics was as organised, competitive, and linked to party politics as were the more conventional functional associations – that allowed the state to avoid 'capture' by powerful interests opposed to the introduction of policies deemed synonymous with good governance. Fixated on promoting the emergence of modern solidarities – in fact, pursuing a thinly veiled modernisation agenda by other means[17] – aid agencies' conceptions of civil society do not allow for the practical utility of such hybrid forms of democratic politics, *even when these are instrumental in effecting their preferred outcomes.* Conceiving of politicised identities as an integral part of democratic civil society undermines too many assumptions about the meaning of modernity.

Another of the reasons why the Indian government was able to succeed in introducing market-oriented reforms also flies in the face of USAID's strategy for promoting civil society. The extent to which trade union

---

[17] See David Williams and Tom Young, 'Governance, the World Bank and Liberal Theory', *Political Studies*, vol. 42 (1994), pp. 84–100.

organisations were integrated into the networks of influence constructed around individual leaders within political parties helped to defuse the resistance of organised labour to a number of important reform measures. While, as with other reforms, the Indian government did not take as bold a stance on labour issues as some neo-liberal advocates might have wished, it did (as we saw in Chapters 5 and 6) take a number of actions that were previously considered unthinkable given the extent of trade-union power. It was not only the Congress Party, but also centre-left and communist parties ruling at the state level, that reined in their affiliated trade unions, limiting the impact of anti-reform protests by independent labour organisations. While donor agency rhetoric condemns the establishment of such strong links between civil society organisations and political parties – their concern is with associational 'autonomy' – it fails to recognise the extent to which the ability of governments to achieve policy reforms *which donors themselves deem consistent with good governance* can rely upon the control of political leaders over such interests.

Anticipating the difficulties that emerge when attempts are made to 'consolidate' a newly installed democracy, USAID (like most bilateral donor agencies) explicitly excludes political parties from *all* of its definitions of civil society, terming them part of 'political society'.[18] While there is ample theoretical precedent for such an exclusion, USAID's stated rationale for doing so – that parties seek to capture, rather than to influence the exercise of, state power[19] – is dubious. It is not until this logic is extended to the point of excluding from its operational definition of civil society those organisations with close links to political parties that it becomes manifestly untenable. To assert that political parties can and ought to remain distinct from the social groups it is their function to reconcile is to assign them a role as dispassionate interest aggregators, shorn of ideology and immune to the pressures of power. There is little empirical justification for such a view in either the recent spate of democratisation – the 'Third Wave'[20] – or in the short-lived wave that accompanied post-war decolonisation.

The account provided in Chapter 5 of the role played by the informal political networks maintained by India's governing elites furnishes a useful perspective from which to assess other cases. For instance, Poland's Solidarity movement, perhaps the greatest single inspiration for the renewed interest in civil society among the donor community during the 1990s, rested upon a complex web of relationships between groups with

---

[18] USAID, Center for Development Information and Evaluation, Programme and Operations Assessments Division, 'Civil Society and Democratic Development: A CDIE Evaluation Design Paper', 24 February 1994, p. 5.

[19] USAID, 'Constituencies for Reform', p. 3.

[20] Samuel P. Huntington, *The Third Wave: Democratization in the Late Twentieth Century* (London: University of Oklahoma Press, 1991).

overlapping memberships, cemented together by charismatic individuals operating networks of influence that transcended organisational boundaries. While Solidarity did not begin life officially as a 'party', it effectively became one, and well before the transfer of power was complete. And it was the links between the movement's political core and its organisational satellites that transformed it into such a formidable political force.[21]

Had USAID's 'strategic logic' criteria been in effect, the party linkages of many of the associations that provided Solidarity its legitimacy would have disqualified them from receiving funding. Fortunately, the collapse of communism did not depend upon the assistance of USAID's democratisation strategists. They are understandably anxious to avoid the co-optation of associations by political organisations that are likely soon to gain control of the state. This is an attempt to prevent the re-emergence of authoritarian rule under another banner, and the capture of state power by rent-seeking interests. The objective is to preserve the fragile creation of civil society so that it may go on contributing to the maintenance of a democratic order and a prosperous (market) economy. However laudable these goals, they in effect put the 'cart' of consolidating market-oriented democracy before the 'horse' of effecting a democratic transition. While the currently fraught relations between the African National Congress and the civic associations and trade unions that fought apartheid in South Africa is a topic of much concern, no one seriously believes that efforts should have been made to cleanse these branches of civil society of their association with the ANC in the period prior to the ending of white rule.[22]

Not only does this excessively cautious approach to civil society risk robbing pro-democracy movements of their force; in its obsession with maintaining the 'autonomy' of centres of social and economic power, it jeopardises the healthy development of 'political society'. Even if the realm of parties and the party system is considered beyond the pale of civil society by aid policy analysts – better left to organisations like the German political foundations[23] and the funding institutes run by the two main

---

[21] See Timothy Garten Ash, *The Uses of Adversity* (Cambridge: Granta/Penguin, 1989).

[22] For an account of the difficulties of this relationship, see Kimberly Lanegran, 'South Africa's Civic Associational Movement – ANC's Ally or Society's "Watchdog"?: Shifting Social Movement-Political Party Relations', *African Studies Review*, vol. 38, no. 2 (1995), pp. 101–26. For an intelligent analysis of how South Africa can reconcile the flaws in both Gramscian and liberal conceptions of civil society (a dilemma which afflicts the aid agency conception as well), see Mark Orkin, 'Building Democracy in the New South Africa: Civil Society, Citizenship and Political Ideology', *Review of African Political Economy*, no. 66 (1995), pp. 525–37.

[23] M. Pinto-Duschinsky, 'Foreign Political Aid: The German Political Foundations and their US Counterparts', *International Affairs*, vol. 67, no. 1 (1991), pp. 33–63.

political parties in the United States[24] – they cannot escape the logical consequences of insisting upon a strict division between political parties and associational entities. Where parties become divorced from either organised sectoral interests or 'principled issue'[25] associations (environmental advocacy groups, women's organisations), the resulting vacuum can often be filled by less appealing forces. Mobilisation around exclusive social identities is certainly not what aid agencies would like to see happen, but in cases such as Kenya and Malawi this is a prominent trend, and has undermined to a significant extent the otherwise welcome ascendancy of civil society. It has been aided by the failure of parties to build strong relations with sectoral interests and principled issue associations.

Developments in Indian politics over the past twenty years represent a similar divergence between high politics and the dynamics of civil society. While this is an extremely complex case, counteracted to a substantial degree by the deep roots that democracy has struck in India over the past half-century, there has been, and continues to be, an alienation of party politics at the national level from specific organised constituencies. The divisive, majoritarian politics of the Hindu nationalist BJP has been a major beneficiary of this trend. Another related phenomenon is what has been termed the 'criminalisation of politics'. This is not merely the corruption of high-level elected and bureaucratic officials, but the wholesale entry into mainstream political parties of notorious underworld figures, who are welcomed by established party bosses because of their hold over formidable political networks. Organised crime syndicates have proved easily adaptable as adjuncts of party machines where party links with trade unions, farmers' organisations and other, more conventional groups in civil society have been weakened. We cannot blame aid agencies for India's political afflictions. But their sanitised vision of civil society, composed of public-spirited watchdogs quarantined from political society, indicates a failure to learn from such lessons. It is certainly not a recipe for the establishment of democratic politics in countries with fewer institutional endowments than India.

In his analysis of why communism failed to provide the basis for a lasting political order in east and central Europe, Ernest Gellner pointed specifically to the absence of civil society.[26] But that which he considered lacking was not what aid-agency policy has created by the same name.

---

[24] Thomas Carothers, 'The N.E.D. [National Endowment for Democracy] at 10', *Foreign Policy*, no. 951 (1994), pp. 123–38.

[25] This term is drawn from Kathryn Sikkink, 'Human Rights, Principled Issue Networks and Sovereignty in Latin America', *International Organization*, vol. 47, no. 3 (1993), pp. 411–41.

[26] Ernest Gellner, *Conditions of Liberty: Civil Society and Its Rivals* (London: Hamish Hamilton, 1994).

The latter vision is too clean-cut and invested with unambiguous virtue to perform the functions to which Gellner was referring. Gellner depicted a more sensible dichotomy: 'In an important sociological and non-evaluative sense, the Bolshevik system did constitute a moral order. By contrast, and this is perhaps one of its most significant virtues, *Civil Society is an a-moral order*'.[27] It is the latter version which we find flourishing in India today. To neglect its profound contribution to facilitating change is to seek answers to questions of power where they are least likely to be found – in the realm of virtue. In what should be their moment of triumph, the west's development professionals are in danger of repeating the errors of the communists by attempting, in Gellner's words, to 'sacralize' the social and political order. To invest civil society with a moral dimension is not only to misrepresent its historical role in the regulation of social and political life, but also to deprive it of its capacity to express, and thereby paradoxically to contain, aspirations for power over resources, which are the stuff of politics. Indian democracy may be messy and sometimes lacking in virtue, but like the market it is currently learning to accommodate, it generates hidden forms of discipline.

The consequences of political management, Indian style: sustaining democracy amidst economic reform

Though this book has attempted to identify the main reasons why a reorientation of development strategy has been possible in India, it would be foolish to consider liberalisation irreversible. The objective has been to explain this major transition of the 1990s, not to predict the shape of the new millennium. The analysis in the preceding chapters has steered clear of either policy prescriptions or assessments of economic impact. Still, it is worth asking whether the means adopted by India's governing elites to overcome political resistance to reform may come back to haunt them – as threats either to the further elaboration of a functioning market economy, or to the health of Indian democracy itself. Precisely because democratic institutions and practices have so profoundly influenced the shape of Indian economic policy – both before and since the advent of liberalisation – it is difficult to treat these two potential threats in isolation from one another. Breakdown in one area will likely spread to the other. In the necessarily brief and tentative analysis that follows, an attempt will be made to spell out such connections, though for purposes of clarity it will be helpful to treat the two issues sequentially.

There are two main aspects to the 'threat to democracy' hypothesis.

[27] Gellner, 'Conditions of Liberty', p. 137 (emphasis added).

First, it is possible that the preoccupation with placating and outman-oeuvring powerful interests has led to a relative neglect of the concerns facing India's poor.[28] If India's brand of economic reform leads to greater social and economic disparities among individuals or social groups – or is seen to have done so, as it already is in many quarters – this may imperil the basis upon which Indian democracy has, in part, rested. Second, disparities between India's regions may also grow far worse as a result of the scaling-back of central planning and the failure of many state govern-ments to adapt to the new realities. The potential scenario worth high-lighting here is not secessionism and the rupturing of India's national unity. Rather, it is the fading of the long-cherished promise that formal, 'procedural' democracy could give way to a more meaningful, 'substan-tive' form of democracy for ordinary people. This is less likely when governments of states which have not seen many economic rewards from India's liberalised economy begin to wither. The first casualty in such circumstances is the rule of law, the loss of which robs people of even the formal trappings of democratic governance.

Both of these issues bear watching. But there are reasons to believe that neither will seriously undermine the essential political stability upon which Indian democracy rests. Whether liberalisation will widen gaps between rich and poor social groups is an empirical question which requires further data, and which will in any event be hotly contested among economists. Should such a chasm emerge, it is also by no means certain that it will result in the sort of political instability capable of overwhelming India's democratic institutions. If most people's well-being is enhanced, widening gaps might not threaten the fabric of democ-racy. India has long challenged the notion that democracy and socio-economic inequality cannot co-exist. The 'why' question, however, has been remarkably under-researched. And, indeed, if liberalisation *does* generate a long-term trend of greater inequality, and yet does *not* result in concerted political action among economically underprivileged groups, the arguments advanced in this book about the functionality of India's federal system might assist in developing hypotheses to explain such a phenomenon. For instance: though economic liberalisation increased disparities in wealth, the threat to political stability was actually reduced because liberalisation also contributed significantly to the decentralisa-tion of economic decision-making to the state level, where strategies to

---

[28] In a slightly different context, these have been termed 'mass politics' and 'elite politics'. See Ashutosh Varshney, 'Mass Politics or Elite Politics? India's Economic Reforms in Comparative Perspective', paper presented for the conference, 'India's Economic Reforms', Centre for International Affairs/Harvard Institute for International Develop-ment, Harvard University, 13–14 December 1996.

avert a revolt among the poor are best devised. In this connection, one might also investigate whether and how the regionalisation of politics, to which economic reform is a major contributor, helps to strengthen the 'tidal barriers' between states, which according to Subrata Mitra were undermined during the 1970s and 1980s by the over-centralisation of the Indian political system. These are, of course, speculative explanations to hypothetical questions. They are introduced here as an illustration of the types of issues that may in future arise, and the ways in which arguments advanced in this book might help to frame fruitful research questions.

As for the issue of regional disparities, the fact is that despite the impression that private investment is flowing only to a few industrially advanced states, poorer states like Orissa and Rajasthan are receiving levels of inward investment which *by their own standards* – and in some cases by national standards as well – are extremely high. In fact, one reason why they are considered substantial is that the record of central planning in preventing the enlargement of inter-regional disparities inherited from the colonial period, to say nothing of actually reversing them, was hardly unimpeachable. The regions that feel cheated by liberalisation are largely the same ones that felt cheated by central planning.[29] As we saw in Chapter 5, leaders of some of these states have themselves adopted liberal policies, and justified their tentative embrace of economic reform by emphasising the extent to which the market could set them free from the even more constraining clutches of New Delhi's mandarins. Whether their states will be worse off – in absolute terms or relative to other regions – is an empirical question, which it is still too early to answer. The political impact of such distributional concerns is even harder to predict, but is worthy of detailed study. To the extent that it reduces the opportunities for state-level political elites to continue blaming the bogeyman of New Delhi, it is quite possible that this process will bring accountability much closer to ordinary people. Or perhaps not. Since landed interests are often in much greater command at state and local levels, it might result in the further restriction of the democratic

---

[29] The state of Orissa, in eastern India, is a case in point. It is one of the least industrialised in India. But in recent years its mineral wealth, including 1.7 million of the world's total 23 billion tonnes of bauxite reserves, has attracted a range of domestic and international investors. While it is unclear how much of the nearly \$20 billion in investment proposals will actually materialise in concrete form, even if only a relatively small fraction does it will transform Orissa from an economic backwater into a major industrial player. Orissa chief minister J. B. Patnaik cited central government control over investment decisions as the key factor which retarded Orissa's economic growth. And this is a man who represented the Congress Party, which has ruled India's central government for all but seven years since independence. See 'Special Report: A Powerhouse in the Making?' *Business World*, 10–23 July 1996, pp. 60–4.

space to which participation in a larger, outwardly oriented national political community gives access.

Beyond these relatively straightforward concerns, there is a potentially more serious consequence which the means employed to ensure liberalisation's sustainability may hold for Indian democracy. This concerns the fate of its informal political institutions. Much has been made in this book of the flexibility and adaptability of the networks of influence to which Indian parties give rise. The operation of these networks has facilitated the arrangement of a great many political accommodations. But as we have seen, governing elites have, in many cases, deployed political skills to exploit the expectations of stability among interest groups which have come to rely upon these 'regularised patterns of interaction'. Governing elites in India, like the redistributive reformers of Latin America studied by William Ascher (and cited in Chapter 3), have lulled many potential opponents of reform into a false sense of security by seeming to observe the informal rules under which these political relationships have functioned, while in a fair number of instances subverting established norms of reciprocity. In other words, they have expended a good deal of their institutional capital to solve short-term problems associated with economic reform. The question is: how much? It is a question that might not have arisen had we not focused on the value of such informal institutions in explaining the sustainability of adjustment.

For instance, many of the dilemmas which faced the United Front and BJP-led coalition governments were by-products of the political strategy employed during the preceding years under Narasimha Rao. The *modus operandi* was for the central government to make vague assurances to various interests, while placing state governments in the position of having to do the dirty work. The Narasimha Rao government, for instance, steadfastly refused to risk a direct confrontation with labour, and in a sense the strategy paid off politically, though the economic jury is still out. But whatever degree of success it achieved was due largely to the institutional endowments of its initially reluctant accomplices at the state level. The point worth bearing in mind is that this may be a finite resource. The combined effect of national neglect and state-level intimidation and cooptation has, for instance, clearly chipped away at the capacity of the trade union movement to resist what may prove to be far more radical policy change in the future – but at what cost to the institutionalised relations that have been assiduously cultivated in this area over the past fifty years?

Since this book has delineated its analytical boundaries rather narrowly, it would be justifiable to step back and revert to the scholarly disclaimer that such questions are 'beyond the scope' of its concerns. But if one believes that asking the right questions can draw attention to the issues of greatest significance, then it is vital at least to consider how findings from the present study might inform such an inquiry. It is essential, in fact, to begin by asking whether India's politicians have, in the process of making reform politically sustainable, recklessly expended the country's institutional capital. India's institutions are not only the bedrock of its democracy, providing an ordered process for the politicisation of previously marginalised groups, but also, as this book has argued, the means by which democracy's change-resistant tendencies are overcome. In short, the hope that India will be able to adapt to future shifts rests largely on the shoulders of its institutions.

Returning to the issue of industrial relations might help to illustrate this point. There is growing impatience among trade unions with the failure of elected and bureaucratic officials in both the central and state governments to live up to their promises. In response to the many examples of what they consider government treachery, trade unions have hardened their positions, and the much-vaunted flexibility among certain segments of the trade-union movement may be giving way to old-style rigidity, of the sort which is good for neither labour nor the economy, nor, for that matter, democracy.[30] The abuse of trust which has characterised the government's approach to interest-group negotiation may have fatally undermined its capacity to evolve the more formal institutions which in many countries have stabilised the labour-relations regime. The tripartite negotiating structures developed in countries like South Africa not only address wages and working conditions, but help to generate a consensus on a range of policy issues. Despite the language of inclusion, such institutions can of course privilege some interests at the expense of others – most notably, the employed at the expense of the unemployed, by erecting barriers to entering the labour market. But they can also lower costs to the society as a whole, by avoiding open conflict, increasing predictability, and smoothing the path of difficult transitions. Though this book has argued that evasion and duplicity have been key factors in making reform politically sustainable in India, it does not consider them optimal means. They were expedients, supported by a democratic framework, which bought reformers the precious commodity of time.

But developing institutions such as formal, regularised, legally sanctioned tripartite negotiating frameworks requires a high degree of trust

---

[30] In mid-1996, a senior official at the International Labor Organization (ILO) in New Delhi stated privately that trade union leaders affiliated to all of the major national parties are planning to oppose virtually any proposals that emerge from the privatisation (or 'disinvestment') commission appointed by Deve Gowda. Interview, 6 September 1996, New Delhi. See also, *Frontline*, 6 September 1996, pp. 107–8.

among elites, which is built up over time through the operation of informal institutions. When these have suffered wilful neglect and deliberate damage, as they have in India, the basis for creating suitably adapted *formal* institutions is thus critically undermined as well. Were India's governing elites to attempt to develop formal tripartite structures, they would most likely find themselves hampered by a situation of their own making. There is widespread and mutual suspicion between leaders of different unions and deep distrust between union leaders and rank-and-file members. Neither union leaders nor ordinary workers, for that matter, trust politicians. And to make things worse, a large section of the general public considers the labour movement captured by advocates of sectarian hatred. Corporatist structures would find such circumstances infertile ground, to say the least. Much of the problem, it must be stressed, has been created by the underhanded means employed by governing elites to undercut political resistance to economic reform. Even if one is not won over by the case for tripartite institutions, it is possible to see the point of this example: short-term expedients, by running down fragile reserves of institutional capital, can harm the prospects for the more difficult types of adaptive reform that a more complex and internationalised economy will, in one form or another, inevitably require.

The silver lining in all of this is that institutional capital is, under certain conditions, a renewable resource, though (as with financial capital) depletion beyond a certain level can make replenishment extremely difficult. Unexpected circumstances, for instance, can provide opportunities for moribund institutions to be resuscitated, and these can help to rebuild some of what has been destroyed in yet other institutions. This has certainly been the case with respect to India's federal system since 1991. This study's focus on the value of a revived form of federalism provides us with some of the perspective necessary to ask whether economic reform and the regionalisation of Indian politics will continue to reinforce one another.

Again, this is a question that will require in-depth empirical research. But thus far such a trend seems to be in evidence. Far from bringing a provincial mindset to New Delhi, Deve Gowda's United Front government – the first in which regional parties played such a large role – injected new life into a flagging reform process. It immediately restructured the Foreign Investment Promotion Board (FIPB), which then went on to approve foreign investment proposals worth more than $5.5 billion in its first three months of operation.[31] Significantly, a good deal of the increased activity on this and other fronts could be traced to the coalition's

---

[31] 'Survey: India', *Financial Times*, 19 November 1996, p. 1.

roots in India's regions. Ministers sitting on the FIPB and other powerful decision-making bodies – whether in the United Front or BJP-led coalitions – hailed from regional parties, and were politically answerable to party bosses sitting in state capitals. The industry minister in the United Front government, Mr Murasoli Maran, belonged to the Dravida Munnetra Kazagham (DMK), the ruling party in the southern state of Tamil Nadu. The DMK's leader, Tamil Nadu Chief Minister Mr M. Karunanidhi, wanted to see new industrial projects sprouting up in his fiefdom. The decision of Ford, in a venture with its Indian partner Mahindra, to produce Fiestas at a greenfield plant in Tamil Nadu rather than at a site it had been studying in Maharashtra was considered a major coup for the state when it was announced by Karunanidhi's predecessor as chief minister in January 1996, and Karunanidhi was keen not to be outdone.

The key point is that Mr Maran answered to Mr Karunanidhi, just as central government ministers from the Telugu Desam Party, another component of the United Front coalition, answered to Andhra Pradesh chief minister Mr Chandrababu Naidu – also a pragmatic provincial politician keen to attract private investment in sectors where public resources are no longer adequate. New Delhi began dancing to the tune of state governments. This is a very significant departure from the past twenty-five years, if not longer. During Narasimha Rao's tenure, for instance, Congress chief ministers could lobby their party chief and his ministerial colleagues in New Delhi for action on pressing economic policy matters. But the centralised Congress would respond in its own time, if at all. Congress chief ministers, in almost all cases, owed their jobs to the prime minister, and kept them at his pleasure. They were in no position to lobby effectively for investment approvals, more autonomy over policy-making, or reforms to the rules governing other economic matters. The new clout of regional parties in central coalitions – which is likely to remain for the foreseeable future – changed all of that. Chief ministers from United Front parties called many of the shots, as did those allied with the subsequent BJP-led coalition. They can threaten to bring down the government if they do not get what they want. While they inevitably lobby for increased funds to grease their election machines, in many instances, rather than asking for the brakes to be put on economic restructuring, they are demanding additional action.

The central government has shown itself capable of responding. For all his flaws, Deve Gowda, as a former chief minister, understood the need to tailor the reforms process to the problems facing state governments. Shortly after taking office, he stated that funds for centrally sponsored schemes for providing 'basic minimum services' would be disbursed through state governments.[32] He announced in September 1996 that the government was considering a proposal to permit state governments to authorise power projects up to a value of Rs. 10 billion.[33] They would no longer need to approach the central government for approval, a process which had delayed many projects. From January 1997, renovation and modernisation schemes of Rs. 5 billion or less no longer required approval from the Central Electricity Authority.[34] In late October 1996, Deve Gowda's government fulfilled a longstanding demand of state governments by initiating a process to give them greater control over granting mining concessions.[35] The government also planned to introduce a bill to amend the Urban Land (Ceiling and Regulation) Act of 1976, which restricts what state governments can do with vacant urban land desperately needed for redevelopment.[36] Though many of these promises were not fulfilled before the United Front government met its premature end, they symbolised a process that any subsequent government would find difficult to reverse. And, indeed, when the Vajpayee government took power in early 1998, in coalition with an even greater variety of regional parties, action on each of these specific policy areas extended what Deve Gowda had initiated.

It is also worth noting that all of these reforms not only have implications for how state governments might make the most of a liberalised economic environment, but also have the potential to assist state-level politicians in building up new pork-barrels to replace those – like public-works patronage – which liberalisation has eroded. A central government inclined to support such activities – because it answers to regional parties – is building a larger and deeper political consensus in favour of reform, making it more politically sustainable in the process. It is also contributing to the strengthening of the many other institutions that emanate from the federal division of power, such as the National Development Council and the Finance Commission. Thus, at least one form of institutional capital is being replenished – through bizarre and unpredictable sequences, to be sure. But it is a side of the balance sheet that it would be wrong to neglect.

The deep roots of both the United Front and BJP-led coalitions in regional politics – and the extent to which even a future Congress government will require alliances with regional parties – may act as a spur rather than a brake on new reforms. In early November 1996, for instance, a leading industrialist personally told Deve Gowda that Indian business was united in its opposition to the government's decision to allow major-

[32] *The Hindu*, 6 July 1996.   [33] *The Pioneer*, 11 September 1996.
[34] *Asian Age*, 10 January 1997.   [35] *Asian Age*, 18 October 1996.
[36] *India Today*, 15 October 1996, p. 61.

ity equity holdings by foreign investors in a range of new industries – that is, beyond those that had been previously justified on the grounds that foreign technology and capital were desperately required. The prime minister was said to be unfazed by this display. The capacity of the Indian government to resist this kind of pressure stems largely from the fact that the traditionally dominant business houses have in the past relied on a close relationship with the Congress Party, which operated a top-down form of federalism. Most of these business houses neglected to build political alliances at the regional level – precisely the level from which power is flowing in today's bottom-up political environment. The business links of the parties ruling in most Indian states are with smaller, but more outwardly oriented regional business groups. Their backers do not in general share the aversion to foreign investment voiced by the traditionally dominant north Indian business houses. The point is that Deve Gowda, as well as ministers in the Vajpayee government from regional parties, precisely because of their provincial backgrounds, may not be as beholden to traditional big business as the leadership of the Congress was. India's big business houses were concerned about the United Front government's approach to economic policy not because Deve Gowda and his cabinet were abandoning liberalisation, but because they were pursuing it more zealously, particularly with respect to foreign investment. Despite the BJP's swadeshi rhetoric, business leaders have the same fear under Vajpayee. Ironically, the diplomatic conflict with the United States over nuclear testing served only to further isolate the swadeshi lobby. Eager to counteract the potential for economic sanctions to hurt India's foreign-exchange position, the Vajpayee government relaxed guidelines on portfolio investment, and worked hard to court European and other investors capable of filling any gap the departure of US firms might create.

In a country of India's diversity, the fact that its federal system is healthier now than it has been for at least two decades, and that the new approach to economic policy is a vital part of its renaissance, is not without important implications. Indeed, after almost thirty years of increasing centralisation of political authority, we may be travelling 'back to the future' – for, as Clifford Geertz recognised in the early 1960s, it is at 'the state level that perhaps the bulk of the bitter hand-to-hand clashes that form the everyday substance of Indian domestic politics are coming to take place, and where the adjustments of parochial interests are coming to be effected'.[37]

[37] Clifford Geertz, 'The Integrative Revolution: Primordial Sentiments and Civil Politics in the New States', in Clifford Geertz, *The Interpretation of Cultures: Selected Essays* (New York: Basic Books, 1973), p. 291. This is a reprint of an article originally published in 1963.

The recasting of centre–state relations should foster cautious optimism about India's capacity to meet its most pressing political challenge – institutional renewal. Samuel Huntington's analogy of almost thirty years ago captured this dilemma: 'Just as economic development depends, in some measure, on the relation between investment and consumption, political order depends in part on the relation between the development of political institutions and the mobilisation of new social forces into politics'.[38] Given the extent to which the dramatic emergence of lower-caste groups from the social margins to political centre-stage is occurring within state-level political arenas, the federal revival assumes even greater significance. It may be just a part of a larger pattern of institutional regeneration – involving judicial activism, tribal self-government, and more sensible arrangements for the operation of coalition governance.

Before getting over-enthused about such a prospect, it would be worth recalling the catalogue of underhanded tactics detailed in this book. If political institutions are revitalised in India – by whatever means – they are as likely to serve narrow, selfish ends as any other.

[38] Huntington, *Political Order in Changing Societies*, p. vii.

Bibliography

Alesina, Alberto, 'Macroeconomics and Politics', *NBER Macroeconomics Annual* (Cambridge, Mass.: National Bureau of Economic Research, 1988), pp. 13–52

'Political Models of Macroeconomic Policy and Fiscal Reform', in Stephan Haggard and Steven B. Webb (eds.), *Voting for Reform: Democracy, Political Liberalization, and Economic Adjustment* (New York: Oxford University Press/ The World Bank, 1994), pp. 37–60

Allison, Graham, *Essence of Decision: Explaining the Cuban Missile Crisis* (Boston: Little, Brown, 1971)

Ascher, William, *Scheming for the Poor: The Politics of Redistribution in Latin America* (Cambridge, Mass.: Harvard University Press, 1984)

Ash, Timothy Garten, *The Uses of Adversity* (Cambridge: Granta/Penguin, 1989)

Asilis, Carlos M. and Gian Maria Milesi-Ferretti, 'On the Political Sustainability of Economic Reform', *Paper on Policy Analysis and Assessment*, IMF Research Department (Washington, DC: January 1994)

Bardhan, Pranab, *The Political Economy of Development in India* (Oxford: Basil Blackwell, 1984)

'Dominant Proprietary Classes and India's Democracy', in Atul Kohli (ed.), *India's Democracy: An Analysis of Changing State-Society Relations* (Princeton: Princeton University Press, 1988), pp. 214–24

'The "Intermediate Regime": Any Sign of Graduation?', in Pranab Bardhan, Mrinal Datta-Chaudhuri, and T. N. Krishnan (eds.), *Development and Change: Essays in Honour of K. N. Raj* (Bombay: Oxford University Press, 1993), pp. 341–52

Baru, Sanjaya, 'Continuity and Change in Indian Industrial Policy', paper presented at the conference, 'Terms of Political Discourse in India', York University, September 1990

Bates, Robert, 'The Reality of Structural Adjustment: A Sceptical Appraisal', in Simon Commander (ed.), *Structural Adjustment and Agriculture: Theory and Practice in Africa and Latin America* (London: Overseas Development Institute, 1989)

Bates, Robert H. and Anne O. Krueger, 'Generalizations Arising from the Country Studies', in R. H. Bates and A. O. Krueger (eds.), *Political and Economic Interactions in Economic Policy Reform: Evidence from Eight Countries* (Oxford: Blackwell, 1993), pp. 444–72

Bates, Robert H. and Anne O. Krueger (eds.), *Political and Economic Interactions in Economic Policy Reform: Evidence from Eight Countries* (Oxford: Blackwell, 1993)

Baviskar, B. S., 'Leadership, Democracy, and Development: Cooperatives in Kohlapur District', in B. S. Baviskar and Donald W. Attwood (eds.), *Finding the Middle Path: The Political Economy of Cooperation in Rural India* (Boulder, Colo.: Westview Press, 1995), pp. 157–75

Bayart, Jean-François, *The State in Africa: The Politics of the Belly* (Harlow: Longman, 1993)

Bhaduri, Amit and Deepak Nayyar, *The Intelligent Person's Guide to Liberalization* (New Delhi: Penguin, 1996)

Bhambhri, C. P., 'The Politics of Manmohanomics', *Financial Express*, 23 July 1993

Bharati, Vivek, 'Corruption and Reforms: Cutting the Unholy Links', *Times of India*, 16 July 1993

Bhargava, Sandeep, 'Industrial Liberalisation in India: Policy Issues at the State Level', *IDS Working Paper* (Jaipur: Institute of Development Studies, January 1995)

Bhatt, Mayank, 'Clutching at Straws', *Business India*, 9–22 March 1998, pp. 218–25

Bidwai, Praful, 'May Day! May Day!', *Times of India*, 1 May 1994

Blair, Harry W., 'Success and Failure in Rural Development: A Comparison of Maharashtra, Bihar and Bangladesh', paper presented at the annual meeting of the Association of South Asian Studies, San Francisco, 25–27 March 1988

Bollom, Michael W., 'Capturing Ideas: Institutions, Interests and Intellectual Property Rights Reform in India', paper presented at the Annual Meeting of the American Political Science Association, Washington, DC, 28–31 August 1997

Brass, Paul, 'Pluralism, Regionalism and Decentralising Tendencies in Contemporary Indian Politics', in A. Jeyaratnam Wilson and Denis Dalton (eds.), *The States of South Asia: Problems of National Integration* (London: Hurst and Co., 1982)

The New Cambridge History of India, IV-1: The Politics of India Since Independence, 2nd edn (Cambridge: Cambridge University Press, 1994)

Bresser Pereira, Luiz C., Jose Maria Maravall, and Adam Przeworski, *Economic Reforms in New Democracies: A Social Democratic Approach* (Cambridge: Cambridge University Press, 1993)

Brown, Judith M., *Modern India: The Origins of an Asian Democracy* (Delhi: Oxford University Press, 1985)

Bujra, Janet, 'The Dynamics of Political Action: A New Look at Factionalism', *American Anthropologist*, vol. 75 (1973)

Cable, Vincent, *China and India: Economic Reform and Global Integration* (London: Royal Institute of International Affairs, 1995)

Carothers, Thomas, 'The N.E.D. [National Endowment for Democracy] at 10', *Foreign Policy*, no. 951 (1994), pp. 123–38

Centre for the Study of Society and Secularism, *Communalism and Industrial Workers* (Bombay, 1994)

232   Bibliography

Chakraborty, Pinaki, 'Growing Imbalances in Federal Fiscal Relationship', *Economic and Political Weekly*, 14 February 1998, pp. 350–4

Collier, David and Ruth Collier, *Shaping the Political Arena* (Princeton: Princeton University Press, 1991)

Cornelius, Wayne A., Ann L. Craig, and Jonathan Fox, 'Mexico's National Solidarity Program: An Overview', in Wayne A. Cornelius, Ann L. Craig, and Jonathan Fox (eds.), *Transforming State-Society Relations in Mexico: The Solidarity Strategy* (San Diego: Center for US-Mexican Studies, University of California, 1994), pp. 3–26

Crook, Richard and James Manor, 'Democratic Decentralisation and Institutional Performance: Four Asian and African Experiences Compared', *Journal of Commonwealth and Comparative Politics*, vol. 33, no. 3 (Nov. 1995), pp. 309–34

Dalal, Sucheta, 'Why Aren't the Institutions Accountable?', *Times of India*, 6 July 1995

Dalmia, Gaurav, 'Reforms and Indian Businessmen', *Economic Times*, 10 November 1993

Dandavate, Madhu, 'Patronage to Maruti: Government's Policy of Double-Faced Liberalisation', *Indian Express*, 1 December 1993

Darman, Richard, *Who's in Control? Polar Politics and the Sensible Center* (New York: Simon and Schuster, 1996)

Datta-Chaudhuri, Mrinal, 'The New Policy', *Seminar* (December 1985), pp. 18–22

'Liberalisation without Reform', *Seminar*, no. 437 (January 1996), pp. 32–5

Deshpande, Charudatta, 'The Man Behind Maharashtra Inc.', *Economic Times*, 4 March 1994

Dhar, P. N., 'The Political Economy of Development in India', *Indian Economic Review*, vol. 22, no. 1 (1987), pp. 1–18

Dreze, Jean and Amartya Sen, *Hunger and Public Action* (Oxford: Clarendon Press, 1989)

India: Economic Development and Social Opportunity (Oxford: Oxford University Press, 1996)

Dubery, Amaresh and Shubhashis Gangopadhyay, 'Poverty and Economic Reforms', *Economic Times*, 23 February 1998

Economist Intelligence Unit, *Country Forecast – India* (London, quarterly), various numbers

Country Report – India (London, quarterly), various numbers

Faruqee, Rashid and Ishrat Husain, 'Conclusions', in Ishrat Husain and Rashid Faruqee (eds.), *Adjustment in Africa: Lessons from Country Case Studies* (Washington, DC: The World Bank, March 1994)

Foulds, Russell, 'NDDB's Loss Could be Oil Lobby's Gain', *Deccan Herald*, 17 April 1995

Frischtak, Leila L., 'Governance Capacity and Economic Reform in Developing Countries', *World Bank Technical Paper No. 254* (Washington, DC: The World Bank, 1994)

Gaiha, Raghav, 'Structural Adjustment, Rural Institutions and the Poor in India: A Comparative Analysis of Andhra Pradesh, Maharashtra and Karnataka', paper prepared for the UN Food and Agricultural Organization, 27 September 1994

Gavaskar, Mahesh, 'Labouring Over a Capital Task', *Humanscape*, May 1997, pp. 17–19

Geddes, Barbara, *Politician's Dilemma: Building State Capacity in Latin America* (Berkeley: University of California Press, 1994)

Geertz, Clifford, 'The Integrative Revolution: Primordial Sentiments and Civil Politics in the New States', in Clifford Geertz, *The Interpretation of Cultures: Selected Essays* (New York: Basic Books, 1973)

Gellner, Ernest, *Conditions of Liberty: Civil Society and Its Rivals* (London: Hamish Hamilton, 1994)

Gellner, Ernest and John Waterbury (eds.), *Patrons and Clients in Mediterranean Societies* (London: Duckworth, 1977)

Ghosh, Arun, '"Rent-Seeking" and Economic Reform', *Economic and Political Weekly*, 1–8 January 1994

Ghosh, Madanmohan, 'Fiscal Management at the Cost of the States?', *Mainstream*, 14 May 1994, pp. 17–18

Gills, Barry, Joel Rocamora, and Richard Wilson (eds.), *Low Intensity Democracy: Political Power in the New World Order* (London: Pluto Press, 1993)

Gladney, D. C., 'Unity vs. Diversity in China', *Asian Age*, 6 March 1995 (originally published in the *International Herald Tribune*)

Gourevitch, Peter A., 'Democracy and Economic Policy: Elective Affinities and Circumstantial Conjunctures', *World Development*, vol. 21, no. 8 (1980), pp. 1271–80

Government of India, Finance Ministry, *Economic Survey 1994/95* (New Delhi: Government Printing Office, 1995)

Economic Survey 1996/97 (New Delhi, 1997)

Government of India, *National Report on Tax Reform* (New Delhi: Government Printing Office, 1993)

Government of India, Office of the Comptroller and Auditor General, *State Report – Maharashtra* (New Delhi: Government Printing Office, April 1993)

Report on the Disinvestment of Public-Sector Enterprises, 1991–92 (New Delhi: Government Printing Office, 1993)

Government of Maharashtra, 'New Industrial Policy for Maharashtra, 1993' (Bombay: Government Central Press, 1993)

Government of Rajasthan, 'Budget Speech of Rajasthan Chief Minister Bhairon Singh Shekhawat for Fiscal Year 1993–94' (Jaipur: Government Publications Office, March 1993)

Graham, Carol, *Safety Nets, Politics, and the Poor: Transitions to Market Economies* (Washington, DC: Brookings Institution, 1994)

Gramsci, Antonio, *Selections from the Prison Notebooks*, edited and translated by Quinton Hoare and Geoffrey Nowell Smith (New York: International Publishers, 1971)

Gray, Cheryl, 'In Search of Owners: Privatization and Corporate Governance in Transition Economies', *World Bank Research Observer*, vol. 11, no. 2 (August 1996), pp. 179–97

Guhan, S., 'Centre and States in the Reform Process', in Robert Cassen and Vijay Joshi (eds.), *India: The Future of Economic Reform* (Delhi: Oxford University Press, 1995), pp. 71–111

Gulati, Ashok, 'Agricultural Sector and Liberalisation', *Economic and Political Weekly*, 13 April 1996, pp. 929–30

Gulati, Ashok and Shashanka Bhide, 'What Do the Reformers Have for Agriculture?', *Economic and Political Weekly*, 6–13 May 1995

Gurumurthi, S., 'Sales Taxation: Evolution and Reform – Lessons from Tamil Nadu' (Part I of II), *Economic and Political Weekly*, 18 January 1997, pp. 111–26

Haggard, Stephan and Robert R. Kaufman, 'Institutions and Economic Adjustment', in Stephan Haggard and Robert R. Kaufman (eds.), *The Politics of Economic Adjustment: International Constraints, Distributional Conflicts, and the State* (Princeton: Princeton University Press, 1992)

Haggard, Stephan and Robert R. Kaufman (eds.), *The Politics of Economic Adjustment: International Constraints, Distributional Conflicts, and the State* (Princeton: Princeton University Press, 1992)

   The Political Economy of Democratic Transitions (Princeton: Princeton University Press, 1995)

Haggard, Stephan and Steven B. Webb, 'What Do We Know About the Political Economy of Economic Policy Reform?', *The World Bank Research Observer*, vol. 8, no. 2 (July 1993), pp. 143–68

Haggard, Stephan and Steven B. Webb (eds.), *Voting for Reform: Democracy, Political Liberalization, and Economic Adjustment* (New York: Oxford University Press/The World Bank, 1994)

Hall, Peter A. and Rosemary C. R. Taylor, 'Political Science and the Three New Institutionalisms', *Political Studies*, vol. 44, no. 5 (1996), pp. 936–57

Hall-Jamieson, Kathleen, *Dirty Politics: Deception, Distraction and Democracy* (Oxford: Oxford University Press, 1992)

Hao, Jia and Lin Zhimin, 'Introduction', in Jia Hao and Lin Zhimin (eds.), *Changing Central-Local Relations in China: Reform and State Capacity* (Boulder, Colo.: Westview Press, 1994)

Harriss, John, 'The State in Retreat: Why has India Experienced Such Half-Hearted Liberalisation in the 1980s?', *IDS Bulletin*, vol. 18, no. 4 (1987), pp. 31–8.

Harvey, Charles and Mark Robinson, 'The Design of Economic Reforms in the Context of Political Liberalization: The Experience of Mozambique, Senegal and Uganda', *IDS Discussion Paper*, no. 353 (Brighton: Institute of Development Studies, November 1995)

Heiner, Ronald A., 'The Origins of Predictable Behavior', *American Economic Review*, vol. 73, no. 4 (1983), pp. 560–95

Held, David (ed.), *Prospects for Democracy: North, South, East, West* (Cambridge: Polity Press, 1993)

Herbst, Jeffrey, *The Politics of Reform in Ghana, 1982–1991* (Berkeley: University of California Press, 1993)

Heredia, Blanca, 'The Political Economy of the Mexican Crisis', in Dharam Ghai (ed.), *The IMF and the South* (London: Zed Books/United Nations Research Institute for Social Development, 1991), pp. 117–38

   'Making Economic Reform Politically Viable: The Mexican Experience', in William C. Smith, Carlos H. Acuna, and Eduardo A. Gamarra (eds.), *Democracy, Markets, and Structural Reform in Latin America: Argentina, Bolivia, Brazil, Chile, and Mexico* (New Brunswick, NJ: Transaction Publishers/North-South Centre, University of Miami, 1993), pp. 265–91

Hirschman, Albert O., 'The Case Against "One Thing at a Time"', *World Development*, vol. 18 (August 1990), pp. 1119–22

Hobsbawm, Eric, *Industry and Empire* (Harmondsworth: Penguin, 1968)

Huntington, Samuel P., *Political Order in Changing Societies* (New Haven, Conn.: Yale University Press, 1968)

'The Goals of Development', in Myron Weiner and Samuel P. Huntington (eds.), *Understanding Political Development* (Boston: Little Brown, 1987), pp. 3–32

The Third Wave: Democratization in the Late Twentieth Century (London: University of Oklahoma Press, 1991)

Husain, Ishrat, 'Why Do Some Economies Adjust More Successfully Than Others? Lessons from Seven African Countries', *Policy Research Working Paper*, no. 1364 (World Bank, Africa Regional Office, October 1994)

'The Macroeconomics of Adjustment in Sub-Saharan African Countries: Results and Lessons', *Policy Research Working Paper*, no. 1365 (World Bank, Africa Regional Office, October 1994)

Hyden, Goren and Bo Karlstrom, 'Structural Adjustment as a Policy Process: The Case of Tanzania', *World Development*, vol. 21, no. 9 (1993), pp. 1395–1404

Jeffries, Richard, 'The State, Structural Adjustment and Good Government in Africa', *Journal of Commonwealth and Comparative Politics*, vol. 31, no. 1 (March 1993)

Jenkins, Rob, 'Where the BJP Survived: Rajasthan Assembly Elections, 1993', *Economic and Political Weekly*, vol. 29, no. 11 (12 March 1994), pp. 635–41

'Theorising the Politics of Economic Adjustment: Lessons from the Indian Case', *Journal of Commonwealth and Comparative Politics*, vol. 33, no. 1 (March 1995), pp. 1–24

'Liberal Democracy and the Political Management of Structural Adjustment: Conceptual Tensions in the Good Government Agenda', *IDS Bulletin*, vol. 26, no. 2 (April 1995), pp. 37–48

'The Politics of Protecting the Poor During Economic Adjustment in India: The Case of Maharashtra', in Usha Thakkar and Mangesh Kulkarni (eds.), *Politics in Maharashtra* (Bombay: Himalaya Publishing, 1995), pp. 195–212

'The Continued Democratization of Indian Democracy: Regionalization, Social Change and the 1996 Elections', *Democratization*, vol. 3, no. 4 (Winter 1996), pp. 501–16

'Rajput Hindutva: Caste Politics, Regional Identity, and Hindu Nationalism in Contemporary Rajasthan', in Christophe Jaffrelot and Thomas Blom Hansen (eds.), *The BJP and the Compulsions of Politics in India* (Delhi: Oxford University Press, 1998)

'Mistaking Governance for Politics: Foreign Aid, Democracy, and the Construction of Civil Society', in Sudipta Kaviraj and Sunil Khilnani (eds.), *Civil Society: History and Possibilities* (Cambridge: Cambridge University Press, forthcoming)

Jian, Tianlun, Jeffrey D. Sachs, and Andrew M. Warner, 'Trends in Regional Inequality in China', *Working Paper 5412* (Cambridge, Mass.: National

Bureau of Economic Research, January 1996)

Joshi, Vijay and I. M. D. Little, 'Macroeconomic Stabilisation in India, 1991–93 and Beyond', in Robert Cassen and Vijay Joshi (eds.), *India: The Future of Economic Reform* (Delhi: Oxford University Press, 1995)

Kaviraj, Sudipta, 'A Critique of the Passive Revolution', *Economic and Political Weekly*, Special Number, vol. 23 (November 1988), pp. 2429–44

'Dilemmas of Democratic Development in India', in Adrian Leftwich (ed.), *Democracy and Development: Theory and Practice* (Cambridge: Polity Press, 1996), pp. 114–38

Keohane, Robert, *After Hegemony: Cooperation and Discord in the World Political Economy* (Princeton: Princeton University Press, 1984)

Khare, Harish, 'Beyond Congress Infighting: Dilemma of Sustaining the New Order', *Times of India*, 12 January 1994

'Ten Headlines in Search of a Regime', *Seminar*, no. 437 (January 1996), pp. 26–31

Khare, R. S., *Culture and Democracy: Anthropological Reflections on Modern India* (London: University Press of America, 1985)

Kingstone, Peter R., 'Corporatism, Neoliberalism, and the Failed Revolt of Big Business in Brazil: The Case of IEDI', paper presented at the Annual Meeting of the American Political Science Association, Washington, DC, 28–31 August 1997

Kirkow, Peter, *Russia's Provinces: Authoritarian Transformation versus Local Autonomy* (Basingstoke: Macmillan, 1998)

Klaus, Vaclav, 'So Far, So Good', *Economist*, 10 September 1994, p. 45

Kochanek, Stanley, *Business and Politics in India* (Berkeley: University of California Press, 1974)

'Briefcase Politics in India: The Congress Party and the Business Elite', *Asian Survey*, vol. 27, no. 12 (December 1987)

Kohli, Atul, 'The Politics of Liberalisation in India', *World Development*, vol. 17, no. 3 (1989)

Democracy and Discontent: India's Growing Crisis of Governability (Cambridge: Cambridge University Press, 1990)

Lal, Deepak, *The Hindu Equilibrium* (Oxford: Clarendon Press, 1988)

Landell-Mills, Pierre, 'Governance, Civil Society and Empowerment in Sub-Saharan Africa', paper prepared for the Annual Conference of the Society for the Advancement of Socio-Economics, 1992

Landell-Mills, P. and I. Serageldin, 'Governance and the External Factor', *Proceedings of the World Bank Conference on Development Economics* (Washington, DC: The World Bank, 1991)

'Governance and the Development Process', *Finance and Development*, vol. 29 (1991), pp. 14–17

Lanegran, Kimberly, 'South Africa's Civic Associational Movement – ANC's Ally or Society's "Watchdog"?: Shifting Social Movement-Political Party Relations', *African Studies Review*, vol. 38, no. 2 (1995), pp. 101–26

Lemarchand, René, 'The Dynamics of Factionalism in Contemporary Africa', in Zaki Ergas (ed.), *The African State in Transition* (Basingstoke: Macmillan, 1987), pp. 149–65

Li, Linda Chelan, *Centre and Provinces: China 1978–93* (Oxford: Oxford University Press, 1998)

Lindblom, Charles E., *Politics and Markets* (New Haven, Conn.: Yale University Press, 1977)

Lindemann, Marcus, 'The Licence-Raj Revisited: The Political Economy of Changing State-Business Relations', unpublished MA dissertation, Department of Government, University of Essex, September 1995

Lowi, Theodore J., 'Think Globally, Lose Locally', *Boston Review*, April/May 1998

McKinnon, Ronald I., 'Market-Preserving Fiscal Federalism', *Working Paper*, Department of Economics (Palo Alto, Calif.: Stanford University, 1994)

Mani, Mohan, 'New Attempt at Workers' Resistance: National Centre for Labour', *Economic and Political Weekly*, 7 October 1995, pp. 2485–6

Manor, James, 'Indira and After: The Decay of Party Organisation in India', *The Round Table* (October 1978), pp. 315–24

'Pragmatic Progressives in Regional Politics: The Case of Devaraj Urs', *Economic and Political Weekly*, annual number, vol. 15 (1980)

'The Electoral Process amid Awakening and Decay', in Peter Lyon and James Manor (eds.), *Transfer and Transformation: Political Institutions in the New Commonwealth* (Leicester: Leicester University Press, 1983), pp. 87–116

'India's States, China's Provinces and the Question of Central Autonomy', paper presented to the China-India Seminar, Fairbank Centre for East Asian Studies, Harvard University, 1986 (typescript)

'Tried, then Abandoned: Economic Liberalisation in India', *IDS Bulletin*, vol. 18, no. 4 (1987), pp. 39–44

'How and Why Liberal and Representative Politics Emerged in India', *Political Studies*, vol. 38, no. 1 (March 1990)

'The Political Sustainability of Economic Liberalization', in Robert Cassen and Vijay Joshi (eds.), *India: The Future of Economic Reform* (Delhi: Oxford University Press, 1995)

March, James and Johan P. Olsen, 'The New Institutionalism: Organizational Factors in Political Life', *American Political Science Review*, vol. 78 (1984), pp. 734–49

Mathur, Ajeet N., 'The Experience of Consultation During Structural Adjustment in India (1990–92)', *Occasional Paper No. 9* (Geneva: International Labor Organization, April 1993)

Meier, Gerald (ed.), *Politics and Policy Making in Developing Countries: Perspectives on the New Political Economy* (San Francisco: ICS Press, 1991)

Misquitta, Lynus Paul, *Pressure Groups and Democracy in India* (New Delhi: Sterling, 1991)

Mitra, Partha Pratim, 'Economics of Food Security: The Indian Context', *Social Action*, vol. 46 (July–Sept. 1996), pp. 279–95

Mitra, Subrata Kumar, 'Crisis and Resilience in Indian Democracy', *International Social Science Journal*, no. 129 (August 1991)

Moe, Terry M., *The Organization of Interests: Incentives and the Internal Dynamics of Political Interest Groups* (Chicago: University of Chicago Press, 1980)

Montinola, Gabriella, Yingyi Qian, and Barry R. Weingast, 'Federalism, Chinese

Style: The Political Basis for Economic Success in China', *World Politics*, vol. 48, no. 1 (October 1995), pp. 50–81

Moon, Chung-in, 'The Politics of Structural Adjustment in South Korea: Analytical Issues and Comparative Implications', *Korea Journal*, Autumn 1991, pp. 54–68

Moore, Mick, 'Economic Liberalisation versus Political Pluralism in Sri Lanka', *Modern Asian Studies*, vol. 24, no. 2 (1990), pp. 341–83

Moore, Mick and Ladi Hamalai, 'Economic Liberalisation, Political Pluralism and Business Associations in Developing Countries', *Discussion Paper 318* (Brighton: Institute of Development Studies, 1993)

Mosely, Paul, J. Harrigan, and J. Toye, *Aid and Power: The World Bank and Policy-Based Lending in the 1980s* (London: Routledge, 1991), two volumes

Muralidharan, Sukumar, 'Paying the Price', *Frontline*, 3 October 1997, p. 37

Nag, Kingshuk, 'CII's Dilemma: To Speak or Not to Speak', *Times of India*, 21 April 1996

Nair, Janaki, 'Predatory Capitalism and Legalised Landgrab: Karnataka Land Reforms', *Economic and Political Weekly*, 3 February 1996, pp. 251–2

Nandy, Ashis, *The Intimate Enemy: Loss and Recovery of Self under Colonialism* (Delhi: Oxford University Press, 1983)

    At the Edge of Psychology: Essays in Politics and Culture (Delhi: Oxford University Press, 1990)

National Council of Applied Economic Research, *Ninth Survey on Business Attitudes* (New Delhi, March 1994)

Nayar, Baldev Raj, *India's Public Sector* (New Delhi: Popular Prakashan, 1990)

Neale, Walter, 'Congress Presiding Over Progress and Change: State Governments and the Indian Economy', in Mike Shepperdson and Colin Simmons (eds.), *The Indian National Congress and the Political Economy of India, 1885–1985* (Aldershot: Gower Publishing Co., 1988)

Nelson, Joan M., 'The Politics of Pro-Poor Adjustment', in Joan M. Nelson (ed.), *Fragile Coalitions: The Politics of Economic Adjustment* (New Brunswick, NJ: Transaction Books, 1989), pp. 95–113

    'The Politics of Economic Transformation: Is Third World Experience Relevant in Eastern Europe?', *World Politics*, vol. 45 (April 1993), pp. 433–63

    Fragile Coalitions: The Politics of Economic Adjustment (New Brunswick, NJ: Transaction Books, 1989)

    Economic Crisis and Policy Choice: The Politics of Adjustment in the Third World (Princeton: Princeton University Press, 1990)

    'Organized Labor, Politics, and Labor Market Flexibility', *World Bank Research Observer*, vol. 6, no. 1 (January 1991), pp. 37–56

Nordlinger, Eric A., *On the Autonomy of the Democratic State* (Cambridge, Mass.: Harvard University Press, 1981)

Noronha, Ernesto, 'Trade Unionism: Changing Slogans', *Humanscape*, May 1997, pp. 8–12

    'Wages of Globalisation', *Humanscape*, March 1998, pp. 11–13

O'Connor, J., *The Fiscal Crisis of the State* (New York: St. Martin's Press, 1973)

O'Donnell, Guillermo, 'On the State, Democratization and Some Conceptual Problems: A Latin American View with Glances at Some Postcommunist

Countries', *World Development*, vol. 21, no. 8 (1993), pp. 1355–76

'Delegative Democracy', *Journal of Democracy*, vol. 5, no. 1 (January 1994)

Olson, Mancur, *The Logic of Collective Action* (Cambridge, Mass.: Harvard University Press, 1965)

Orkin, Mark, 'Building Democracy in the New South Africa: Civil Society, Citizenship and Political Ideology', *Review of African Political Economy*, no. 66 (1995), pp. 525–37

Overseas Development Administration (UK), Government and Institutions Department, 'Taking Account of Good Government', *Technical Note No. 10* (London, 1993)

Packenham, Robert A., 'The Politics of Economic Liberalization: Argentina and Brazil in Comparative Perspective', *Working Paper No. 206*, Kellogg Institute for International Studies, University of Notre Dame, April 1994

Pai, Sudha, 'Elections and Fiscal Reform', *Economic and Political Weekly*, 13–20 January 1996, pp. 142–7

Pani, Narendar, *Redefining Conservatism: An Essay on the Bias of India's Economic Reform* (New Delhi: Sage Publications, 1994)

'The Services Factor', *Economic Times*, 21 April 1995

'Rural Banks without Patronage', *Economic Times*, 6 September 1996

'When Farm Policies Turn Suicidal', *Economic Times*, 3 April 1998

'Political Economy of Karnataka – 1950–1995: An Overview', *Journal of Social and Economic Development*, vol. 1, no. 1 (Jan.–June 1998), pp. 64–84

'The Modernisation of Corruption in Karnataka' (typescript, n.d.)

Parekh, Bikhu, 'The Cultural Particularity of Liberal Democracy', *Political Studies*, vol. 40, Special Issue (1992), pp. 160–75

Patnaik, Prabhat, 'New Turn in Economic Policy: Context and Prospect', *Economic and Political Weekly*, vol. 21, no. 23 (1986)

Pederson, J. D., 'Complexity of Conditionality: The Case of India', *European Journal of Development Research*, vol. 5, no. 1 (June 1993)

Pierson, Paul, 'When Effect Becomes Cause: Policy Feedback and Political Change', *World Politics*, vol. 45, no. 3 (July 1993), pp. 595–628

Dismantling the Welfare State (Cambridge: Cambridge University Press, 1995)

Pinto-Duschinsky, M., 'Foreign Political Aid: The German Political Foundations and their US Counterparts', *International Affairs*, vol. 67, no. 1 (1991), pp. 33–63

Przeworski, Adam, *Democracy and the Market: Political and Economic Reforms in Eastern Europe and Latin America* (New York: Cambridge University Press, 1991)

Rajagopal, Arvind, 'Ram Janmabhoomi, Consumer Identity and Image-Based Politics', *Economic and Political Weekly*, 2 July 1994, pp. 1659–68

Raman, P., 'Political Fallout of the Budget', *Business Standard*, 7 March 1994

Rego, Stephen, 'Pall of Doom', *Humanscape*, May 1997, pp. 13–15

Reserve Bank of India, *Bulletin*, Supplement: 'Finances of State Governments – 1996–97' (February 1997)

Bulletin, Supplement: 'Finances of State Governments – 1997–98' (February 1998)

Report on Currency and Finance, 1992 (New Delhi, 1992)

Richardson, Neil R., 'International Trade as a Force for Peace', in Charles W. Kegley, Jr. (ed.), *Controversies in International Relations Theory: Realism and the Neoliberal Challenge* (New York: St. Martin's Press, 1995), pp. 281–94

Roberts, Kenneth M., 'Neoliberalism and the Transformation of Populism in Latin America: The Peruvian Case', *World Politics*, vol. 48, no. 1 (October 1995), pp. 82–116

Robison, Richard, *Power and Economy in Suharto's Indonesia* (Manila: Journal of Contemporary Asia Publishers, 1990)

Rodrik, Dani, 'How Should Structural Adjustment Programs be Designed?' *World Development*, vol. 18, no. 7 (1990), pp. 933–47

Rothchild, Donald and Michael W. Foley, 'African States and the Politics of Inclusive Coalitions', in Donald Rothchild and Naomi Chazan (eds.), *The Precarious Balance: State and Society in Africa* (Boulder, Colo.: Westview, 1988), pp. 233–64

Roy, Rathin, 'State Intervention, Interest Groups and the Politics of Fiscal Policy', *Discussion Paper No. 36*, Institute for Development Policy and Management, University of Manchester, 1994

Rubin, Barnett R., 'Economic Liberalization and the Indian State', *Third World Quarterly*, vol. 7, no. 4 (October 1985), pp. 942–57

Rudolph, Lloyd I. and Susanne Hoeber Rudolph, *The Modernity of Tradition* (Chicago: University of Chicago Press, 1967)

In Pursuit of Lakshmi: The Political Economy of the Indian State (Chicago: University of Chicago Press, 1987)

Saberwal, Satish, 'Democratic Political Structures', in T.V. Sathyamurthy (ed.), *Social Change and Political Discourse in India: Structures of Power, Movements of Resistance – Volume I: State and Nation in the Context of Social Change* (Delhi: Oxford University Press, 1994), pp. 174–97

Sardesai, Rajdeep, 'Machiavellian Politics: Maharashtra Congress in a Bad Way', *Times of India*, 4 March 1993

Saxena, Kiran, 'The Hindu Trade Union Movement in India: The Bharatiya Mazdoor Sangh', *Asian Survey*, vol. 33, no. 7 (July 1993), pp. 685–96

Scaritt, James R. and Shaheen Mozaffar, 'Toward Sustainable Democracy in Africa: Can US Policy Make a Difference?' *Working Paper No. 171*, African Studies Centre, Boston University, 1993

Schmitter, Philippe C., 'The Consolidation of Democracy and Representation of Social Groups', *American Behavioral Scientist*, vol. 35 (1992), pp. 422–49

Serra, Jose, 'Three Mistaken Theses Regarding the Connection between Industrialization and Authoritarian Regimes', in David Collier (ed.), *The New Authoritarianism in Latin America* (Princeton: Princeton University Press, 1979), pp. 99–164

Shin, Doh Chull, 'On the Third Wave of Democratization: A Synthesis and Evaluation of Recent Theory and Research', *World Politics*, vol. 47 (October 1994)

Sikkink, Kathryn, 'Human Rights, Principled Issue Networks and Sovereignty in Latin America', *International Organization*, vol. 47, no. 3 (1993), pp. 411–41

Singh, Gurbir, 'Who Needs an Exit Policy Anyway?', *Economic and Political Weekly*, 10 June 1995, pp. 1359–60

Singh, Mahendra Prasad, 'Political Parties and Political Economy of Federalism: A Paradigm Shift in Indian Politics', *Indian Journal of Social Science*, vol. 7, no. 2 (1994), pp. 155–77

Singh, Satyajit, *Taming the Waters: Political Economy of Large Dams in India* (Delhi: Oxford University Press, 1997)

Skalnes, Tor, 'The State, Interest Groups and Structural Adjustment in Zimbabwe', *Journal of Development Studies*, vol. 29, no. 3 (April 1993), pp. 401–28

Skocpol, Theda, 'Wallerstein's World Capitalist System: A Theoretical and Historical Critique', *American Journal of Sociology*, vol. 82, no. 5 (March 1977)

Slider, Darell, 'Russian Economic Reform: Regional Policies and Market-Distorting Federalism', paper presented at the Annual Meeting of the American Political Science Association, Washington, DC, 28–31 August 1997

Sridharan, E., 'Economic Liberalisation and India's Political Economy: Towards a Paradigm Synthesis', *Journal of Commonwealth and Comparative Politics*, vol. 31, no. 3 (November 1993), pp. 1–31

Srinivasulu, K., 'Handloom Weavers' Struggle for Survival', *Economic and Political Weekly*, 3 September 1994, pp. 2331–3

Suarez, Sandra L., 'Interest Learning: Explaining the Political Behaviour of Business', paper presented at the Annual Meeting of the American Political Science Association, Washington, DC, 28–31 August 1997

Subbarao, Duvuuri, 'Inter-state Disparities and Reform', *Economic Times*, 6 February 1998

Swaminathan, Padmini, 'Liberalisation, Market Concentration and Prospects for Growth: A Study of the TVS Group of Companies', *Economic and Political Weekly*, 14 May 1988, pp. 1026–31

Tanzi, Vito, 'Fiscal Federalism and Decentralization: A Review of Some Efficiency and Macroeconomic Aspects', *Proceedings of the Annual World Bank Conference on Development Economics*, 1995, pp. 295–316

Thapar, Romila, *Cultural Transaction and Early India: Tradition and Patronage* (Delhi: Oxford University Press, 1994)

Thomas, John W. and Merilee S. Grindle, 'After the Decision: Implementing Policy Reforms in Developing Countries', *World Development*, vol. 18, no. 8 (1990)

Tilak, Jandhyala B. G., 'The Pests are Here to Stay: Capitation Fee in Disguise', *Economic and Political Weekly*, 12 February 1994

Toye, John, 'Political Economy and the Analysis of Indian Development', *Modern Asian Studies*, vol. 22, no. 1 (1988), pp. 97–122

'Interest Group Politics and the Implementation of Adjustment Policies in Sub-Saharan Africa', *Journal of International Development*, vol. 4, no. 2 (November 1992), pp. 183–97

USAID, Center for Development Information and Evaluation, Programme and Operations Assessments Division, 'Civil Society and Democratic Development: A CDIE Evaluation Design Paper', 24 February 1994

Center for Development Information and Evaluation, 'Civil Society and Democratic Development in Bangladesh: A CDIE Assessment', *USAID*

Working Paper No. 212, August 1994

Center for Development Information and Evaluation, 'Constituencies for Reform: Strategic Approaches for Donor-Supported Civic Advocacy Programs', *Program and Operations Assessment Report No. 12*, February 1996

Van de Walle, Nicolas, 'Political Liber[aliz]ation [sic] and Economic Policy Reform in Africa', *World Development*, vol. 22, no. 4 (1994), pp. 483–500

Varshney, Ashutosh, 'Self-Limited Empowerment: Democracy, Economic Development and Rural India', *Journal of Development Studies*, vol. 29, no. 4 (July 1993), pp. 177–215

'Mass Politics or Elite Politics? India's Economic Reforms in Comparative Perspective', paper presented for the conference, 'India's Economic Reforms', Centre for International Affairs/Harvard Institute for International Development, Harvard University, 13–14 December 1996

Vijayaraghavan, R., 'Corruption is a Cost of Production', *The Hindu*, 5 July 1993

Weiner, Myron, 'The Indian Paradox: Violent Social Conflict and Democratic Politics', in Myron Weiner (ed.), *The Indian Paradox: Essays in Indian Politics* (New Delhi: Sage Publications, 1989)

Weingast, Barry R., 'The Economic Role of Political Institutions: Market-Preserving Federalism and Economic Growth', *Journal of Law, Economics, and Organization*, vol. 11 (Spring 1995)

Weir, Margaret and Theda Skocpol, 'State Structures and the Possibilities for "Keynesian" Responses to the Great Depression in Sweden, Britain and the United States', in Peter B. Evans *et al.* (eds.), *Bringing the State Back In* (Cambridge: Cambridge University Press, 1985), pp. 107–63

White, Gordon, 'Market Reforms and the Emergence of Civil Society in Post-Mao China', *IDS Working Paper*, no. 6 (Brighton: Institute of Development Studies, 1994)

'Towards a Democratic Developmental State', *IDS Bulletin*, vol. 26, no. 4 (April 1995), pp. 27–36

Widner, Jennifer, 'Reform Bargains: The Policies of Change', in D. Lindauer and M. Roemer (eds.), *Asia and Africa: Legacies and Opportunities in Development* (Cambridge, Mass.: Harvard Institute for International Development, 1994)

Williams, David and Tom Young, 'Governance, the World Bank and Liberal Theory', *Political Studies*, vol. 42 (1994), pp. 84–100

Williamson, John (ed.), *The Political Economy of Policy Reform* (Washington, DC: Institute for International Economics, 1994)

Williamson, John and Stephan Haggard, 'The Political Conditions for Economic Reform', in J. Williamson (ed.), *The Political Economy of Policy Reform* (Washington, DC: Institute for International Economics, 1994), pp. 527–96

Wills, Gary, 'A Tale of Two Cities', *New York Review of Books*, vol. 43, no. 15 (3 October 1996)

World Bank, *Sub-Saharan Africa: From Crisis to Sustainable Growth* (Washington, DC: The World Bank, 1989)

Governance and Development (Washington, DC: The World Bank, 1992)

Adjustment in Africa: Reforms, Results and the Road Ahead (New York and Oxford: The World Bank/Oxford University Press, 1994)

Governance: The World Bank's Experience (Washington, DC: The World Bank, 1994)

Country Operations, Industry and Finance Division, India Country Department, South Asia Region, *India: Recent Economic Developments and Prospects* (27 May 1994)

Country Operations, Industry and Finance Division, Country Department II, South Asia Region, *India: Country Economic Memorandum – Five Years of Stabilization and Reform: The Challenges Ahead* (8 August 1996)

India: Sustaining Rapid Economic Growth (Washington, DC: The World Bank, 1997)

World Development Indicators 1998 (Washington, DC: The World Bank, 1998)

Wyplosz, Charles, 'After the Honeymoon: Economics and Politics of Economic Transformation', *European Economic Review*, vol. 37 (April 1993), pp. 379–86

Zhou, Kate Xiao and Lynne T. White III, 'Quiet Politics and Rural Enterprise Reform in China', *Journal of Developing Areas*, vol. 29 (July 1995), pp. 461–90

INDIAN NEWSPAPERS AND MAGAZINES

Asian Age
Business India
Business Standard
Business Today
Business World
Dateline Business
Deccan Herald
Economic and Political Weekly
Economic Times
Financial Express
Frontline
The Hindu
The Hindu – Business Line
Hindustan Times
Humanscape
The Independent
India Today
Indian Express
Observer of Business and Politics
Outlook
The Pioneer
Rashtriya Sahara
The Statesman
Sunday
The Telegraph
The Times of India
Tycoon
The Week

OTHER NEWSPAPERS AND MAGAZINES

African Business
The Boston Review
The Economist
Financial Times
The Guardian
International Herald Tribune
The New York Review of Books

Index